A Critique of Pure Teaching Methods and the Case of Synthetic Phonics

Bloomsbury Philosophy of Education

Series editor: Michael Hand

Bloomsbury Philosophy of Education is an international research series
dedicated to the examination of conceptual and normative questions
raised by the practice of education.

Forthcoming in the series

Cherishing and the Good Life of Learning, Ruth Cigman
Philosophical Reflections on Neuroscience and Education, William Kitchen

Also available from Bloomsbury

Does Religious Education Work?, James C. Conroy
Educational Assessment on Trial, Andrew Davis and Christopher Winch,
edited by Gerard Lum
Educating the Postmodern Child, Fiachra Long
Dyslexia: Developing the Debate, Julian Elliott and Rod Nicolson,
edited by Andrew Davis

A Critique of Pure Teaching Methods and the Case of Synthetic Phonics

Andrew Davis

BLOOMSBURY ACADEMIC
LONDON • NEW YORK • OXFORD • NEW DELHI • SYDNEY

BLOOMSBURY ACADEMIC
Bloomsbury Publishing Plc
50 Bedford Square, London, WC1B 3DP, UK
1385 Broadway, New York, NY 10018, USA

BLOOMSBURY, BLOOMSBURY ACADEMIC and the Diana logo
are trademarks of Bloomsbury Publishing Plc

First published 2018
Paperback edition first published 2019

Cover design: Clare Turner

A catalogue record for this book is available from the British Library.

Library of Congress Cataloging-in-Publication Data
Names: Davis, Andrew, 1948- author.
Title: A critique of pure teaching methods and the case of synthetic phonics
/ Andrew Davis.
Description: London, UK ; New York, NY : Bloomsbury Academic, 2017. | Series:
Bloomsbury philosophy of education | Includes bibliographical references
and index.
Identifiers: LCCN 2017019296| ISBN 9781474270670 (hb) |ISBN 9781474270687
(epub)
Subjects: LCSH: Reading–Phonetic method.
Classification: LCC LB1050.34 .D38 2017 | DDC372.46/5–dc23 LC record
available at https://lccn.loc.gov/2017019296

ISBN: HB: 978-1-4742-7067-0
    PB: 978-1-3501-1094-6
    ePDF: 978-1-4742-7069-4
    ePub: 978-1-4742-7068-7

Typeset by Deanta Global Publishing Services, Chennai, India

To find out more about our authors and books visit
www.bloomsbury.com and sign up for our newsletters.

For Margaret, without whom this book would not have existed

Contents

List of Figures

Series Editor's Foreword

Bloomsbury Philosophy of Education is an international research series dedicated to the examination of conceptual and normative questions raised by the practice of education.

Philosophy of education is a branch of philosophy rooted in and attentive to the practical business of educating people. Those working in the field are often based in departments of education rather than departments of philosophy; many have experience of teaching in primary or secondary schools; and all seek to contribute in some way to the improvement of educational interactions, institutions or ideals. Like philosophers of other stripes, philosophers of education are prone to speculative flight, and the altitudes they reach are occasionally dizzying; but their inquiries begin and end on the ground of educational practice, with matters of immediate concern to teachers, parents, administrators and policymakers.

Two kinds of question are central to the discipline. *Conceptual* questions have to do with the language we use to formulate educational aims and describe educational processes. At least some of the problems we encounter in our efforts to educate arise from conceptual confusion or corruption – from what Wittgenstein called 'the bewitchment of our intelligence by means of language'. Disciplined attention is needed to such specifically educational concepts as learning and teaching, schooling and socializing, training and indoctrinating, but also to the wider conceptual terrain in which educational discourse sits: what is it to be a person, or to have a mind, or to know or think or flourish, or to be rational, intelligent, autonomous or virtuous? *Normative* questions have to do with the justification of educational norms, aims and policies. What educators do is guided and constrained by principles, goals, imperatives and protocols that may or may not be ethically defensible or appropriate to the task in hand. Philosophers of education interrogate the normative infrastructure of educational practice, with a view to exposing its deficiencies and infirmities and drawing up blueprints for its repair or reconstruction. Frequently, of course, the two kinds of question overlap: inappropriate aims sometimes rest on conceptual muddles, and our understanding of educational concepts is liable to distortion by ill-founded pedagogical norms.

In terms of scholarly output, philosophy of education is in rude health. The field supports half a dozen major international journals, numerous learned societies and a busy annual calendar of national and international conferences. At present, however, too little of this scholarly output finds a wider audience, and too few of the important ideas introduced in journal articles are expanded into fully developed theories. The aim of this book series is to identify the best new work in the field and encourage its authors to develop, defend and work out the implications of their ideas, in a way that is accessible to a broad readership.

It is hoped that volumes in the series will be of interest not only to scholars and students of philosophy of education and neighbouring branches of philosophy, but also to the wider community of educational researchers, practitioners and policymakers. All volumes are written for an international audience: while some authors begin with the way an educational problem has been framed in a particular national context, it is the problem itself, not the local framing of it, on which the ensuing arguments bear.

Michael Hand

1

Setting the Scene

Introduction

Research-based or research-informed teaching approaches have a high profile in much of the developed world at the beginning of the third millennium. Apparently, we can discover effective methods, and their universal implementation in schools is long overdue. In the UK, the success of ResearchEd, started in 2013 by Tom Bennett, and other similar movements have drawn many teachers into the business of mining research for the purposes of improving practice. The authority of science lurks in the background, to be invoked when necessary to enhance the status and credibility of school teachers. The latter are now expected to base their classroom activities firmly on relevant evidence. Support for this posture is especially strong in the secondary sector, but it can be found across all phases of schooling. Politicians claim to favour research-based social policy.

Teaching reading to young children has not been immune from these trends. There are now a number of groups out there who think they know how this should be done, that their knowledge has its source in appropriate research and that the right ways should be mandatory for all teachers and children. Supporters include some with very considerable financial interests and certain English politicians.

Such is the context for the writing of this book. There are some positive aspects of the current movements that focus on evidence. However, as regards the teaching of reading, I believe there are also some disturbing and potentially destructive consequences for schools pupils and their teachers, especially in the Early Years. On my view, this is because putative evidence-based methods threaten to interfere with teaching, properly so called. At least, they constitute a threat if attempts are made to impose them on all teachers and young children on the grounds that they are endowed with 'scientific' authority. These so-called methods prove to be singularly elusive on closer examination, and policy based on empty constructs can be especially dangerous. It attempts to force teachers to engage comprehensively in certain specific kinds of classroom practices when there is no justification for doing so and when the very notion of a specific practice is sometimes opaque. To set the scene, let us rehearse a little history.

The Reading Wars

The Reading Wars have raged for decades in many parts of the world, and continue while fashions for particular teaching approaches have come and gone. In England, up to and during the 1950s, versions of phonics were influential. The splendid publication illustrated below appeared in 1929.

By the 1960s, an approach known as 'Look and Say' was widespread in the UK. Recently, phonics has re-emerged in various guises. Certain other countries are moving strongly towards phonics too, including Australia at the time of writing.

The varieties of phonics concerned include Analytic, Synthetic and Linguistic. Sometimes 'systematic' is added to these descriptions. I give more detail of some of them later. At this early stage, before inevitable complications emerge, let us understand 'Look and Say', a method associated with 'Whole Language' approaches to reading, as concentrating on pupils 'recognising' words as wholes. 'Synthetic Phonics' is about learning the sounds linked to letters and groups of letters, and blending them to form a longer sound that might represent a word as

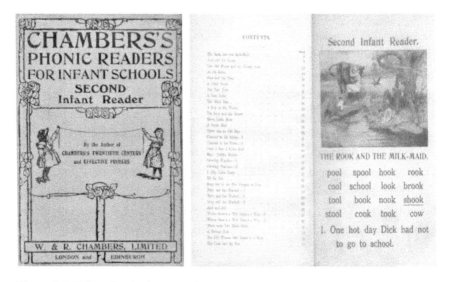

Figure 1.1 Infant phonics between the wars

it could be heard in speech. A very basic example would be blending the sounds associated with the letters 'd', 'o', 'g' to compose the sound that we can hear when someone says 'dog'. 'Systematic' presumably is added to the descriptions to indicate teaching that is carefully structured and organized, rather than phonics content being offered in a random and impulsive fashion.

I began primary teaching in the early 1970s when, according to some commentators, 'Whole Language' approaches prevailed. They may well have done, though I found some phonics materials in my grossly under-resourced school and made extensive use of them. One day, perhaps, social scientists may be able to account for the political support for Synthetic Phonics. It certainly needs explaining. For even if 'scientific' research could, in principle, show that Synthetic Phonics is particularly effective, the results of such research to date are less than overwhelming. (For a measured review, see Wyse and Goswami 2008.) Yet education policy that thinks of itself as strongly backing this so-called method is implemented in a number of countries. In the absence of a rational explanation for these extremes, something other than reason and evidence must be at work. I have my suspicions, but a complete solution to the mystery eludes me, and is certainly outside the scope of this book.

In any case, I will be developing an argument that conventional quantitative empirical research into specific teaching approaches is often hedged about with deep conceptual obstacles, and that the idea that such research should be 'scientific' is problematic. Those attempting such inquiries often model them on natural science. The contention that much of educational research cannot and should not resemble natural science practice too closely is, of course, very familiar. In this book I develop what I believe is a distinctive line of argument for this widely held view.

A few happy readers may still be oblivious of the so-called Reading Wars. For their sake, I am forced to venture into this unlovely territory. Wars need 'sides' to oppose. In the First World War, the Allies encouraged widespread stereotypes of Germans. British citizens were told, among other things, that the 'Hun' cut off the hands of children and used priests as clappers in bells. This was to stimulate hatred of the 'other' and to encourage the growth of patriotic feeling. For the 'other' to be imagined, the main tool is stereotyping. Stereotypes, by definition, overlook the fine-grained-ness of reality. They collect together into a falsely homogenous class, an otherwise inconvenient variety of individuals and their detailed characteristics. Even if any Germans were cutting off the hands of children, those appropriately labelled 'German' lacked any kind of common essence involving the disposition to cut off children's hands.

Some aspects of the 'Reading Wars' echo these phenomena. Laughably inadequate stereotypes of how reading is taught, such as 'Whole Language', 'Look and Say', and of phonics varieties such as Systematic, Analytic or Synthetic have been constructed and used as weapons to demonize opponents. Yet, in reality, those deemed to fall under any one of these labels would rarely be doing exactly the same as each other. Later, I will argue that, as true teachers, it would be a matter of some concern if they *were* too similar to each other.

Some people seem to think that much research on an international scale points unambiguously to *one* of these approaches (Synthetic Phonics) and to the terrible effects of using 'mixed methods' – the 'false balance' option. This triggers thoughts of US controversies about the teaching of evolution and creationism. Most scientists are infuriated by the demands by certain religious fundamentalists that state-funded schools should offer a 'balanced' treatment of the virtues of evolutionary theory on the one hand, and creationism on the other. Scientists know that creationism is not a viable scientific theory, whatever else it may be, and so striking a 'balance' would be to depart from the truth. It is to be hoped that phonics supporters do not think their position resembles that of these scientists. If they did, they would, in effect, be comparing all approaches other than theirs to creationism.

Synthetic phonics followers have been enraged because Higher Education Initial Teacher Training courses continue to mention a range of approaches to the teaching of reading. Yet in England, higher education (HE) institutions are required to inform their students about Synthetic Phonics, and are subjected to high stakes Ofsted inspections that incorporate a verdict on whether this is being delivered to standard. When that is pointed out, phonics adherents have been known to reinforce their criticism by doubting Ofsted's competence to judge the quality of initial teacher training phonics provision. I could not possibly comment on this. Most, if not all HE institutions continue to teach their students to engage in careful critical evaluation. Hence their reading lists will include treatments of 'Whole Language', phonics in its various guises, Reading Recovery (RR) and many other perspectives.

Another project that was drawn into the Reading Wars was the National Literacy Strategy. It began in England in 1997, and applied to all state schools. It ran for many years, and its 'Searchlight' model for the teaching of reading involved pupils using at least four strategies. In the Phonics route, pupils were supposed to use the initial letter to help them think of a word that made sense, to try blending the relevant sounds, and to look for familiar letter clusters associated with particular sounds. A second aspect of the model involved drawing on knowledge of grammar. Children were encouraged to go back to the beginning of the relevant sentence and use their awareness of grammar to try to make sense of the piece of text they were tackling, attending to punctuation, relevant prefixes and suffixes, and the rest of the sentence for further clues. In the third strategy, described in the Searchlight model as 'context', children were urged to consider any pictures supplied, to have the confidence to make a guess and then to check that it made sense in the context of the sentence as a whole. (We will need to return to that word 'guess', and the misuse of it made by those I am disposed to call 'phonics fundamentalists'.) Further, where necessary, pupils were to take account of wider elements of content and genre. Finally, under the heading of 'graphic knowledge', children were encouraged to note the shape of the word concerned, to look for words within words and blend them together, to discover familiar words and to use analogies with known words to read new words.

For a time, the National Literacy Strategy had a high profile in education policy. While not statutory, it was thought by many schools to be one of the lenses through which they would be examined by Ofsted. Yet I began to be aware of the increasing stridency of phonics advocacy. Ruth Kelly, one of the Secretaries of State for Education during New Labour's terms of office, was an explicit supporter, mentioning Synthetic Phonics in her 2005 letter to Rose setting up his report on the teaching of reading. That same government funded a systematic review of the same topic. Its published version is known as the Torgerson Report (Torgerson et al. 2006). Its conclusions were modest, mildly favouring phonics in general, but not 'Synthetic Phonics' in particular. Bizarrely, the government-initiated Rose Report that immediately followed Torgerson, ignored its very cautious conclusions, and gave strong support to Synthetic Phonics. Meanwhile, the National Literacy Strategy has been withdrawn. The multi-cuing strategies for young readers that the Strategy supported are detested by phonics supporters.

The official policies apparently bearing down on teachers and the consequences of these for young children are important elements in the motivation for this book. I am going to include some extensive quotations from government documents, since adherents of Synthetic Phonics frequently contend that it is 'flexible', and should be taught within a rich literacy programme. I agree with them. Yet many personal messages attest to the fact that, for some schools, phonics 'taught within a rich literacy programme' is understood to legitimate a very rigid 'first and fast' delivery for *all* pupils. That is not exactly what some of us thought 'within a rich literacy programme' meant.

The Year 1 Programmes of Study are statutory and so, presumably, must be addressed by all primary schools. The wording is open to interpretation. Here is a relevant extract:

Pupils should be taught to:

apply phonic knowledge and skills as the route to decode words respond speedily with the correct sound to graphemes (letters or groups of letters) for all 40+ phonemes, including, where applicable, alternative sounds for graphemes read accurately by blending sounds in unfamiliar words containing GPCs that have been taught read aloud accurately books that are consistent with their developing phonic knowledge and that do not require them to use other strategies to work out words re-read these books to build up their fluency and confidence in word reading. (Department for Education 2013)

Written requirements are one thing, and their applications in practice are quite another. I returned to the Rose Report to seek out what the above could possibly mean. It was pretty clear, or so it seemed to me, about what the above was excluding. After all, Rose does go out of his way to make that wholly explicit: 'A model of reading which encourages switching between various searchlight strategies, particularly when phonic work is regarded as only one such strategy, all of equal worth, risks paying insufficient attention to the critical skills of word recognition which must *first* be secured by beginner readers' (Rose 2006, para 116) (my italics).

That italicized word 'first' in the above quotation from Rose must be noted when reflecting on the claims of synthetic phonics supporters that their approaches are 'of course' embedded in rich literacy programmes. Just in case you were in the slightest doubt about the implications, Rose also said: 'This means teaching relatively short, discrete daily sessions, designed to progress from simple elements to the more complex aspects of phonics knowledge, skills and understanding' (ibid., para 36). Rose describes what looks very like a recommended teaching *method,* in addition to sketching what he sees as desirable content. I will be returning to this issue.

Clear direction for trainee teachers is contained within the Teachers' Standards, which stipulate that trainees must, if teaching early reading, 'demonstrate a clear understanding of Systematic Synthetic Phonics' (DfE 2012a, p. 7).

Is there any flexibility in that word 'demonstrate'? Sean Harford, HMI, Ofsted's National Director, Education, said recently (social media) that Synthetic Phonics is *not* a teaching style but is part of 'Teaching Standards'. In a separate comment, he added that Synthetic Phonics was a 'body of knowledge', and that teachers should teach it as they saw fit (Twitter comments, 25 October 2015). Now what is the difference between a teaching style and a teaching 'Standard'?

I have also studied the official guidance for schools, where it sets out the criteria that programmes must meet to secure matched funding for their phonics materials. To be deemed 'high quality' programmes must:

> be designed for the teaching of discrete, daily sessions progressing from simple to more complex phonic knowledge and skills and covering the major grapheme/phoneme correspondences; demonstrate that phonemes should be blended, in order, from left to right, 'all through the word' for reading; ensure that as pupils move through the early stages of acquiring phonics, they are invited to practise by reading texts which are entirely decodable for them, so that they experience success and learn to rely on phonemic strategies. (Department for Education 2011)

'Discrete daily sessions' sounds remarkably like a teaching style, yet school inspectors in England are now enjoined not to expect to see any particular style. Anyhow, an evaluation by the DfE of Sounds-Write, a government-approved phonics scheme, is consistent with the above requirements. It is always good to have an example of how criteria are actually applied in practice so that we can understand at least some of their possible interpretations. The DfE characterizes the first criterion against which schemes are judged as follows: 'The training promotes high quality systematic synthetic phonic work as the prime approach to decoding print i.e. a phonics "first and fast" approach' (Department for Education 2012b). The said evaluation made the following comment against this criterion about the Sounds-Write training: 'The disadvantages of alternative strategies such as whole-word learning were exemplified and discussed' (ibid.).

Later in the evaluation it is noted that 'the materials in the Sounds-Write programme are clearly designed for regular, short, periods of discrete teaching' (ibid.). Is this a 'style', a 'strategy', or something else altogether?

Finally, another example indicates the exacting requirements emanating from the DfE. Two or three years ago, a well-established and apparently well-regarded reading programme with a strong phonics element called 'THRASS' (Teaching Handwriting, Reading and Spelling Skills) was deemed by the Department for Education to be unworthy of matched funding. Apparently, it included some elements of 'analytic phonics', meaning, in this context at least, that pupils were encouraged at times to look at the text versions of whole words and how they were spelt, identifying sound families such as 'wail', 'fail', 'jail', 'mail', 'tail' and 'nail'.

In 2013, I published a short book entitled *To Read or Not to Read: Decoding Synthetic Phonics*, objecting to the rigid imposition of Synthetic Phonics on all teachers and pupils. My focus was on, among other things, those aspects of the statutory requirements opposing 'mixed methods' or 'multi-cuing'. These are very explicit, and have been there at least since the Rose Report itself. The fact that the approach known as 'Reading Recovery' countenances multi-cuing means that it is often the target of hostile treatment by synthetic phonics supporters. I return to RR later.

Interestingly, one place where the wording in relation to the potential prescription of teaching approaches is much more circumspect is the training materials for Ofsted inspectors themselves, where it says:

> the research evidence for 'what sort' of phonics teaching is simply insufficient to provide a basis for choosing between 'analytic' or 'synthetic' phonics. It is better, therefore, to have systematic phonics teaching than unsystematic or no phonics teaching and to give children the knowledge, skills and understanding they need to move forward confidently as readers and (writers). (Ofsted 2014, p. 50)

Did some Ofsted personnel, however briefly, distinguish between the 'knowledge, skills and understanding' that children need in order to read, and the necessary teaching methods to bring this knowledge about? At the end of this chapter, I look at the knowledge-method issue in some depth.

In England, the final tool in the hands of those seeking to impose Systematic Synthetic Phonics is the Phonics Check. All Year 1 pupils (5–6-year-olds) must take the test. It features twenty so-called real words and twenty 'pseudo-words' (the official term), all of which can be sounded out by blending the sounds that are standardly linked to the letters and letter combinations in the text concerned. The alleged words are presented in isolation. They are not part of meaningful sentences.

The Check is marketed as being outside our high stakes assessment system. Such a stance is wildly implausible. Ofsted take account of the results. Parents are informed of their children's performances. Pupils failing to reach the required standard retake the test in Year 2, and there are now proposals for further retakes still. The schools minister, Nick Gibb, actually writes special letters to primary schools who have done 'well' in the Check. Some schools are pleased to receive these communications, and even advertise them on social media as a kind of badge of honour. One commercial provider of synthetic phonics materials also writes letters to schools of this kind, and some of these are also put into the public arena.

Scientism

As I indicated at the beginning of this book, policy makers, some educational researchers and some teachers now embrace with much enthusiasm the idea of evidence-based practice. In turn, whether explicitly or otherwise, the authority of 'science' is invoked. Now I have long understood the prestige of science in popular culture. I have scientist friends, and love their enthusiasm, passion for truth and pursuit of rigour in their disciplines. Unfortunately, the legitimate authority of the subject has been extended to domains where it has no place. Popular culture, and even educational research sometimes endorse this aberration. Supporters of Synthetic Phonics often appeal to 'science' in attempts to ensure that their favoured methods are universally applied.

'Scientism' says that science is the *only* tool that is suitable for discovering whether a claim is true. Some critics of my phonics interventions in Davis 2012 and 2013 appeared to be strongly influenced by such a view. It is hardly new. Yet I was still surprised by how widespread and unthinking were the attitudes concerned. The scientism now abroad takes its model from natural science. But Wellington (2015) observes: 'There has been a persistent illusion that there is something called "the scientific method" which "scientists" follow and which should be adopted by educational research. There is no *one* scientific method: there are as many methods as there are sciences and scientists' (p. 12). Perhaps Wellington overstates his case. Nevertheless, he does have a point.

Examples may help here. Some sciences, especially physics at key moments in its history, do seem to proceed along the lines that Popper (1963) suggests. Popper's view of the scientific method is the following: the scientist puts forward a hypothesis or conjecture. Information about items to which the hypothesis would apply is fed in. A prediction of observable phenomena is deduced. Then observations are carried out to see whether the prediction is confirmed or falsified. Einstein's theory of relativity represents one such 'conjecture' here. Data is fed in about astronomical bodies to which the conjecture applies. One prediction is that light from specified stars will be bent in certain ways. The Eddington solar eclipse observations in 1919 were thought to support this prediction.

However, other examples in natural science depart from this well-worn paradigm case. Consider scientific 'histories' of, for instance, the origins of the solar system, of why some valleys are 'U' shaped or the narratives involved in Darwinian evolution. These look very different from the relativity case, even if there are some 'conjectures' embedded in these narratives.

All this has to be said about natural science before we even begin to touch on scientism's ignorance of the significant and legitimate differences between natural science and at least some of the inquiries within the broad category of 'social science'. These differences will be important later when I examine, in particular, contrasts between classifications characteristic of the natural sciences, and of those of the social sciences. The most profound problem here is that scientism fails to grasp that empirical evidence cannot *on its own* settle a whole host of claims, many of which are of vital importance to the health, well-being and flourishing of the human race. I want to spend a few moments defending this assertion.

If someone says 'science is the only discipline for discovering what is true', we assume that they would not assert this unless they believed that what they have said is true. How do they know that? They cannot now have recourse to science itself to establish their assertion. Hence they aspire to at least one truth in their portfolio of truths that undermines their scientism.

A common response is that once accepted, the scientism mission statement operates at a second-order level. As soon as the expression of an overarching commitment is established, then the scientism show is on the road, so to speak. So it can be implemented without undermining its own credentials.

This reply is unconvincing. Such a crucial act of faith by those espousing scientism is substantial, yet, we are being told, is beyond the reach of science. However, once such a move is allowed, it is, surely, the thin end of the wedge. It only has to be pushed a little way to reveal a gaping hole in scientism.

Nevertheless, much more needs to be said. Consider a claim such as 'a person comes into existence at the moment of conception'. This familiar, high stakes assertion may be encountered in debates about the morality of abortion. Its crucial obscurities and ambiguities are also familiar and contentious. I hope that what is *not* contentious is that science alone cannot settle whether this assertion is true. Evidently science can make important contributions to the debate, one way or another. Yet at the heart of the claim are rich notions such as 'person'. People debating the claim will argue over the meaning of 'person'. Their discussions may involve some sterile semantic disputes about how the term 'person' should be used, and that can often be frustrating. A good debate, however, even it does begin by arguing about meaning, will not rest there. It will go on to engage in important kinds of reasoning about the *nature* of personhood, and these will look beyond biology and chemistry, and transcend superficial discussions of word meaning. Such reasoning would not draw directly on the discipline of natural science.

Goldbach's conjecture says that every even number greater than 2 is the sum of two prime numbers. This has never been proved. If either its truth or falsity could ever be shown, it would not be a matter for science, but rather for logical and mathematical reasoning. No reference would be made to the empirical world, observation or laboratory experiments. No one is going to walk down the street searching for even numbers greater than 2 in order to test out Goldbach. The claims of mathematics are not the business of science. Science makes crucial *use* of mathematics to develop and to express its theories, but that is quite another matter. The fact that 2 + 3 = 5 is *not* established as true on the basis of evidence from a physics laboratory.

I have a hazy memory of my finals papers including a question that went something like this: "'A man-made device could never feel pain.' Discuss'. You may well think that this is an arcane topic, fit for nothing except ivory tower academic inquiry. Perhaps you have a point, though I seem to remember enjoying trying to tackle it. In any case, some high stakes contemporary issues involve closely related philosophical debates. There is continuing controversy over whether lobsters and other crustaceans feel pain, and, in particular, whether they feel pain when boiled alive, which is apparently a good way of cooking them. A few years ago I remember reading that a group of scientists had 'proved' that they (the lobsters, not the scientists) do not feel pain. As with the person conception example touched on just now, it is evident that science is *relevant* to this question. It is far less clear that science could actually *settle* the matter. Biologists might discover the presence or absence in lobster nervous systems of phenomena similar to those observed in other organisms where scientists are pretty certain that pain is occurring. Such discoveries might well point quite strongly in one direction or another. Yet pain may well be 'multiply realized'. That is to say, there may be many ways in which neural processes provide the bases for pain experiences. Hence, the absence of certain processes often typical of animal pain might not establish that lobsters were not feeling pain.

To understand further how matters would still not be settled definitively, imagine that, in a few years' time, Microsoft issues Windows 20. In their wisdom, they have arranged that when you press a special pain button on the keyboard or screen, events take place inside the computer that, in some way, mimic the neural events observed to be associated with pain in creatures. These special internal events bring about observable computer phenomena, including high pitched screaming sounds and flickering screens. Microsoft is convinced that this would appeal to computer users. Would this definitely mean that computers could feel pain when loaded with this operating system, to the joy of frustrated users yearning to exact revenge on their recalcitrant devices? Surely, we cannot quickly move to a definitive verdict. I would contend that the question is still open for debate, and the protagonists on either side would not simply be demanding more scientific investigation and information to establish their positions.

Science cannot *settle* normative and political issues either. Consider this claim: 'In a liberal democratic society, the state should not criminalize homosexual relationships.' A scientifically minded commentator might argue that evidence about the extent to which people can 'help' their sexual orientation could be adduced in relevant discussions. Even if such a controversial point were conceded, it does little to establish appropriate responses to the said claim. Exchanges about it would probably turn on the meaning of 'liberal democracy', the link between that and ideas about fundamental human rights, and much else. As with earlier examples, there would be some element of dispute over the meaning of key terms. Nevertheless it is to be hoped that discussions would transcend mere disagreement about word use. They should embrace explorations about the nature of a good society and human flourishing more generally. Much of this is of profound importance for all human beings, and little of it has anything to do with science or scientific method.

My final example consists of a question: 'What caused the First World War?' As with the other examples, the meaning of the key term 'caused' should be discussed. Furthermore, science may be deployed in all sorts of ways to establish facts about the nation states involved. At the heart of this question, however, are matters of complex and rich interpretation. In human affairs involving action, meaning, motive, reason and intention, verdicts cannot simply be 'read off' from reality as revealed by natural science. The social domain is a hugely important and all-embracing aspect of human existence, which resists any kind of strict scientism. At least, this is true, if we take scientism to mean the idea that the methods of natural science, understood in a rather particular fashion, are appropriate for the resolving of all truth claims. Differences between some versions of the social sciences and natural sciences re-emerge in Chapter 2.

Scientism does influence the approaches of some educational researchers. For instance, those educational researchers wedded to a broadly natural science perspective will usually insist that, although we can have reliable judgements that are not valid, we certainly cannot have valid judgements that are not reliable. There are a variety of conceptions of reliability in the research literature. One that is important for the argument of this book is the following: the degree of reliability of a judgement, say, about the nature of a teaching episode, is the extent to which observers reaching this judgement agree with each other. Validity will be construed as the extent to which the judgement actually succeeds in capturing what it is supposed to be capturing. As far as a teaching episode is concerned, if an observer's judgement about it is valid, this means that the judgement has succeeded in registering its characteristics in an accurate or appropriate fashion.

The thought behind 'no validity without reliability' is, I take it, that we simply cannot be measuring anything at all unless our procedures glean consistent results. This very basic point must be conceded immediately when we are in the natural science domain. If a scientist is measuring temperature, or mass, or light intensity, then we expect that the same results will be obtained (within a standard margin of error) no matter what instruments are used or which observer is employed.

Accordingly, the use of the term 'measurement' gives a strong steer on the kind of perspective adopted, for instance, within the psychometric tradition in psychology. According to this tradition, we can 'measure' intelligence, or creativity, or other constructs favoured by researchers of this kind. However, I will be arguing in what follows that when reaching verdicts on complex and value-ridden social phenomena such as teaching approaches, such notions of measurement are wholly inappropriate. It may well be, given this point, that applying notions of reliability and validity to judgements about these situations makes a kind of category mistake. The idea of a category mistake has been widely deployed in analytic philosophy since Gilbert Ryle (1949) first developed it. Ryle's familiar examples include one where a foreigner visiting Oxford sees the colleges, libraries and all the main university buildings. He then asks where the University is. Ryle comments that he was mistakenly allocating the University to the same category as that to which the other components belong.

To say that Theresa May is a square root, or that emotion is a petrol engine would be further surreal examples of category mistakes. Scientists can measure mass and temperature, for example. Yet these are in radically different categories from a so-called method of teaching using Systematic Synthetic Phonics. So, according to the category mistake argument, teaching interventions are in the wrong category to be measured according to the standards appropriate in natural science.

My treatment of scientism is likely to attract 'Straw Man' type criticisms. No one, it will be objected, believes that the methods of the natural sciences, taken alone, are the appropriate tools with which to investigate the social and normative complexities of school classrooms. Moreover, the endless debates between quantitative and qualitative research in the social sciences, and in educational research in particular, are only too familiar. This shows that many educational researchers are well-aware of the shortcomings of scientism, and do not espouse it in their inquiries.

In response, I can only offer some examples. I am not trying to show that scientism infects all educational research. It is very clear that it does not. The cases I now quote seem broadly to assume scientism rather than explicitly endorsing science as the only route to truth.

The frequently cited report from the American National Reading Panel (2000) on reading instruction is entitled *Teaching Children to Read: An Evidence-based Assessment of the Scientific Research Literature on Reading and its Implications for Reading Instruction*. Hattie's (2009) widely cited *A Synthesis of Over 800 Meta-analyses Relating to Achievement* refers to a natural science model when he cites a familiar passage from Popper:

> Bold ideas, unjustified anticipations, and speculative thought, are our only means for interpreting nature: our only organon, our only instrument, for grasping her. And we must hazard them to win our prize. Those among us who are unwilling to expose their ideas to the hazard of refutation do not take part in the scientific game. (Popper 1968, p. 4, 280)

Yet the 'hazard of refutation' may well be entirely irrelevant to some perfectly legitimate social science research. An unwary Hattie reader may worry that, were her approach to teaching not to mirror Popper-style scientific method, she would be open to the most serious criticism. She could fear, quite without justification, that she has given way to the forces of unreason.

However, an advance organizer for later discussion, so to speak is this: educational research is often not doing anything like 'interpreting nature'; sometimes it is probing aspects of *social* reality, and that can be a very different matter.

The United States (2001) No Child Left Behind legislation favours 'scientific, research-based programmes'. The definition of these includes the requirements that they are replicable in schools with diverse settings and that they are able to demonstrate evidence of effectiveness.

Note the prevalence of the idea of 'evidence-based policy' in policy documents issuing from the DfE, and the practices and 'philosophy' of bodies such as the Education Endowment fund. Despite attempts to replace 'evidence-based policy' with the expression 'evidence-*informed* policy', the former continues to figure in much discourse about education. 'Evidence-*based*' is an unhelpful phrase that ignores the fact that education policy will nearly always incorporate or assume value judgements. The questionable wording gives the impression that we *only* need evidence before us when making educational decisions.

I mention a few more examples here: 'Should science guide practice in special education? Most individuals would say "Yes".... Major initiatives in other disciplines such as medicine, the allied health professions and psychology are attempting to identify and disseminate practices that have scientific evidence of effectiveness' (Odom et al. 2005). A 2014 paper is entitled *Is Scientifically Based Reading Instruction Effective for Students With Below-Average IQs?* The very title implies the possibility of rigorous scientific support for a specific approach to instruction. Buckingham, Wheldall and Beaman-Wheldall (2013) assert: 'There is a large and robust body of scientific evidence on how children acquire reading skills early and quickly' (p. 22). Their offering is entitled *Why Jaydon Can't Read: The Triumph of Ideology Over Evidence in Teaching Reading*. Moats (2014) gives us another contribution from a similar stable: 'Coursework for teachers has remained impervious to scientific evidence regarding the nature and treatment of reading disabilities … Seidenberg (2013) … accurately portrays deep differences between the cultures of reading science and reading education, the anti-intellectual and anti-science bias in our schools of education.... Many are actively taught to be suspicious of scientific research.'

I did much in Davis (2013) that I believed to be legitimate, yet was obviously and explicitly unrelated to empirical evidence. For instance, when I dissected the relationship between 'decoding' words and reading for meaning, I was engaged in conceptual analysis and the careful scrutiny of examples. My argument that the very idea of clear specifiable teaching interventions whose causal role could be assessed by quantitative empirical research into early reading, was a myth, involved analytical and conceptual discussions. I take up this argument once more in the present work, and develop it in far more depth than was possible in *To Read or Not To Read*. I do not anticipate a consensus on whether this argument is sound, but the correct view of much of it depends in no way on empirical evidence or scientific method, however interpreted.

In the drive for evidence-based practice modelled on 'scientific' method, comparisons are frequently made with medical research. Such moves have triggered disputes between those who claim that educational research is clearly unlike medical research, and others who contend that the contrast has been oversold. The latter group is likely to hold that educational research highlights approaches likely to be effective for *most* students, rather than claiming infallibly effective methods for *all*. Yet, they may say, this should not be held to be any kind of defect. After all, they can argue, much medical research is in exactly the same position. In either case, it would be irresponsible of practitioners not to pay careful attention to relevant research results (see, for example, Cook, Smith and Tankersley 2012). Later, I will return to the medical versus educational research theme.

Meanwhile, my provisional conclusion from these reflections about scientism is the following: the emphasis on 'science' in connection with evidence-based practice is often overblown, and in many cases distorts the direction of appropriate research together with the understanding of how it might apply to classroom practice.

This is a suitable point at which to outline the agenda for the rest of the book. In the final section of this first chapter I show that the nature of the content to be taught, considered independently of any other factors, does not itself determine a suitable pedagogy. Chapter 2 begins by noting that standard quantitative empirical research into whether a teaching method is effective requires a robust account of its character. A reasonable level of consistency in verdicts about whether it is being used must be achievable, and this cannot happen if we have not succeeded in identifying *what it actually amounts to*.

Accordingly, I proceed to investigate certain features of the way we *classify* in social science. Our characterizations of teaching approaches are then explored in particular depth. This issue is first pursued by comparing the status of natural science and social science classifications in general. The fruits of this comparison pose serious challenges for the cogency and stability of at least some teaching methods classifications across time, place and culture. In Chapter 3 I concentrate on generality and specificity in our teaching method categories. I argue that some classroom practices aspiring to the status of 'pure teaching methods' turn out to be less than pure. I explain how this sets limits to the possibility of reliable judgements about whether a particular teaching episode exemplifies a given method. This in turn limits the scope of standard empirical research into that method's effectiveness.

The approach to helping struggling readers known as RR is often targeted by synthetic phonics proponents, but in a section dedicated to RR, I show that it cannot be regarded as a specific teaching method per se and hence cannot be sensibly compared with other approaches using standard quantitative empirical research. RR has some elements of an ethical position focusing on respecting pupils, and what that entails in terms of devising specific programmes in the light of individual reading difficulties.

Suppose, nevertheless we could set aside the profound problems associated with the search for teaching method identity. Imagine, in addition, that empirical research could establish the 'effectiveness' of a given method, and that we could agree on the meaning of 'effectiveness' and what should count as the method 'working'. Even then, I will argue, it does not follow that teachers should implement the method without carefully considering the relevant moral and value issues that nearly always impinge on educational decisions. The final section of Chapter 3 looks in great detail at the problems associated with the Phonics Check for all English 5–6-year-olds, this being a paradigm case of an attempt to force teachers to employ a specific teaching method.

Chapter 4 demonstrates that pupil-proof methods are not consistent with a defensible constructivist account of learning and the proper conception of teaching that this account entails. Overcoming method 'purity' problems in a way that would render the methods available for rigorous empirical research is incompatible with teaching. This is so, if a necessary condition for an activity to count as teaching comprises appropriate elements of interaction between adult and students. An appropriate constructivist understanding of learning entails the necessity for interaction of this kind.

A key component of a method for teaching young children to read is, of course, the nature of reading itself. Chapter 5 explores some fundamental concepts involved in the analysis of reading, including the idea of the phoneme and the very notion of 'word' I challenge the versions of these ideas that are assumed or needed by Synthetic Phonics. A 'pure' Synthetic Phonics method requires a concept of 'word' that does not sit easily, to say the least, with the fact that words are denizens of the realm of meaning.

Chapter 6 broadens the inquiry to embrace reading for meaning in general. A significant problem with synthetic phonics adherents' conception of reading is that they hold that decoding is a necessary condition for *any* process to count as reading. They deem anything outside this when dealing with text to be 'guessing'. I explain that such a move on their part is emotive and fails to do justice to the family of processes that reading comprises.

One inadequate conception of 'word' is closely linked to the so-called Simple View of Reading (SVR), beloved of phonics defenders and associated empirical researchers such as Tunmer. I explain that SVR is flawed, and perhaps should be renamed 'the over-simple view of reading'. SVR is untenable, because it overlooks the basic point that reading involves an interaction between 'decoding' and the realm of meaning. I also explore some abstract and difficult philosophical theory to probe more deeply into the nature of the gulf between speech sounds and written text, on the one hand, and the realm of meaning on the other.

Recently, phonics adherents have taken to mining the research literature about educational neuroscience to support views about the effectiveness of their teaching methods. I glance at one or two of the recent studies in this area, and argue that there is much less here than meets the eye.

In Chapter 7, I return to a theme explored in both studies, Davis (2012, 2013). This concerns the fate of a small percentage of 4-year-olds who arrive at school already able to read, or, at least, well on their way to reading, understood as extracting real meaning from text. The very existence of children with these achievements should make us question the existence of 'pure' methods of teaching reading, and question them in a very particular way. Some advanced young readers will have had a rich and nourishing experience of sharing story books at home with their families. These children are rapidly developing their identities as persons, and in particular, as agents who interact with others and who can take account of others' thoughts and feelings. These developments can have important implications for what should and should not feature in how children are taught reading in the first year or so at school. In particular, I contend, what *should not* be part of their experience is a rigidly imposed, 'first and fast' dose of Synthetic Phonics. Or, at least, their teachers should retain professional autonomy in this area, so that they can make decisions about just how far, in what way and when such advanced readers will be 'injected' with Synthetic Phonics. Professional autonomy would serve to diminish the 'purity' of synthetic phonics teaching methods, and I believe that teachers should retain or regain such autonomy.

I draw on and develop in much more depth, themes first explored in my paper *A Monstrous Regimen of Synthetic Phonics* (Davis 2012) and my short book *To Read or Not To Read: Decoding Synthetic Phonics* (Davis 2013). There was a brief but quite extensive outbreak of national publicity early in 2014 in connection with the latter, and I say more about this at the end, where I offer a brief history of events up to the time of writing this book.

Teaching content and teaching method

As the title of this book suggests, I intend to focus very closely on the very possibility of a 'pure' teaching method and the problems about researching its effectiveness. However, to do this without distractions requires a certain amount of conceptual cleansing and tidying. In many discussions about effective teaching methods, a key distinction is not always observed. It is this. There is a distinction to be made between, on the one hand, *methods* of teaching reading and, on the other, the nature of reading processes themselves. The latter amounts to the content or knowledge that will be taught in reading lessons. Defenders and opponents of particular approaches sometimes run method and content together. They think, for instance, that someone who opposes a given 'pure' method for the teaching of reading fails to appreciate the importance of the knowledge that method might involve. So, someone opposing Systematic Synthetic Phonics as a method is credited with the view that phonics knowledge for pupils is not important.

Accordingly, before moving to the first of my main projects, that of critiquing the very idea of a pure teaching method, it is essential to reflect on this distinction between method and what is taught, and how the relationship between these two things is properly to be conceived. I believe that progress cannot be made without doing this first.

Let us start with a musical example. A facility in playing scales and arpeggios on the violin may be a necessary condition for playing anything beyond the most elementary of compositions. (I understand that this is contestable, but I will assume it for the sake of argument.) Some violin teachers conclude from this that it is essential to teach scales and arpeggios very early in their pupils' development. Whether this is 'effective' is, no doubt a matter for empirical investigation. Anecdotally, as a parent of musicians, I am quite certain that it is not effective for *all* pupils, for various reasons. Motivation and engagement will be important considerations, even though some teachers will be very skilled in making those scales 'fun'. For some young learners, playing real tunes as early as possible is a powerful and indispensable motivator. This may not always sit easily with the strongest emphasis on scales and arpeggios. It is evident, then, that, were scales and arpeggios successfully argued to be an essential component of violin playing, this would fail to settle how and when such a component should figure in a teaching method.

Continuing for a moment with the music theme, there is a long-standing debate about whether it is ever educationally satisfactory to teach children approximate or even partially false 'knowledge' early on, and at an appropriate later time to 'put them right'. Many feel very strongly that this can never be educationally benign. Yet some musicians are encouraged by their teachers to play certain passages incorrectly, as steps towards playing them correctly. For example, perhaps a focus on deliberately performing with the wrong rhythm somehow readies the performer to move on to the correct rhythm later. Now I am neither supporting nor objecting to these kinds of practices. They merely demonstrate one way in which it is possible to separate *what* is to be taught from the method used to teach it.

Consider another example. If I am teaching English to primary children and, among other things, need to teach them to punctuate dialogue properly, I could adopt a very simple and direct view about how to do it. I could concentrate on the appropriate knowledge and skills. The children really do need to know where to place the speech marks, commas and new lines when punctuating dialogue. Therefore I must teach that knowledge 'directly'. (I will say much more about forms of 'direct' teaching later, but for now I hope I can rely on the reader's intuitive understanding of such a strategy.)

Nevertheless, in theory at least, a teacher could approach matters in a different way. For instance, she might give the children simple passages of punctuated dialogue, invite them to write some of their own dialogue and then to punctuate it on similar lines to the examples supplied to them. She can circulate and offer help while the children are carrying out this task. Now, this second strategy may well not be a good one, or at least, not a good one for all the pupils. The point here is that it is surely perfectly legitimate for it to be considered *as a possibility*. It might be entertained as a possibility because the teacher has made a judgement about how to catch the pupils' attention and interest. She could think it easier to motivate them using these 'indirect' methods. Of course, even reflections of this kind may provoke controversy, with objectors insisting that motivation should not be something the teacher should worry about. She should just teach, they might insist!

When choosing how to teach a topic, teachers may sometimes consider how the resulting pupil knowledge is likely to be 'owned' by their students. The point of punctuating dialogue is to render writing about people talking to each other accessible by any reader. The end-in-view is to communicate writing that incorporates characters talking. This transcends the merely conventional and technical use of punctuation. In the light of this, teachers might decide, rightly or wrongly, to select more pupil-centred and indirect approaches.

Consider another example that highlights the importance of distinguishing between the nature of what is taught and the appropriate methods for teaching it. During the 1960s in UK primary schools, various kinds of 'New Mathematics' flourished. Curricula were transformed: exciting content including aspects of shape and space, data handling and probability was introduced, and the emphasis on traditional arithmetic was reduced. Novel conceptions relating to sets began to appear in schemes, teacher education and Continuing Professional Development. (Even at the time, some educators thought such conceptions were arcane and irrelevant.) Many infant children were introduced to 'logic' by means of games played with materials such as 'logi-blocks'. These were sets of coloured bricks in geometrical shapes. The activities were supposed to help children develop very basic conceptions of set relationships such as intersection, union, disjoint sets, and logical operators such as 'not', 'or' and 'and'. The extent to which these small children were expected to use the jargon explicitly varied a good deal, though I have a clear memory of a 6-year-old coming up to me and claiming that he had displayed on his desk 'a union of disjoint sets'. I smiled warmly in response to this information, unable to think of a response that would give due value to his splendid achievement.

The theory behind this was that mathematics was based on, or somehow 'included' logic or set theory. Hence it should be taught (and taught first). Ormell (1967) observed: '"Logical sequence" may be defined as a way of ordering the main steps in a mathematical curriculum (especially in the early years) which broadly follows the hierarchy of formal concepts used by professional pure mathematicians. Such a curriculum sequence commonly begins with *sets,* and the *relationships between sets'* (p. 163). He proceeded to argue, with some plausibility, that logical sequences do not of themselves determine appropriate learning sequences. In a classic remark about this issue, Hirst (1967) commented: 'To insist that this sequence of truths can only be grasped as truths, by temporally building on previously adequately established truths, is to take the characteristics of what is to be achieved as an end for the characteristics of the process by which the end is achieved' (p. 55). I understand Hirst to say, in his inimitable fashion, something like the following: the character of what you are trying to teach need not and should not determine *how* it is taught at every point in the process, and need not and should not determine the *order* in which elements of the content should be taught.

The logic activities that were so widespread at one time forty or fifty years ago may have been valuable educationally in many ways, whether or not they enhanced pupils' mathematical learning in particular. Education fashions have changed, and the boxes of logi-blocks have long since disappeared, incomplete and crumbling, into school cupboards and probably in time to the tip. So history informs us that 'wiser' counsels came to prevail. After some years had passed, it came to be felt that pedagogical decisions should not be entirely determined by the character of what was being taught (even if we assume, for the sake of argument, that mathematics is 'based' on set theory in any sense. Russell argued that it could not be, but I must go no further down that road). Fashions may change yet again, of course, and activities concerning sets could return to the infant years.

What ground has been covered so far? Content to be taught does not, of itself, foreclose the teaching methods to be used. Teachers' decisions about classroom approaches should, of course be richly informed by their grasp of the relevant knowledge content, including key aspects of its conceptual and logical structure. There are many other factors they should also take into account. Some of these will vary over time, and from one group of pupils to another.

Let us take stock, and apply the argument to the teaching of reading. Suppose that learning about the sounds associated with letters and letter combinations, and about how to 'blend' these sounds together when encountering some text, proves to be an indispensable aspect of reading. Imagine, that is to say, that you cannot be said to be reading if you are not, among other things, making use of letter–sound correspondences. (I question this later, but let us stay with it for the time being.) *It simply does not follow from this that all pupils should be taught about this at a particular time, and in a fashion that excludes other aspects of reading.* One of the many extraordinary features of the current versions of the 'Reading Wars' is that this straightforward logical point rarely, if ever, surfaces.

Here is just one example of the logic failure (there are hosts of examples in the literature), from Cook, Holland and Slemrod (2014): 'Strong reading comprehension cannot occur unless decoding skills, oral language comprehension and reading fluency abilities are all strong. From this model, it is clear that educators must teach students to decode proficiently as early as possible' (p. 200).

Yet it just is not 'clear' that decoding must be taught as early as possible. The authors of this study present us with a simple non sequitur. I would not want to argue that it is 'clear' from this that decoding should not be taught early, either. We cannot conclude, from considering the relevant knowledge by itself, anything about when or how it should be taught.

The argument so far has revolved around the relationship between pupil knowledge and teaching approaches. Suppose we move the focus to teacher knowledge. Let us begin with a mathematical example, before we apply the results to the specific issue of reading and phonics.

Research could be carried out on whether there is a relationship between teacher knowledge of the traditional long division algorithm and pupil knowledge of that algorithm (see below).

If we wanted to pursue this idea in any depth, we would need to elaborate in detail what amounted to knowledge here. Before such explication, it is tempting to assert *a priori* that a teacher *lacking* knowledge cannot play a causal role in pupils acquiring it.

We should be cautious, however, about giving into that temptation. We need to consider carefully the potent role of the coach. A tennis champion has knowledge of how to play so that she wins a tournament. Her coach could well lack the skills required to win.

I think that there are at least two stories that can be told about this. In the first, the coach plays a causal role in the champion acquiring the relevant tournament winning knowledge. The coach has a significant level of tennis knowledge. This can be separated from the winning skills possessed by her pupil. The coach has at least as much tennis knowledge as the pupil even though lacking the winning skills. If this is the right story about coaching a champion, the prima facie paradox of the coach helping her pupil to gain knowledge that the coach lacks has been dissolved. Coach and champion pupil have comparable knowledge bases about tennis.

However, this is not the only story we might tell about such a coaching example. In the second story, the pupil's winning skills are impossible without knowledge. The 'knowledge' versus 'skills' theme in educational debate shows little sign of disappearing any time soon, and many argue that knowledge cannot, conceptually speaking, be separated from skills. If we accept that argument, the implication would now be that high skill levels bring in their train high levels of knowledge. In this alternative story, it is arguable that, if

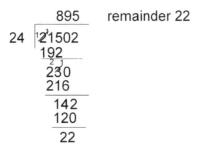

Figure 1.2 Example of the traditional long division algorithm

the pupil has greater skills than her coach, then this implies that she has more knowledge as well. Accordingly, she surely *does* develop knowledge lacked by her coach. The paradox is reinstated. On this alternative perspective, then, a coach with knowledge at level X can help her champion pupil advance and acquire knowledge at level X+1.

I am not able to pronounce definitively on the respective virtues of the two perspectives just rehearsed. Working from the point of view of the second perspective for a little longer, we could grant this point, perhaps, in connection with sport, but resist the thought that teachers of mathematical knowledge could play the role of a coach. In the tennis case, the coach can describe to the champion desirable moves, skills and exercises even where these could not be directly demonstrated. Yet in the mathematics case, if the teacher lacks knowledge of the procedures for long division, she cannot do anything whatever in the way of causing pupils to know those procedures. There is nothing equivalent to the role of a coach that is possible for her.

The debate becomes more interesting when we postulate that she has knowledge of the procedures but lacks understanding of why they make sense in terms of the nature of arithmetic, and of division in particular. In that situation, can she, in principle, play a causal role in the pupils' acquisition of the long division algorithm? Since some pupils *do* 'fill in the gaps' long after they have been taught a procedure, and come to have a good understanding of it, then she may in a sense be acting as 'coach'. She offers something and some of her pupils go beyond it.

Let us now return to reading and phonics. Imagine that research is carried out on the degree to which teacher knowledge of phonics is associated with (and so, presumably in some sense helps to cause) young readers to make progress in reading. At first sight there is nothing particularly problematic about this. This is simply a brief thought experiment, so evidently I have little idea about how it would turn out. It leaves teachers the freedom to *teach* reading in all sorts of different ways. Hence, if the said research were carried out, and demonstrated a significant association between teacher phonics knowledge and pupil progress in reading, this might go at least some way towards justifying an insistence that teachers are provided with appropriate phonics knowledge during their training. As such, it would not support the implementation of specific teaching methods. It is interesting to note in passing that the framework for core content for Initial Teacher Training in England, published in July 2016, says: 'If teaching early reading, demonstrate a clear understanding of systematic synthetic phonics.' It does *not* say that students in training must demonstrate a clear understanding of a method of *teaching* Systematic Synthetic Phonics.

Incidentally, there is recent empirical research (Andrews and Lo 2011) demonstrating that some mature skilled readers do not have accurate orthographic representations of words they can actually read: 'Many skilled readers have relatively imprecise lexical representations that do not accurately discriminate between orthographically similar words' (p. 161). This might make us wonder about what all mature and competent readers *must* know of decoding.

Imagine for a moment that it really is possible to identify a synthetic phonics skill or set of skills and to demonstrate that it is an integral part of reading. In such a circumstance, why *not* teach it directly and independently from the rest of reading, at least to some pupils? We have just seen that content being essential to a subject does not determine how it should be taught. Nevertheless, this question is worth confronting directly.

Would the situation be comparable, for instance, with teaching the skill of bowling in cricket? For it might be perfectly sensible for the latter to be taught directly. A would-be cricketer could be trained to bowl, before applying that skill intelligently in real cricket matches. This is surely so, despite the fact that it is the latter that gives bowling real meaning and purpose. Or, consider another example from learning to play a musical instrument. Acquiring the skill of playing scales and arpeggios on the piano or the violin may be a powerful route into the ultimate achievement of performing a demanding piece of Beethoven. Accordingly, might this not be a reasonable demand to make of pupils, despite the fact that learning and practising scales is not usually motivating for young learners?

However, the decoding skills involved in reading are very different. They are inherently interrelated with grasping the meanings of texts and linking those meanings to readers' existing knowledge and understanding. Later, I show in detail how, when reading for meaning, there are continual *interactions* between decoding and making interpretations from the context. By way of contrast, sounding out 'a rat ran at a ham', outside the context of some kind of narrative that might give it sense, is not a truly meaningful human activity.

Yet is the sport example really so different from the reading case? Is bowling a ball particularly meaningful outside the context of a proper cricket match? Perhaps not, but I suggest that it has rather more meaning and potential for motivating learners than blending letter sounds. It is a complete activity in itself, whereas decoding is not. Now consider the case where advanced early readers are subjected to a universal first and fast phonics programme. The phonics mechanism in which they engage is, to a degree distinct from the process of reading for meaning which they have shared with their families outside school. The school programme, rigidly applied, poses a threat, and I return to this theme in the final chapter. By way of contrast, practising scales does not per se detach an element of music performance from that performance as a whole in a fashion that has any potential for undermining it.

Delivering a phonics 'skill' in isolation resembles teaching a would-be actor how to represent sadness by showing him how to turn his mouth down. For lip shapes have no significance outside the intricate detail of human interactions. I have no doubt whatever that phonics sessions in the hands of the multitudes of skilled Early Years teachers out there are often motivating, and 'fun'. There are plenty of excellent resources available, some of them produced by those whose ideologies I oppose. Yet the very success of some of this activity should disturb us. The children are being stimulated by the skills and sheer charisma of the teachers. This teacher magnetism is essential if the pupils are to be motivated. This puts decoding in a very different situation from that of reading proper, where, arguably, an intrinsic motivation to read should derive directly from the process of uncovering the meaning in the text.

2

A Critique of Pure Teaching Methods

Introduction

Suppose, for the sake of argument, that a heavily 'phonics' saturated account of reading is correct. Should the teaching *method* ever be restricted to phonics decoding instruction? To what extent and in what senses, if at all, should the decoding lessons consist of 'Direct Instruction'? How far, if phonics is in some sense being taught 'directly', might timing and sequencing be subject to legitimate variation by teachers? Should *all* pupils be taught phonics in a particular way at any one time? How systematic should the teaching be, and in what sense? It may look as if these questions should be addressed by some kind of empirical research into these kinds of methods. However, this chapter will be devoted to problematizing the very notion of a teaching 'method' in connection with reading.

'It worked there. Will it work here?' is repeated like a mantra throughout Cartwright and Hardie's book on evidence-based policy (2012). If their focus is important, and I think it is, it should be applied to education policy. For instance, the 'it' in question could be a so-called effective teaching approach. It worked in that classroom, at that time, in that school, in that country and in that culture. Will it work here? They offer a convincing account of the complexities involved in addressing this question, but I concentrate here on a basic conceptual issue that it raises.

A researchable approach needs a clear identity. What counts as a teacher employing a particular method today, and applying that *same* method next week? For several teachers to adopt the *same* approaches in *different* classrooms, contexts, cultures and even countries? Without satisfactory answers, a reasonably high level of agreement between observers about whether the approach is being implemented in any one lesson cannot be secured. Lacking that, robust empirical research into its 'effectiveness' is simply not feasible.

I now show that attempts to characterize a researchable teaching method often confront intractable challenges. Meeting these fully is incompatible with *teaching*, as opposed to performing other classroom activities, whether valuable or otherwise. Hence, educational research purporting to assess the effectiveness of certain teaching approaches is limited in principle. As a result, policy 'based' on this research can be seriously problematic. The limitations which I demonstrate are crucially important for contemporary debates about so-called evidence-based approaches in schools.

Many have argued for related conclusions, urging that aspects of teaching and learning resist some of the standard quantitative empirical methods favoured by educational researchers. I have in mind, for instance, those valuing the importance of teacher *phronesis*, or comparing teaching to an art. Here, I return to conceptual basics, so to speak, in order to support them, following in the footsteps of others from Dewey to Eisner, and especially Biesta (2007).

The argument is developed in this and the following chapter. This chapter contrasts natural science and social science classifications in general. It proceeds to explore some of the implications of these contrasts for teaching method identity and the possibility of agreement about the classification of observed teaching. The following chapter addresses specificity, generality and abstraction in our teaching approach categories. In the light of this, it further strengthens the case for the existence of fundamental problems associated with teaching method identity. I explore attempts to solve the identity and consistency problems. I show that these attempts confront difficulties in principle, if, that is, we wish *teaching* to take place in classrooms rather than the following of rigid procedures or scripts.

Natural science and social science classifications

First, then, let us compare taxonomies typical of natural sciences such as physics, chemistry and biology with those characteristic of the social sciences. Natural science classifications include elements such as gold, silver and hydrogen. Among social science classifications we have the middle class, self-efficacy, culture and types of teaching method.

One approach to conceptualizing at least some science classifications is that they are 'natural kinds'. The status and the very coherence of the latter is still a matter of philosophical dispute. My discussion will avoid this vexed territory. At this point in the argument, I will understand natural kinds to be categories in nature that, for the most part, subsist independently of human activity. They concern how nature is divided up. These categories are there to be discovered. For instance, gold and silver are different types of stuff, regardless of how people deal with them, talk about them or classify them.

Each element has a particular atomic number. This is the number of protons in each atom. Human activities have no influence on these features. Over the centuries, human beings discovered the elements and the periodic table. They have invented languages and symbols in connection with them. Nevertheless, human pursuits have not, and could not affect, for instance, how gold differs from silver. That gold will be liquid at such and such a temperature, and that it is denser than silver, has nothing to do with people, their language, culture or thinking.

Some of the ways we categorize phenomena have important features that are *not* associated with natural kinds as I have just described them. Hacking has long studied what he calls 'interactive' kinds, such as attention deficit hyperactivity disorder (ADHD). How people are classified can influence how they behave, and this in turn has repercussions for how they are classified and the meaning of the labels concerned. Hacking calls these influences 'looping effects'. Hacking 2006 observes: 'We think of these kinds of people as given, as definite classes defined by definite properties... . But ... they are moving targets because our investigations interact with the targets themselves, and change them... . That is the looping effect. Sometimes our sciences create kinds of people that in a certain sense did not exist before. That is making up people.'

The interactions involved in 'making up' people embrace institutions, patterns of behaviour on the part of relevant professionals and much else. Patients with psychiatric disorders become accustomed to certain questions from doctors about their conditions and about how they are reacting to drugs and other treatments. They interact with these, and can respond differently over time as a result of them. In turn, the doctors' perspectives may shift as they digest messages coming from their patients. The parents of children with ADHD or dyslexia read about these conditions online and react in certain ways. Teachers of such children bring conceptions of the conditions to bear on how they treat them as pupils, who, in turn, react to the treatments and this affects their teachers' subsequent behaviour. Charities broadcast content embodying particular perspectives on the learning disorders concerned. These ultimately influence children's behaviour and 'symptoms' because they have effects on parents and teachers.

The phrase 'making up' might seem to suggest a fiction, that is to say, an invention without a basis in reality. Hacking avoids the crude dichotomies which might underlie such thinking. Once constructed, categories acquire an important kind of social reality. The social reality of ADHD makes a significant impact on pupils with that label, on their teachers and on their parents. He also points to cases which are significantly 'made up', but special cases of which might have a biological basis. Obesity, for instance has significant 'made up' features, yet a subset of the 'obese' almost certainly feature medical/biological conditions. In consequence, the claim that interactive kinds differ from natural kinds is really about the conceptions of these kinds themselves, rather than about the cases to which they apply. An 'obese' person may belong *both* to a category that has at least some 'natural kind' features, *and* to a category subject to human construction.

One example of how the looping effects may actually work is termed 'bio-looping', and can be found in Hacking 1999. Suppose someone suffering from depression undergoes a programme of behaviour modification designed to diminish their symptoms and feelings of depression. As a result of the treatment, 'numerous kinds of behaviour are reinforced, all of which run counter to the classification *depressed*' (p. 123). In turn, the patient's underlying neurological conditions and processes are altered. Hacking contends that some psychiatric condition labels such as schizophrenia also resemble obesity. They are to a degree 'biologized', yet there are also looping effects relating to them.

On the face of it, Hacking's elaboration of interactive kinds marks them off from natural kinds, at least as I characterized them above. However, it may be harder than it first appears to make a radical distinction between them in this respect (Khalidi 2013). Khalidi argues strongly that the dependence of a 'kind' on mental attitudes should not lead us to give up on their 'ontological objectivity' (p. 151). Nevertheless, the looping effects Hacking describes are undeniably much more prominent in a range of 'social kinds' than in the conventional examples of natural kinds. These effects must be taken into account when we explore the possibility of empirical research into their effectiveness, as we will see.

When we classify teaching approaches, are we thereby registering that there is something common to *all* the instances of a given approach? The later Wittgenstein taught us to be wary of insisting that everything we place in a given category has at least one property in common. So, for instance, people might assume that the English all share a feature, or that all chairs have a property in common. Wittgenstein says: 'Don't think, but look.' Games lack a common feature, but are linked by 'family resemblances'. This point, he contends, is obvious once you 'look'.

There is a powerful cultural tendency to credit a range of phenomena such as personal traits with 'essences', along the lines of natural kinds. This may be seen as a more extreme version of the thinking Wittgenstein was concerned to oppose, at least outside natural science contexts. The phenomenon arguably underlies varieties of racism, sexism and xenophobia. According to thinking of this kind, all women share, for example, a trait of being emotionally weaker than men, or all the French are cowards. More recently, Bastian and Haslam (2006) explore this point, and Haslam has a long track record of related research into our dispositions to be essentialist about a wide range of social categories. Bastian and Haslam found that the more people held essentialist beliefs, the more they were inclined to explain the persistence of their stereotypes in terms of innate and inherent factors.

I am convinced that essentialist thinking is also applied to at least some social phenomena classifications, including teaching approaches or methods. All instances of 'Direct Instruction' are thought to have something in common, or 'essences' of some kind. Similar thinking may be applied to many other approaches, including 'Discovery Learning', 'Systematic Synthetic Phonics' or 'Whole Language'. Conventional quantitative empirical research into teaching methods needs such essentialist perspectives to be viable yet, as we will see, essentialism and true teaching are not comfortable bedfellows.

Suppose a social scientist wishes to research flirting. What is gold in one culture is still gold in another. However, what counts as flirting in one culture may well not do so in another and, indeed, may vary over time even within one culture. Could this 'problem' be averted by describing flirting in exclusively physical terms? This would, of course be bizarre, but let us pursue this thought experiment for a few moments. There could be descriptions of arm movements, lip twitches, glances and so forth that excluded any references to human intentions, meanings, desires or purposes. Multiple observers should experience relatively little difficulty in reaching consistent verdicts about the character of stand-alone physical events, collections of which would be involved in flirting. Nevertheless, characterizing flirting 'physically' would be an unpromising strategy for social science investigations. For the physical manifestations of flirting are extraordinarily various. It may well be that no specific facial expressions, bodily movements, words and voice tone are common to *all* instances of flirting even within a particular culture at a given time.

Understandably, a social scientist would give short shrift to the project of characterizing flirting physically. Descriptions of that kind could not draw together the disparate phenomena in a way that could enable any kind of theorizing. Our social scientist could appeal at this point to a famous argument developed by the philosopher and cognitive scientist Jerry Fodor (1974). He opposed the attempts to 'reduce' the so-called Special Sciences that included economics, psychology and other social sciences, to physics.

In his anti-reductionist arguments, Fodor shows that even if, in principle, every event can be described in terms of physics, it does not follow that the Special Sciences are *reducible* to physics. He makes a powerful case that this means at least three significant things. First, that important and interesting generalizations 'can often be made about events whose physical descriptions have nothing in common' (Fodor 1974, p. 103). Second, whether these events share common features characterizable in terms of physics has no relevance to those important and interesting generalizations. Third, the Special Sciences focus on making just these kinds of generalizations. They would be needed for characterizations of flirting that could feature in any kind of effective and productive research into this phenomenon.

Meeting a requirement for consistent verdicts on flirting is significantly more difficult than achieving consistent verdicts about physically observable phenomena such as a rain shower. Why is this so? The answer lies in the differences between the roles played by human intentions in the classifications of natural and social phenomena. This claim needs explaining and defending in some detail.

Rain showers are what they are independently of any human intentions. Several observers could easily reach agreement with each other about whether a rain shower was occurring. In contrast, flirting verdicts take us straight to the realms of meaning, intention and informal conventions that can vary from one culture to another, and even from one local group to another. These realms are studied by a range of social sciences. Whether a social phenomenon is flirting is *not* independent of human intentions. Let me explain.

Rawls (1955) distinguished between *regulative* and *constitutive* rules. Regulative rules are those everyday prescriptions with which we are all familiar, such as 'speed limit 30 m.p.h.', 'do not cycle on this footbridge' and so forth. *Constitutive* rules are particularly interesting and important for our understanding of the social world. Soccer rules governing how and when a ball kicked into the net counts as scoring a goal 'constitute' the action concerned. Goal scoring is what it is in virtue of the rules. Football rules are *constitutive*. Without them, kicking the ball into the net would merely belong to a physical category. With them, that same action also belongs to the goal scoring category. Searle (1969) contends that in the case of rules that are purely regulative, 'behaviour which is in accordance with the rule could be given the same description … whether or not the rule existed' (p. 35). Where the rule is constitutive, behaviour in accordance with the rule can be classified in a way that would be impossible were the rule not to exist. Searle goes on to argue that 'constitutive rules are involved in speaking a language' (p. 37). (Some philosophers have criticized the distinction between regulative and constitutive rules, or even argued that all rules have both aspects. It is beyond the scope of this book to settle this, but I do not believe that my argument is significantly affected, even if they are right.)

Searle (1995) had much to say about *collective intentionality*, on which the functioning of constitutive rules depends. We are familiar with individual intentions. I intend to eat my lunch at around 1.00 p.m. and to clean my teeth this evening. In addition, however, there are 'we' or group intentions. We intend the road sign to signal a speed limit, and we intend a £20 note to have its particular meaning and role in our economy. Imagine that creatures from an alien civilization finally arrive in our solar system. The mother ship pauses in a discreet location, while a small module takes a couple of aliens, carefully disguised as human beings, down to earth. They walk along Oxford Street and find a £20 note on the pavement. Intrigued, they return with it to the mother ship and subject it to scientific tests in their laboratories, whose technologies are many millennia in advance of those achieved by human beings. They make a number of discoveries about the chemical and organic properties of the note, the pigments in the print, and so forth. Disappointingly, this tells them little about what the £20 note actually is. The aliens need to return to earth and investigate the complexities of money, value, banks, exchange, economies and too many other things to mention here. These social facts and institutions have a kind of existence that is sustained because people in a society or culture intend this. Such 'we' intentions are often tacit and rarely conscious psychological episodes. They exist for all that.

Group intentions underlie constitutive rules such as those of chess. 'We' intend that chess rules should apply worldwide. As long as we intend this, we sustain in existence those rules according to which, moving that castle-shaped piece in a certain way on the 8 × 8 squared board, just is a rook move. We intend that such and such a road sign means that you must not drive faster than 30 miles per hour, and that the £20 note has such and such a place in our economic and monetary system.

Peter Winch's important and plausible contention in his classic work *The Idea of a Social Science* is, in effect, that virtually all phenomena in the social world belong there because of the existence of classifications governed by collective intentionalities and constitutive rules (though as far as I am aware, he never makes use of these expressions). Perhaps some very primitive actions, such as a baby suckling, are what they are regardless of what any society or community think about them or intend in respect of them. However, most action classifications, from flirting to those involved in teaching, require to be 'constituted' by collective human intentions. That is to say, they acquire classifications that give them status in the social world because of the continuing existence of relevant collective human intentions. This is how it is that moving my arm and hand in a certain way *is* also waving goodbye. It explains how putting my hand on someone's arm can be a comfort gesture. When I close one of my eyes this can also be a deliberate wink. I can vote by writing a cross in a box. My gazing at a pupil can constitute a teacher's 'stare', because she has still not stopped talking at the start of a lesson. Readers can easily continue this list. Relevant intentions also support in existence most social phenomena such as banks, nation states and cultures. They certainly sustain the categories we apply to teaching methods, such as 'Direct Instruction', 'Discovery Learning' and 'Systematic Synthetic Phonics'.

Goldman (1970) developed a rich theory about how actions acquire classifications. In effect, one element of his theory elaborates on what has just been said about social phenomena classifications, action classifications being a subset of these. He dubs the relevant element in his theory 'conventional generation'. This relates to 'the existence of rules, conventions or social practices in virtue of which an act A 'may be ascribed to an agent' (p. 25). He contends that in most instances of conventional generation, certain circumstances must obtain in addition to the relevant conventions for the action classified in a given way to be attributed appropriately to an agent. For instance, someone waving her hand from a car window cannot be signalling that she is going to slow down unless she is actually driving the car. Furthermore at the present time, at least, it has to be a person waving her hand rather than a machine using a robotic 'arm', for the signalling to take place.

The collective intentions discussed above, vary in their stability and in how narrowly they are tied to particular cultures, places and times. For instance, shaking hands is constituted as a greeting in the UK. Yet, even in the UK in certain circumstances, a man shaking a Muslim woman's hand would be offensive and insulting, whatever his intentions might be. A classroom episode of an hour or so comprises a host of teacher actions, pupil actions and teacher–pupil interactions that are interconnected in multiple ways. These include utterances, facial expressions, body language and many other aspects of human behaviour too numerous to mention. The existence of the categories to which all of these sub-components belong, depend at least in part on the collective intentions of the wider society or relevant minority. The very character of these categories themselves also reflects how these sub-components are held to relate to each other by the salient community or communities.

Interpreting teaching and the challenge to consistent classification

When such interrelationships are complex, as they usually are, classifying a social phenomenon incorporating many interrelated elements requires *interpretation*. For the purpose of my argument here, I am going to understand 'interpretation' as a judgement about rich, complex and interconnected social phenomena. As I have already shown, in regard to most taxonomies that apply to human activity, collective human intentions are constitutive. The categories to which teaching approaches are assigned cannot simply be 'read off' from direct observation of classroom phenomena, as if observers could succeed in detecting an inherent character that the said phenomena possessed, a character that obtained entirely independently of human intentions. One observer may well reach a different verdict on how the teaching episode should be classified from another, without it being obvious that one is wholly wrong and the other is entirely right. More than one interpretation of the teaching may have a kind of value and legitimacy and hence succeed in registering something important. In fact, I would argue that it can sometimes be unclear in principle what it would actually amount to for one observer to be 'correct' and another 'incorrect'. It is not the case that *either* that famous picture is a duck, *or* that it is a rabbit.

Bruner (1991), in related thinking, comments: 'Nor is it surprising that anthropologists have increasingly turned away from positivist descriptions of cultures toward an interpretive one in which not objective categories but "meanings" are sought for, not meanings imposed *ex hypothesi* by an outsider, the anthropologist, but ones arrived at by indigenous participants immersed in the culture's own processes for negotiating meaning' (p. 17).

Given that the classification of classroom teaching processes depends in very complex ways on the constitutive intentions of the society in which they occur, the verdicts may sometimes lack the stability of judgements about, for example, whether this material is gold. Returning to Hacking's discussion of interactive kinds and looping effects, those teachers credited with a particular teaching approach will sometimes know of their classification and will respond to this in various ways. These responses may well include modifying how they teach. Some classifications may carry a value loading that reflects views about what is to count as 'good' teaching. Such views may be held by powerful players in the education system. Once teachers have modified their classroom behaviour in the light of how they perceive themselves to be classified, such modifications can, in turn, affect future verdicts on how their teaching is categorized by relevant observers. The allegedly detectable character of a teaching approach can prove to be a shifting target. Those seeking consistency in how teaching episodes are classified cannot ignore these possibilities.

At this point, an objector could accuse me of making empirical claims without evidence. Can I support my contention that teachers will be aware of how they are classified, and hence will become embroiled in Hacking-type looping effects? I concede that this *is* an empirical claim, and that I am not able to offer evidential data in support. I can only say that the phenomena I suggest seem very likely, and further that their very possibility in principle should make us wary of overconfidence about achieving consistency in the classification of teaching episodes. We know, for instance, from Alexander (1992) that some teachers in the Leeds of the 1980s whose approaches were classified as traditional rather than progressive feared that their promotion prospects would be limited. The thought that their practices might have shifted as a result of such apprehensions surely has some plausibility, whether or not those shifts were changes of which the teachers were aware.

Optimists about the possibility of researching teaching approaches, and therefore about the possibility of achieving a reasonable level of observer agreement about their implementation will not let the matter rest here. They would want the analysis taken much further. Surely, they may urge, such approaches *do* have inherent characters that are to a degree, at least, independent of the intentions and conventions of the social groups in which they are embedded.

To deal with this point, I need to say much more about classifications and conventions. Some constitutive rules and their supporting collective intentionalities are more arbitrary than others. So, in some cases, the link between the *physical* characteristics of action, event, process or thing and its classification that is underpinned by certain collective intentions and constitutive rules may be wholly conventional. In other cases, the physical characteristics concerned may serve to constrain the kinds of constitutive rules that could apply, and inform a social classification.

In game examples, the rules are wholly arbitrary and conventional. The piece that can move horizontally and vertically could have had a different shape and name. The constitutive rules and the required associated collective intentionality are *entirely* responsible for the moves of the piece acquiring a new classification. Wittgenstein's idea of a language game is wholly appropriate in this regard, for speech and text are in the same position. With the exception of a tiny number of onomatopoeic words, the particular sounds and spellings of words are arbitrary and conventional.

In contrast to these examples, are there others where matters are 'less' arbitrary? What of the handshake as a form of greeting? Is this wholly arbitrary? There is the actual contact with another person and the feeling of warmth. Does this in some sense justify our intentions that such contact should constitute a greeting? Yet could it not also be argued that the very same features that justify the greeting classification might also justify the handshake being classed as an insult in certain circumstances?

In the light of these points, we should note that Khalidi (2013) thinks that Searle exaggerates the difference between natural kinds and 'social kinds' such as money, marriage, private property and elections (p. 151). He supports Thomasson's criticism of Searle: 'For failing to recognize that many social kinds do not depend for their existence on people's having thoughts about those kinds themselves' (p. 152). Economic recessions, for instance can exist independently of what anyone might think about them.

It does seem to be true that some social kinds are more 'directly' dependent on certain human psychological states than others. Nevertheless, I would still argue that recessions could not exist at all without a whole host of constitutive rules and collective intentionalities being in place concerning money, exchange and many other social phenomena. That there are degrees of conventionality in social kinds does not undermine my argument, nor does the plausible claim, also supported by Khalidi, that they may well have a significant 'reality', and be such that they can 'come to participate in new causal patterns that were not in existence before the creation of the conventional kind' (p. 157).

Let us apply these reflections to teaching itself. As I said above, optimists about the possibility of researching the effectiveness of teaching may well hold that certain classroom performances by adults have intrinsic features that are independent of constitutive rules and collective intentionalities. They might even urge that I have over-complicated the whole issue about method identity and observer consensus about the presence of a method. 'Why not simply ask the teachers concerned what they are doing?' our hopeful researchers might inquire. If teachers say they are implementing Direct Instruction, or Discovery Learning, or Systematic Synthetic Phonics, and can offer a reasonably clear sketch of the relevant approach, then this effectively addresses the classification reliability issue. As actors, they have direct access to the intrinsic features of the teaching methods they are implementing, or so might conclude the optimists.

In the case of single actions performed at a particular moment, such as standing up, saying a word, or waving her hand, matters seem relatively straightforward.

> What did you do just then?
> I stood up!
> What was the last thing you did?
> I said 'Time to pack up'

Even in these examples, of course, she will often 'do' more than she intends. Saying a word may also be upsetting Debbie, even though she did not mean to. Waving her hand could be attracting John's attention, while she actually intended her gesture to signal to Wayne to return to his seat. Furthermore, although the agent has 'direct' access to the character of her own action under at least one description, this access is surely not infallible. She can sincerely claim that she was doing X, when, in fact, she was not. She claims, for instance, to say 'Lunch time', but in fact says 'Home time'. All the pupils assure her that this is what she said. She is convinced that she said 'Lunch Time', but allows herself to be persuaded by her pupils' verdict. She is probably tired. Similarly, she asserts that she nodded just now, but onlookers report that in fact she shook her head. Admittedly such cases are rare. If they happened more often to someone we might begin to be worried about their health.

Let us move on from these 'single action' cases to complex sets of activities comprising a lesson. (The scare quotes are here because what actually counts as just 'one' action is a murky area, and has been the subject of extensive debates in analytical philosophy. The outcome of these debates does not affect my line of argument.) Consider a more complicated case, central to the concerns of this book. At the end of a lesson, the teacher is asked: 'What teaching approach have you just used?' She answers: 'Systematic Synthetic Phonics'. Now we have established that an agent's access to the character of her acts falls short of infallibility. In the case of these complex activity sets, the agent is having to interpret what she is doing in a fashion that, at least to some degree, mirrors the interpretative demands required of someone else observing her teaching. Her personal authorship of the actions fails to endow her with an authority over the nature of her performances that trumps without qualification, verdicts supplied by observers. In effect, she is just another observer. *She* may say that she was teaching Synthetic Phonics. An observer might assert that in fact she was employing Analytic Phonics. Admittedly, being the agent in the case, she may well be able to provide a considered and sophisticated justification for how she characterizes her own teaching. Nevertheless, so might an observer who reaches a different conclusion from the teacher. We really cannot occupy any kind of high ground and pronounce on the 'truth' of either protagonist. It is unclear in principle what would count as the truth of the matter here.

Taylor (1985) makes some related points. When others seek to understand us, they must take the trouble to grasp how *we* would describe what we are doing. That is our self-understanding. However, if they went no further than this they would be seriously astray; they would be adopting what he calls the incorrigibility thesis. This is the mistaken idea that we can, incorrigibly, characterize our own thoughts and actions. It is true that our interpreters must attend to the terms in which we grasp our beliefs and actions. However, they cannot be trapped by *our* terms when trying to make sense of us. How *we* see matters is not the last word on the situation. Moreover, making sense of us, Taylor reminds us, is not always equivalent to our interpreters concluding that we are making sense!

You say that you are passing on information about a work colleague to management to circumvent the possibility that flaws in her department lead to a poor baby food product and damage babies. Nevertheless, what you are really doing is damaging the promotion prospects of your work colleague; you and she have both applied for the same senior post. (It is possible that you are doing *both* of these things.) If a teacher believes that she is teaching according to the tenets of Synthetic Phonics, we must attend carefully to what she thinks about what she is doing. Yet she cannot be regarded as being entitled to the last word on the matter.

If we are seeking to understand teachers' actions and beliefs, we have to grasp what Taylor (1985), following Elizabeth Anscombe, calls the 'desirability characterizations' that are part of how teachers see their classroom activities. We need to comprehend what they care about, value, hate and hope for. Their teaching and educational philosophy will embrace many of these 'desirability characterizations'. Taylor argues that these characterizations 'cannot be intersubjectively validated in an unproblematic way' (p. 119). That is to say, it is not possible for 'scientifically competent observer(s)' (p. 120) to discern the appropriateness of these characterizations in a (technically) reliable fashion. The observers may not be able to reach agreement about classifications of teaching that incorporate such desirability characterizations. In part, this is because they may not be able to grasp the relevant 'fine sensibilities' being exercised by the teachers concerned. The observers could lack 'certain developments of character and sensibility' 'only recognizable from the standpoint of those who have acquired them' (p. 120). We cannot hope to aspire to fully replicable findings, for these would belong to a kind of social science that would be a universal science of society. Elements of the latter should, if it were possible, consist of appropriate taxonomies of teaching methods that are value free. Taylor shows that this is an impossible aspiration for much of social science. We may not always be able to describe teaching activity in terms that can apply to different teachers in different schools at different times. For the terms a teacher might use to capture her thoughts and deeds in the classroom, will be permeated by 'desirability characteristics'. We have learnt from Taylor that how a particular individual or group sees their actions and beliefs cannot be regarded as the last word on the matter. Yet, to understand them, the terms in which they see things must at least be taken into account.

While outlining Searlian insights about collective intentionalities and constitutive rules, I referred to the complexity of social phenomena such as teaching episodes. However, complexity per se is not the real issue here. Meteorology deals with situations of the greatest complexity: it discerns patterns, regularities, assigns causes and makes predictions. Phenomena are classified, including depressions, fronts, anticyclones and clouds. The language and purposes for which the classifications are constructed are evidently human. Yet the phenomena themselves, such as 'depressions', in an important sense belong to the relevant categories without regard to human intentions. Human intentions are behind the fact that certain taxonomies are *employed* by the Meteorological Office. Yet such intentions do not *constitute* the appropriate ways of classifying depressions, fronts and the like. Were human beings never to have existed, and to have had thoughts about Atlantic depressions, Polar Lows and cold fronts, such phenomena would still have obtained, and belong to the relevant classifications.

I now return to the need for a reasonable level of consistency between observers seeking to classify a teaching episode when its effectiveness is to be the subject of conventional quantitative empirical research. I explore this further by offering a commentary on a couple of examples from Robin Alexander's *Culture and Pedagogy* (Alexander 2001). He analyses lessons in primary classrooms across five countries. He includes the elusive feature of 'pace' as a term used to characterize these lessons. This idea of pace is complex, value laden and contestable. Let us try to understand just how observers legitimately might differ over whether a particular lesson has it.

Alexander offers accounts of the following five kinds of pace: (1) Organizational pace (the speed at which lesson preparations, introductions, transitions and conclusions are handled); (2) task pace (the speed at which learning tasks and their contingent activities are undertaken); (3) interactive pace (the speed of a sequence of classroom exchanges); (4) cognitive or semantic pace (the speed at which ideas are presented and developed, and the demands that this places on the child's thought processes) and (5) learning pace (how fast pupils actually learn).

Would several observers of the same lesson necessarily agree about the presence of pace in any of these senses? For their verdicts cannot be separated from verdicts about the teacher's objectives in the lesson, the kind of classroom control sought and many other things. Even more challenging is the fact that, according to Alexander, some aspects of pace themselves can be in tension with others. In one lesson, a desirable pace of exchanges between pupils was not wholly consistent with covering conceptual ground at a good pace. This is understandable. After all, we can readily imagine a mathematics lesson where a teacher is introducing calculus, and the potential tensions between an objective of rich exchanges about the fascinating yet difficult concepts at the heart of this topic, on the one hand, and covering the ground within a time limit, on the other. Moreover, in complex ways differing verdicts about the presence or absence of pace may reflect the values of the lesson observers.

Consider another lesson feature for which agreement between observers might be sought: the clarity of the teacher's goals. Each of those assessing clarity levels must have an understanding of what is to count as setting given goals with given levels of clarity. Yet the verdict concerned is, once again, complex and contestable. It has important interrelationships with other potentially desirable lesson features. How does it, or should it, relate to *pupils* being clear about the intended learning outcomes? What should count as being clear about these? It might make a difference whether we are considering mathematics, or drama, or creative writing. For instance, perhaps teacher goal clarity in some kinds of drama lessons means that in a certain sense pupils cannot be clear about the intended learning outcomes, at least at the start of the lesson, if it is to succeed. Drama teachers must, of course, have defensible learning outcomes in mind for their lessons. Yet 'being clear' about these, if that meant spelling out the outcomes at the start of the proceedings, might at least be in tension with, for instance, ideas about pupils exploring roles and improvising responses to others in role.

In a mathematics lesson, on the other hand, the teacher's clarity about the learning outcomes might turn out to be inherently linked in some way with the pupils' clarity about the said outcomes. For instance, the teacher might have pursued the classic so-called effective teaching ploy of outlining the intended learning outcomes in a perspicuous manner. If this 'went well', it might result in pupils grasping fully what they were to learn. Of course, this might only be possible if it was sensible to think of the learning as something that really could take place in the space of one lesson. If the learning concerned was a longer term project, it might be much more difficult for pupils to grasp the learning to be achieved in advance of it happening. There is a hint of a paradox here. How *can* pupils fully grasp what they are to learn before they actually learn it? Of course, 'advance organizers' are often possible and even sensible. Yet the question of how the teacher's 'clarity' at the beginning of the lesson is linked to the pupils' clarity at that point looks as if it has a number of legitimate answers. The nature of such linkage should depend on many factors, including context and the nature of the subject matter concerned.

In yet another perspective, could 'being clear' be construed as knowing in advance what actually is to happen during the lesson? That is to say, being informed in detail about the precise nature, timing and sequence of events? For instance, the teacher will talk with pupils from the front for ten minutes, pupils then work in such and such groups on this specific task with those particular resources for twenty minutes, and so on. Yet being clear in *this* way might be in tension with certain kinds of clarity about the intended learning outcomes, in at least some circumstances. To know exactly what is going to happen during a lesson might only be possible if the learning outcomes are left flexible. A very determined effort to ensure that *all* pupils achieve a certain learning outcome by the end of a lesson might require the lesson's precise character, sequencing and timing to be a matter for teacher decision-making during that lesson.

All these possibilities have relationships with other potential lesson objectives. From time to time, teachers might intend that their pupils are given a degree of control over their learning during the lesson. Yet teachers being very clear (in a certain sense) about their *own* goals might be in tension with the objective of ensuring that pupils have some control of their learning during the lesson in question. With a degree of pupil control, the precise sequence of events in the lesson cannot be predicted, and so teachers cannot be clear about these in advance. Pupil control might not always be compatible with covering a precisely delineated area of knowledge. A very tight teacher intention about learning outcomes may not sit easily with pupil control beyond a certain point.

In the light of these points, just how, for instance, could consistency of classifying 'clarity of teacher goals' be secured? Decisions would have to be made about how clarity of lesson goals is to relate to pupil control over learning (among other things). By so doing, are these choices excluding other illuminating interpretations of the lesson concerned? After all, one interpreter might not attach significance to pupil control of learning, the latter itself capable of being understood in a number of ways. Accordingly she will judge goal clarity differently from an interpreter who attached a greater significance to pupil control. Arguably, for a rich picture of the lesson, we need to take account of a range of verdicts. Each verdict highlights facets of the lesson related to each other in different ways. Some or all of these perspectives may be illuminating. These verdicts may well not cohere with each other. Insisting on consistency here would come at a cost. And on what grounds might one particular interpretation be chosen to be *the* story of the lesson, rather than others?

The argument so far runs as follows: the categories to which teaching approaches belong reflect collective intentionalities and constitutive rules on the part of the societies in which these approaches are implemented. Classifications of social phenomena, and of teaching interventions in particular, involve matters of interpretation. Hence, one key requirement for robust empirical research into their effectiveness can be difficult to meet. The said requirement is the *certainty* that different observers can reach reasonably consistent verdicts concerning the appropriate applications of the classifications concerned. Indeed, given that interpretation is at the heart of such verdicts, it can be argued that the *certainty* of consistent verdicts *should* be ruled out.

Critics of scientism in educational research sometimes talk of the value of 'holistic' perspectives on complex social situations, claiming that these perspectives illustrate the gulf between research appropriate here and that applicable in the natural sciences. I now illustrate an aspect of this 'holism' that seems to underlie both the 'clarity of teachers' goals' and 'pace' examples above. In recent decades there has been much discussion of a position in meta-ethics known as 'moral particularism'. It opposes a certain kind of consistency in moral judgements. Such consistency would be exemplified by moral rules like 'taking the property of others is wrong', 'causing suffering is wrong' or 'telling lies is wrong'. Any action featuring removal of someone else's property is wrong, every single action that causes suffering is wrong, and so on. Verdicts will be simple and consistent.

To explain the challenge to consistency and to defend a holistic approach, we again need examples. It would usually be assumed that bringing about pleasure would always count in favour of the goodness of an action, even though we might not support a crude rule to the effect that if an action brings about pleasure it *must* be good. However, the moral particularist (I draw on Dancy 2000) cites instances such as the following: Consider a case where something I do means that people can watch hangings and they get pleasure from doing so. Then, it might be argued, my action is morally worse than it would have been had the pleasure not resulted. Pleasure *and* the witnessing of hanging combine to count against moral goodness in a fashion that is far from straightforwardly additive.

Accordingly, when we are interpreting complex social phenomena, our judgements similarly may be non 'additive'. The constitutive conventions that govern the nature of such phenomena interrelate with each other in ways that cannot be computed definitively in advance. The 'pace' and 'clarity' examples discussed earlier appear to illustrate features of just this kind.

These particularist insights relate to the challenges of interpreting text studied by hermeneutics. Of these, Taylor (1979) observes:

> We are trying to establish a reading for the whole text, and for this we appeal to readings of its partial expressions; and yet because we are dealing with meaning, with making sense, where expressions only make sense or not in relation to others, the readings of partial expressions depend on those of others, and ultimately of the whole. (p. 28)

If 'reading' a social phenomenon such as a teaching activity can appropriately be compared to reading a text, we can appreciate yet again how it might be that no sense can be attached to the claim that just one interpretation is 'correct'. Several interpretations, not all of which are obviously consistent with each other, may have some degree of legitimacy.

At this point, I need to give serious consideration to what may seem to be an obvious objection. Is confidence that we can reach reasonably consistent verdicts really so misplaced? Have I exaggerated the difficulties here? After all, when investigating the effectiveness of a given teaching method, we could train observers to be consistent, or so it might be argued. In any one culture, at any one time, constitutive rules and collective intentionalities may be perfectly stable. Surely, unambiguous teaching classification criteria that reflected these rules and intentionalities could be framed. Observers could be schooled in their application. If teaching method classifications succeed in reflecting the collective intentions of the social groups within which the methods are implemented, then it is perfectly possible for researchers to ensure that these intentions are clarified and classification consensus achieved.

Yet such careful crafting of the classification seems to set it at some distance from the rich and *inherently interpretable* character of the social phenomena concerned. The alleged story is that the phenomena can now be 'read' in just one way. However, the true story here is that we have lost sight of the phenomena altogether. In this thought experiment, criteria now determine 'correctness' in the classification of a teaching episode. So why are *these* the 'correct' set? What counts as correctness here, and why? If the criteria fit a particular culture's intentions at a particular time, what makes them so salient? Why might it be supposed that *all* the teaching conforming to a classification according to *these* criteria embodies features worth subjecting to empirical research, rather than an alternative set? Unless the choice of particular criteria can be supported with suitable justification, the move to produce them appears to introduce an element of 'mere' construction into the taxonomy. The very possibility of such justification seems to be ruled out by the fact that at least *some* possible criteria other than those featured in our thought experiment seem just as legitimate as those that made it to the starting line. This in turn undermines any sense that a method identity could be appropriately achieved by implementing 'top-down' unambiguous criteria.

3

Describing Teaching: The General and The Specific

In this chapter, I continue to develop an argument that unambiguous criteria for classifying methods would often be incompatible with teaching per se as opposed to other activities, valuable or otherwise, that adults might carry out in classrooms. This argument will be completed by the end of Chapter 4. Our attention now turns to issues connected with how specific or general we are in our descriptions of the teaching methods that we might seek to research.

The term 'method' immediately presents our understanding with some challenges. What is its relationship to a 'practice', for example? I ask this partly because of the ubiquity of phrases such as 'evidence-based practice' and 'evidence-informed practice'. In the UK, determining just how these phrases will be interpreted can be high stakes indeed. Ofsted are now going out of their way to claim that during school inspections there are no expectations that any particular 'style' of teaching will be favoured. I mentioned earlier that Sean Harford, HMI, Ofsted's National Director, Education, has recently distinguished between a teaching style on the one hand, and Synthetic Phonics as a body of knowledge on the other. It is difficult to predict whether such observations will begin to change the culture, and to distance what is expected of schools from the recommendations of the Rose Report.

Classification of teaching: The general

Before tackling those very special complexities associated with early reading and phonics, consider some *very* broad ways of describing teaching. It is now fashionable to extol the virtues of 'Direct Instruction', and to claim that empirical research often supports this teaching style, as opposed to those methods associated for many decades with 'progressive' and 'child-centred' education. Unsurprisingly, characterizations of Direct Instruction vary, and are open to interpretation. Consider one from Cook, Holland and Slemrod (2014). Their version is fairly typical of what is on offer about Direct Instruction at the time of writing: 'Lesson objectives that are clear and communicated in language students are able to understand ... . An instructional sequence that begins with a description of the skill to be learned, followed by modeling of examples and non-examples of the skill ... shared practice ... and independent demonstration of the skill ... . *Instructional activities that are differentiated and matched to students' skill levels to the maximum extent practicable* (my italics) Choral response methods in which all students respond in unison to strategic teacher-delivered questions' (p. 202).

Needless to say, some of this is open to interpretation. (This is not a criticism of the authors. *Of course it is open to interpretation!*) What does 'clear' mean? The phrase 'language students are able to understand' implies that the clarity concerned relates to how the students receive the instruction. So does it mean 'clear' to *all* the students? How does the teacher know what they can 'understand'? Is the teacher making a very general judgement about what pupils of that age and stage are likely to understand? Or are her decisions about the nature of her instruction drawing on some kind of assessment of this particular group of students? Or some combination?

There are a variety of possible (and, arguably, legitimate) answers to all these questions, depending in part, of course on what counts as understanding and what would be regarded as appropriate ways of detecting it. In any case, not all Direct Instruction lessons will begin with a skill description, since some Direct Instruction lessons will not concern skills, even if many will. (The distinction between skills and other possible learning outcomes may itself be contested, and afford tricky border line cases, but I am going to sidestep such debates here.)

Some versions of Direct Instruction are more extreme. Take (Flores and Ganz 2009), for instance:

> The researchers implemented instructional procedures and instructor behaviors as directed in the instructor's manual. These procedures and behaviors consisted of: (a) following the given script; (b) choral student responses; (c) the use of a clear signal to elicit student responses; (d) correction procedures for incorrect responses or responses that were not in unison; and (e) modelling skills, guiding students by responding with them, and asking students to respond independently (42).

This may seem to be less open to interpretation than the first example. Yet 'modelling skills' could mean all kinds of different things, depending on the curriculum area, the age and stage of the pupils, and the variety of actions and activities the teacher might employ to 'model'. 'Modelling' how to solve a quadratic equation with thirteen-year-olds would surely have little in common with modelling the decoding of some simple pieces of text with five-year-olds, or how to make good use of metaphor and simile in creative writing with eleven-year-olds. Furthermore, as with the first example, 'skills' might not feature at all. A key question about this extreme version of Direct Instruction is whether it should be counted as teaching at all. I will pursue this point further later in the discussion.

Direct Instruction[1] is sometimes characterized as 'opposite' to Discovery Learning. In the former approach, teachers are usually described as teaching content 'directly', rather than creating contexts in which pupils are supported in discovering the material for themselves. For instance, a teacher can inform pupils that the internal angles of a triangle always add up to 180 degrees. I imagine that supporters of Direct Instruction would count this as a short and unambitious instance of their commodity. In an allegedly contrasting 'discovery' lesson, the teacher asks pupils to cut out triangles, to tear off their corners and then place them together to form a straight line. Pupils would need to try this for several cases, before 'seeing' that this result would be obtained for any triangle.

Of course, they would need to 'know' that the angle at a point on a straight line is equivalent to 180 degrees. This would have to be so, if the knowledge they acquire is to be equivalent to the learning they acquire as a result of successful 'Direct Instruction'.

(Incidentally, our imaginary scenario might be modified, so that the teacher declines to let pupils loose on scissors and papers, but demonstrates 'from the

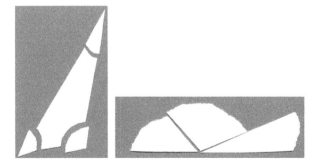

Figure 3.1 Tearing the corners off triangles

front' the process of tearing the corners from triangles and putting them together to form 'straight line angles'. Does *this* still count as Direct Instruction?)

We need to pause for breath for a moment. Just *how* might pupils come to know that a straight angle is equivalent to 180 degrees? Pupils could not possibly 'know' that without being told this directly. They could never discover it for themselves. The very nature of the relevant content rules this out. Measuring angles in degrees has a venerable history, but is, of course, a matter of human convention. It is not written somehow into the fabric of a platonic mathematical reality, awaiting human discovery.

Of course, when the teacher asks pupils to cut out triangles, they cannot do so unless they already know that 'triangle' is the appropriate label for shapes with certain properties. They also need to grasp an implication of this point, namely, that the word 'triangle' does not label an *image*.

The appearance of triangles varies. The term 'triangle' is defined in terms of certain properties of 2D plane shapes. Moreover, how 'triangle' is written and pronounced is a matter of convention. Again, pupils cannot discover this unaided. Nevertheless, there might be certain steps they could be encouraged to take that could enable them to 'realize' that 'triangle' is the label being applied to shapes with three straight sides and three corners. For instance, they could be shown a computer animation in which a pile of shapes were sorted into several sets. They could then be asked to look and see what was common to the shapes in one of these sets. If they were able to point out that all the shapes in that set had three straight sides and three corners, they could then be told that all of these were called triangles.

Such examples drive a coach and horses through a simple binary opposition between 'Direct Instruction' and 'Discovery Learning', and any claim that either of these approaches is capable of a simple and pure characterization. The devil is always in the detail.

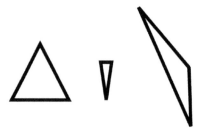

Figure 3.2 The appearance of triangles varies

Consider another mathematics example. Pupils, Year 6 or Year 7, perhaps, are shown one case of a triangle that can be formed on a 3 × 3 pin board, and then asked to investigate how many different triangles can be made on such a board. The students are told that corners of triangles must be pins and that no corners should be placed anywhere on the board other than on pins.

This instruction is, of course, deliberately ambiguous. The class is divided into groups, each of which is to work together, but independently of the others. Several pupils are likely to protest, early in their inquiries, that they have not been told by the teacher what 'different' is supposed to mean. The teacher can respond that they must agree together on a definition of the term, and then investigate accordingly. After a period of investigation, the teacher draws all the pupils together, and asks them to report back. It is probable that a range of answers to the original question will be offered, depending on whether, for instance, triangles in different positions or orientations on the board are counted as 'different', whether similar triangles are counted as different, and so on. ('Similar' triangles have identical angles but can come in different sizes.)

Triangles are *congruent* if they have exactly the same three sides and exactly the same three angles. One can be made to fit on the other, though rotation and reflection might be needed.

One obvious way in which the phrase 'different triangle' might be interpreted is as 'non-congruent triangle' (see illustration overleaf) yet there is nothing sacred about this particular account. The intended learning outcome here is a sophisticated one, namely that pupils begin to learn that mathematical 'truths' depend in part on the definitions given to the relevant terms and symbols.

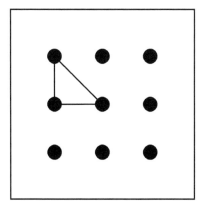

Figure 3.3 One example of a triangle on a 3 × 3 pin board

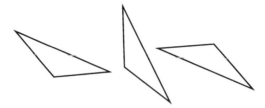

Figure 3.4 Three congruent triangles

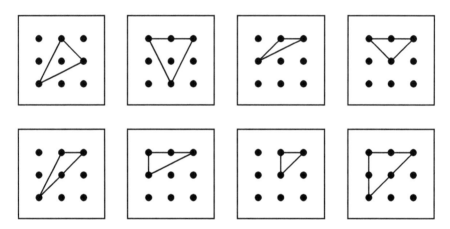

Figure 3.5 Eight non-congruent triangles on 3 × 3 pin boards

Now, the children need not be left to themselves to decide on the meaning of 'different'. The teacher could have explained the importance of establishing this meaning by talking through the pin-board investigation from the front. Even here, however, the detail could vary. The teacher could just tell the group directly about the situation. Or she might teach from the front, but interact with the pupils by for example, asking for views about possible meanings for 'different' in this context. On the face of it, then, there are a variety of possible lessons that might reasonably be referred to as cases of Direct Instruction.

To counter this inconvenient variety, could 'Direct Instruction' be *defined* as consisting of an adult simply saying things? This is a very broad characterization. As it stands, it is open to serious criticism, because it would include all sorts of examples that would be wholly inappropriate. Much more detail would need to be built in. In the face of difficulties in so doing, we might employ the expedient of looking instead at what is being ruled out. Among other things, Direct Instruction would obviously exclude teaching scenarios in which pupils are largely left to their own devices. Yet this move would not amount to any real progress. We would not have succeeded in capturing a 'method' that a teacher could decide to adopt or to reject on the basis of empirical research. It is far too all-embracing to constitute an approach that a teacher could possibly implement in a constructive fashion. Furthermore, at least *some* defenders of Direct Instruction are likely to regard the 'telling from the front' characterization as a crude caricature, and unworthy of further attention.

A defender of Direct Instruction might say at this point: 'Of course lessons exemplifying Direct Instruction vary. This is not news. We can easily define Direct Instruction. Many researchers have done just that, and produced respectable data as a result of their investigations.'

I am not sure *what* criterion for Direct Instruction our protagonist might have in mind when offering such an observation, but whatever it might be, let us suppose that it is framed at a significant level of generality in order to encompass at least some apparently legitimate variations. If a teacher wished to take seriously research demonstrating the effectiveness of Direct Instruction, she might be quite confused at this point. 'What can I draw from your research?' she might be forgiven for asking. 'You may be ruling some things out, but the sheer generality of your criterion leaves me with all the professional autonomy I had before I spoke to you. I continue to make decisions in the classroom, and your research gives me minimal guidance beyond the injunction that I should refrain from leaving the pupils alone to "do their own thing" right through the lesson. I do not think I needed your research to tell me that.'

If generality on the scale discussed above should be avoided, how can either of 'Direct Instruction' or 'Learning by Discovery' achieve a researchable identity? How might consistency in judgements about whether a teaching performance constitutes Direct Instruction or Learning by Discovery be achieved?

Describing teaching: The specific

Descriptions of 'Direct Instruction' and 'Discovery Learning' would normally cover various possibilities. It might be thought that we have artificially created for ourselves a 'method identity' problem by considering classifications of such generality and abstraction. Suppose, then, we resort to far more specific ways of classifying approaches. How far should the move in the direction of precision go?

An example of such precision in medicine might be 'point scalpel at an angle of 45 degrees. Insert x centimetres'. This, needless to say, is far too specific. It would be impossible, for instance, for empirical research to be carried out on the efficacy of precisely delineated scalpel moves. For patients would be likely to die during the research.

Medicine draws on biology and chemistry. The surgeon will be well-versed in these disciplines, among other things. Nevertheless, she will have professional autonomy over the detail of how to act when operating. She will have a repertoire of skills, knowledge and previous experience on which she will draw when deciding, for instance, precisely what to do with that scalpel from moment to moment. A Randomized Control Trial might establish, for instance, that it was a good idea to remove an appendix in certain conditions. That trial would go nowhere near establishing very precise rules about what the surgeon should do with that scalpel. Her informed professional autonomy concerning how to handle that tool is crucial. 'Removing the appendix' embraces a range of actions, depending on many factors. These include the health and age of the patient, the state of the appendix itself, how long the patient has been suffering from appendicitis and the patient's reactions to drugs, antibiotics and anaesthetics.

Recently I visited Iceland and took part in a walk on a vast glacier. Our small group was supplied with ice axes and crampons by a young instructor who guided us with great enthusiasm. Nevertheless, I attended carefully to what he said about how to travel on the ice. 'Walk with feet apart, except when going downhill.' 'If walking sideways along a slope, keep the foot on the downward side slightly pointing in that direction.' 'Don't use just part of the foot – ensure that you are using all the crampons as far as possible.' 'Don't bend forwards – and if going downhill and using a stick or ice axe for support, keep it a little behind you.' (Expert ice walkers may wish to dismiss this as amateurish nonsense. Please bear with me, because the precise details do not have to be 'correct' for the point I hope to make with this example.)

So I had, for good or ill, absorbed some fairly general principles that would improve my chances of surviving the glacier 'hike'. The principles were framed at a low level of specificity, on the assumption that I would exercise significant (and hopefully, intelligent) autonomy in how I applied them. While we followed the guide in single file (more or less), there were many moments when the character of the ice I was traversing diverged from that covered by the guide, or even the person immediately in front of me. My body and my habitual walking habits are to a degree idiosyncratic, even though there will have been much in common with others in the group. I wear glasses with varifocal lenses, and I suspect that what I saw sometimes differed from my fellow hikers (which is not to imply that they were all seeing the same things as each other either). Needless to say, the guide had no idea of all these idiosyncrasies, but he had no need to know given, as I say, that he took it for granted that I would make my own applications of his guidance. Certain things had been ruled out in advance – for instance, we would not have been allowed on the ice if we had medical conditions that were serious beyond a certain point. Nevertheless, we had considerable freedom of action. We did not behave exactly the same as each other in terms of how we used our feet, our crampons and our bodies more generally.

Freedom was essential for the guidelines to work. Our guide could not have offered more specific rules. As with the above scalpel example, over-prescription might increase the probability of death. We would have been unable to walk on the ice at all if attempting to follow very specific injunctions.

Compare the freedom needed here with that which a teacher should enjoy, even if seeking to follow guidelines closely. Teachers need more freedom than I had on the ice. Pupils make choices about responding to their teachers during exchanges, and also, if the teacher permits, about how to respond to fellow pupils. Teachers choose how, if at all, to react. Guidelines are of no use whatever to teachers unless offered at a level of generality that affords teachers significant scope to make decisions with students 'on the hoof'. Once we take account of these decisions, we begin to lose an identifiable approach whose success in promoting learning could possibly be supported by research evidence. There will be nothing that remotely corresponds with, say, the drugs that are legitimately and rigorously tested with randomized controlled trials. While the contexts for drug administration vary, the dosage, frequency and chemical constitution can be tightly specified and user agreement on this is readily attainable.

Imagine that a state Department of Health began to treat surgeons in the same way as, at the time of writing this, Nick Gibb treats primary teachers. Gibb 'knows' that Synthetic Phonics First and Fast is *the* way to teach early reading. Similarly, a health minister might claim to 'know' precisely how the scalpel should be wielded. Hence government might decide to put in place a 'scalpel effective use' check, to be taken by all would-be surgeons. Those failing the check might be obliged to retake it. Meanwhile, patients would continue to die.

Describing approaches to the teaching of reading

Turning now to early reading, consider some attempts to characterize 'Direct Instruction' in this area. Some are very precise indeed. Consider, for example Snel et al. 2012: 'The instruction is highly structured and describes or even scripts classroom activities in considerable detail. The emphasis is squarely on the systematic teaching of the written language code. Direct Instruction addresses both "what" to teach (i.e., the content of a curriculum) and "how" to teach (i.e., specific techniques)' (p. 356). A similar version can be found in Allor et al. (2014) who observe, in connection with the notion of 'Direct Instruction': 'Lessons are highly detailed to make instruction explicit' (p. 293).

Incidentally, some of those researching approaches to the teaching of reading have long been aware of the challenge posed by attempts to pin the methods down. For instance, Pinnell (1994) observes of:

> research-based rules for practice. These rules do not always apply within the complex environment of the classroom and do not provide teachers with the flexibility they need to make good judgments while teaching … handing down rules dangerously oversimplifies the process of making teaching decisions and does not account for the on-the-spot decisions that teachers need to make. (p. 10)

The desire for intervention identities is understandable, despite its incompatibility with teaching as a significantly interactive process. Cowen and Cartwright (2015) observe: 'Some commercial suppliers of reading and other policy packages insist that the package be implemented exactly as the supplier says. … Suppliers cannot be responsible for failure if their instructions are not followed. "The cake won't rise if you don't follow the recipe"' (p. 12).

Pinnell's sentiments are echoed by Bodmin, Taylor and Morris (2012), who add: 'The linear professional learning in SSP (Systematic Synthetic Phonics) has emphasised replicative and applicative types of knowledge' (p. 18). But Shulman (1999) observed: 'Education is not a science; it is a complex set of practices that is grounded and principled but not rule-governed.'

Biesta (2015) observes, 'When we make education less open, when we limit the possibilities for interpretation and when we guide the thinking of the actors in education in particular directions, the system will slowly begin to function in more patterned and predictable ways' (p. 16). I understand Biesta here as commenting ironically, in the sense that 'patterned and predictable ways' may be convenient for policymakers of a certain temper, but 'limiting the possibilities for interpretation' amounts to inflicting serious damage on education.

Let us now confront the challenge head on. What actually counts as a synthetic phonics teaching method? How general should the characterization be? How specific? There are 'principles', of course. At the beginning of the book, I quoted some of these, insofar as they are enshrined in the Programmes of Study, the government criteria for matched funding for phonics schemes, and the Rose Report. For expository convenience, I will now reproduce some of the principles as they are expressed in Ofsted's *Reading by Six* (2010). They are certainly from the same hymn sheet as my earlier sources.

> Present high-quality systematic, synthetic phonic work as the prime approach to decoding print, i.e. a phonics 'first and fast' approach.
>
> Be designed for the teaching of discrete, daily sessions progressing from simple to more complex knowledge and skills and covering the major grapheme-phoneme correspondences; Demonstrate that phonemes should be blended, in order, from left to right, 'all through the word' for reading Ensure that children apply phonic knowledge and skills as their first approach to reading and spelling, even if a word is not phonically regular.
>
> Ensure that as pupils move through the early stages of acquiring phonics, they are invited to practise by reading texts that are entirely decodable for them, so that they experience success and learn to rely on phonemic strategies. (p. 42)

But abstract principles such as these are open to a great variety of interpretations. That is not because they are badly expressed, or, in any fundamental sense ill defined. Nevertheless, they do not serve to specify a method that can be researched like a drug or a fertilizer. If they did, they would sideline a whole series of important questions that surely *ought* to be faced and acted on by teachers if seeking to follow such guidelines. Here are just some of these questions:

What exactly happens at the beginning of the systematic intensive teaching? Imagine that the three letter sequence 'sat' is being used with a group. Imagine further that one or more children immediately recognize 'sat' as a whole shape and can say it. Or instead, perhaps a child has blended it once, and then encounters it again, recognizing it immediately. There are, presumably, a variety of pedagogically sensible things that the teacher might do in this situation, depending on the context, the immediate teaching and learning history, what the teacher knows about the children who are able to offer a sensible pronunciation of a letter sequence when glancing at it as a whole, and so on.

Similarly, we can contemplate what teachers might do when there are a range of accents in the class, or when some or even all of the pupils' accents differ from that of the teacher's. Aitken and Beardmore (2015) discuss the case of a Year 1 child who reads to her parents in a different accent from the one she normally uses in speech. The child explains that she needs a reading voice and a voice with which she can talk at home. We can think of a range of class scenarios in which this situation might arise, and a variety of appropriate strategies on the part of the teacher, depending on the child's maturity, sophistication and a whole range of other factors.

Suppose one or more children can read on arriving at school, and can even read silently. Perhaps they now find the demand to sound out and blend, those steps deemed part of the normal progress towards reading aloud, a real challenge. This might be a cognitive issue. Or it might be that the child is shy, self-conscious and, in a sense, worried about already being able to read. By way of contrast, another advanced early reader who already reads silently might feel that 'school reading' (that she has rapidly learnt to think of as reading out loud) is somehow more 'grownup' and 'important', so she tries to repress her tendencies to read text silently. What is the appropriate response here from the teacher? Should she reassure the pupil, and allow her to be excused at least temporarily from any kind of teaching where she would be required to read aloud? Or rather, should she try to explain to the pupil that reading silently really is the most grownup and mature way of reading, and that the reading aloud phase is a stage on the way. The pupil might need to be helped to grasp that 'school reading' is not the ultimate goal at all. Such an attempt at explanation is unlikely to succeed with some young children. The teacher will have to make a judgement based on her knowledge of the personality of the child concerned. There is, surely, no *rule* about what ought to be done here. We must not, as Pinnell 1994 rightly argues, dangerously oversimplify the process of making teaching decisions.

At a different stage in a reading lesson, the teacher may be explaining the relation between the results of blending on the one hand, and reading actual words (where reading is understood as *extracting the meaning from text)* on the other hand. There would be a difference between blending the letters of a piece of text presented in isolation and blending the letters of a piece of text which occurred in the middle of a meaningful sentence. The teacher will be making decisions (or so it is to be hoped, rather than following some kind of peculiar rule) about what to do with children who have significant experience of sharing books with parents on arrival at school, recognize a number of whole words and are intelligent about working out the meaning of text from verbal and pictorial contexts. Ellis and Moss (2014) observe:

> Wyse (2010) suggests that how phonics knowledge is presented and contextualised in conversations between pupils and teachers may make a significant difference to how children use phonics in their reading. Fine theoretical distinctions are quickly lost in the classroom where a responsive teacher spontaneously

elaborates on children's conversational observations. A teacher slips from synthetic to analytic teaching as soon as he/she makes a sensible response to a child's observation that 'some words rhyme but don't sound like they are spelled' or that 'some words should rhyme but don't'. (p. 252)

Wyse makes an important point, though my reservation about his wording is that it may appear to suppose a clear distinction between 'synthetic' and 'analytic' phonics teaching. However, *we* decide to place some teaching approaches in one category called 'synthetic phonics programmes', and other teaching approaches in a category called 'analytic phonics programmes'. Our labelling decisions are *our* decisions to interpret the cases concerned in a particular way. Distinctions between 'synthetic', 'analytic', 'systematic' and other versions of phonics are difficult to draw, to put it mildly. Wyse and Goswami (2008), in their commentary on Rose's (2006) recommendation that Synthetic Phonics should be adopted, note the 'common ground' between Synthetic Phonics and Systematic Phonics as represented by Rose: 'namely learning grapheme-phoneme correspondences, and learning to blend and segment' (p. 694). Wyse and Goswami criticize the Clackmannanshire Study (Johnston and Watson 2004) for the way it purports to compare Analytic and Synthetic Phonics. Johnston and Watson define Analytic Phonics as 'children [learning] letter sounds in the context of words that they have been taught to recognize by sight' (p. 329). As against their definition here, I would have thought that the stipulation that pupils must recognize words by sight is unnecessarily strong. A weaker requirement, namely that pupils *look* at the textual representations of whole words and that they should be helped to analyse why they are written as they are, seems a reasonable representation of Analytic Phonics.

Would any approach worthy of the classification 'Synthetic Phonics' need to exclude the possibility that the pupils recognized *any* of the texts they were supposed to be sounding out and blending as representations of words with which they were familiar? Analytic Phonics, according to Wyse and Goswami (p. 701), is regarded as going from whole to part, while Synthetic Phonics goes from part to whole. I would argue that, both in practice and in theory these processes are impossible to keep independent from each other. It is scarcely surprising, therefore, that empirical research fails to show that any one 'method' has a significant advantage over another.

To reiterate once again one of the main themes of this book, if the teacher simply ignores the properties of her pupils, one set of concerns about method identity are laid to rest. She could decide that *none* of the questions I set out above, as issues potentially encountered when operating according to the abstract principles, need addressing. She could, in theory, adopt a particular application of a precisely specified script, transmitted in the same way each time. Hence all the instances of her phonics teaching would have something in common – that is to say, the precise type of delivery in question.

Our descriptions of teacher actions can incorporate aspects of their consequences in terms of learning, or they can focus directly and exclusively on what the adult in the classroom actually does. In 'Gerald threw the cricket ball', we have an action description that concentrates largely on observable physical properties. Compare this with: 'Gerald clean-bowled the batsman.' Here we have another description that might be applied to Gerald's throwing action. This second description incorporates a consequence, together with aspects of the social world that are independent of what Gerald does with his arm, physically speaking. Gerald could have performed the 'same' ball-throwing action, but the bail might not have been knocked off (if, for instance, the wind had been stronger, thus altering the ball's flight). That is to say, his arm action could have been identical in terms of its physical characteristics, even had it lacked the property of clean-bowling the batsman.

Are there parallels between the cricket ball-throwing and, for instance, 'the teacher explained to her pupils how to decode a letter sequence?' The latter description of the teacher's action *could* be interpreted as incorporating the consequences for the pupils, namely that the teacher's message is communicated successfully. 'Explaining' would then be functioning as a success or achievement verb. The pupils come to grasp the decoding. So we would not say that the teacher 'explains' it if the pupils fail to grasp it.

But we need not use 'explain' in its success or achievement sense. If we were reluctant to build into the description anything about the consequences for the learners, we could say instead: 'The teacher attempted to explain to her pupils how to decode a letter sequence', thus leaving open whether the explanation is successful.

In principle, the teacher's performance could have possessed many of the same properties, whether or not any or all of the pupils acquired decoding skills. For the sake of argument, let us artificially simplify what the teacher might do, and think of it as the teacher saying some words to a child or to children. (In a realistic scenario, explaining decoding would be a complex interaction between teacher and pupils, but let us stay with the simplistic case for the moment.)

Various explanations for the learning failure might be envisaged. Here are just two possibilities. In the first, the pupils are distracted in a way that the teacher could not have anticipated by a sudden snow storm that they can easily see. In the second, the teacher, who is new, has been misinformed about previous work the children have done on decoding.

The most brilliant (and lucky) teacher is unlikely to install a specific decoding skill in all the pupils as a result of her actions in any one lesson. Even if she does, it can be difficult to tell, at least in the short term. Suppose we thought it possible to identify a research-based method of explaining decoding. Would teaching acts with certain properties be described as explaining decoding, regardless of the actual results in any particular lesson? That would fit with some of the more extreme characterizations of Direct Instruction noted earlier. There would need to be evidence that actions with certain properties (which they can possess whether or not particular performances of them actually bring about learning improvements in particular school contexts) will for the most part cause relevant learning improvements.

Do supporters of evidence-based methods wish them to be used, regardless of whether individual pupils are learning on any particular occasion? As we have seen, some strong versions of Direct Instruction seem to fit the bill. If so, it would follow that teachers should use the methods in question whether or not they *think* that all their pupils are learning at any given time. For even the most ardent supporter of the strongest 'Direct Instruction' version of a phonics method will not claim that it 'works' on every single occasion.

It is a very important issue. If approaches to explaining in the classroom are recommended as being informed by research of this kind, then the teacher cannot be held directly responsible for whether the children learn. She can only be called to account for whether she has used the research-informed method, namely the method which is believed by researchers to bring about more learning than alternative approaches *for the most part*.

Compare the situation with a fertilizer trial. We need a robust account of the chemical features of the particular fertilizer and crop or crops concerned. Just how much fertilizer to use per unit area can be precisely specified. It is true, of course that the contexts in which the fertilizer may be administered are likely to vary a good deal. The terrain will come in different shapes, sizes and aspects, with a range of soils and climates. There could be significant interactions between our fertilizer and at least some of these contextual features. Nevertheless, the fertilizer itself could be specified by means of certain essential properties. These would be like Hacking's 'indifferent kinds', and it would correspond to describing what the teacher must do in terms that are conceptually independent of any learning consequences. If we prescribe the activities of adults in the classroom in this way, we may well construct a procedure that can be subjected to stringent empirical research. However, the question arises as to whether we are now speaking of teaching at all, and, as I have already indicated, I will later tackle this issue head on.

Let us return to our attempts to pin down a synthetic phonics method. What is *essential* to it? If I am an Early Years teacher seeking to implement a synthetic phonics programme, what *must* I do? Ofsted's *Reading by Six* principles are reasonably clear and straightforward but, as we have seen, open to a range of interpretations. In search of a common essence for our synthetic phonics method, we may turn, in desperation, to what is definitely *not* considered desirable. It is fairly easy to glean from synthetic phonics adherents several specific approaches from which the teacher is expected to refrain. These include the following:

> Do not teach an initial sight vocabulary where learners are expected to memorise words as whole shapes. Do not teach or encourage guessing/predicting words from their shape, or from picture, context or initial letter cues (sometimes known as 'multi-cueing or a 'range of reading strategies').

These negatives are quite clear and informative. Yet a great variety of teaching approaches are compatible with these negatives. Surely, attempting to pin down a category of teaching approaches by specifying what teachers should *not* do, fails to identify a researchable method, let alone a method that the committed teacher might aspire to follow.

Some recent empirical research on the use of phonics in English schools in the last few years (Machin, McNally and Viarengo 2016) provides a splendid case study of the teaching methods identification problem. It was hailed both by phonics proponents and by their opponents as providing support for each of their positions, and it is instructive to see why this happened. The researchers refer to the effect of a new 'teaching technology', calling it Synthetic Phonics. The latter method is characterized as involving 'learning to pronounce the sounds (phonemes) associated with letters "in isolation". These individual sounds, once learnt, are then blended together (synthesized) to form words' (p. 6). (I believe that their use of 'phoneme' here is unhelpful, and later I explore this issue in some depth).

They exploit what they see as some recent history of the effects of 'intensive support' provided for some primary schools after policy about teaching reading was given a strong steer in the synthetics phonics direction from the mid-2000s onwards. They report confidently that there are no average effects on children across the board, once they have reached the age of eleven. At the same time, they claim that the synthetics phonics approach *did* have long-term effects on those pupils who were struggling to learn to read early in their time at school. They sketch their version of some recent history of the debates about how to teach reading, in which they offer very broad-brush outlines of different approaches. For instance, 'Whole Language' is described as 'being introduced to language through context (e.g. through stories, picture books, etc.)' (p. 2). Their characterization of phonics is that it is 'a more systematic method of teaching how spelling patterns correspond to sounds' (p. 2).

The 'intensive training', the effects of which they investigate, involves literacy consultants working directly with schools and also helping Local Authorities with training opportunities to 'disseminate best practice' (p. 7). Direct support to schools provided by the consultants included modelling or co-teaching, together with helping the school-based teachers to 'plan further learning and teaching opportunities over the following few weeks' (p. 7).

They conclude that the intensive training in the use of a new pedagogy has effects, and that these cannot simply be the results of the active involvement of the literacy consultant because the effects persisted long after the consultants had left the schools concerned. However, what we lack here is anything approaching blow-by-blow accounts of *what actually happened* in the classrooms concerned. So the actual causes of the observed effects are wide open to interpretation. For example, the consultants might have affected the schools in terms of a long-term focus that involved increased energy and motivation on the part of those teachers who were particularly concerned with early reading. This energy may be broadly spread, and not specifically related to phonics teaching of any kind.

Despite the comments I have just made, it might be thought that the modelling and co-teaching *might* have resulted in something approaching a homogeneous approach to Synthetic Phonics on the part of the teachers. That is perfectly true. Yet we are left to guess here, and it is to be hoped that, if the teachers continued to teach, rather than following any kind of script bequeathed to them by the consultants, strong homogeneity in classroom practices did *not* actually result.

General problems with research into teaching and learning?

Do arguments against the very possibility of identifying specific teaching methods rule out the possibility of decent and valuable research into the teaching of reading? Even more worryingly, do they exclude the viability of research into teaching and learning more generally? For if they do, would this not constitute a reductio ad absurdum of my argument?

Naturally enough, I reject this possibility, and maintain that teachers can gain insights for their practice from a rich variety of educational research. In particular, carefully crafted narratives of Early Years teachers engaged with readers can surely be deeply illuminating. Students can learn from experienced teachers. We know they do, and they say they do. They might be deceived on occasion, but nevertheless, that teachers can learn from other teachers surely is an incontrovertible fact, observable across the world. Needless to say, teachers may be mistaken when they think they are passing on expertise to their young colleagues or students. When the latter claim to have learnt from veteran pedagogues, they may be deluded at times. Yet, or so I am going to assume, these mistakes are the exceptions. Often enough the relevant convictions and claims about learning from senior and experienced colleagues are well-founded and true. Surely, then, it must be possible somehow to characterize the kinds of things that can be learnt.

It may be possible, but it proves to be a challenge when attempted. Students have been known to model their behaviour quite literally on that of an experienced mentor. Doing this may well be wholly ineffective, and experience tells us that naïve modelling is simply not what we are looking for in this regard. For example, one of the problems with the National Numeracy and National Literacy Strategies in England was that they became 'high stakes' in an informal fashion. Their implementation was never statutory. Nevertheless, perceptions of Ofsted inspections were that, though schools were free not to implement the Strategies to the letter, if results were not up to standard then the absence of Strategy recommended 'methods' might be noted, to the schools' discredit. As a result of such perceptions, some schools and teachers were tempted to operationalize aspects of the strategies in such a way that they were able to follow them as a kind of script. When they did this, the teaching that resulted was not necessarily successful.

Teachers who are very concerned to please Ofsted, their Senior Management Teams or to conform to government educational policy might attempt to mirror what they take to be approved styles. Such copying might be very unhealthy for their own classroom practice. They might believe that they should mimic those regarded as experts, but such echoing could well be superficial and inappropriately literal-minded. The expert's approaches might well be 'working there', but have little hope of 'working here', that is to say, small chance of working in other teachers' classrooms and contexts.

Let us return to the possibility of research-based teaching methods. Consider educational research that might be carried out into whether pupils learn better when they are sitting in rows. Observers should be able to agree about whether pupils are doing that, so we apparently have a phenomenon with a clear identity that can be subjected to empirical research. Nevertheless, 'sitting in rows' can cover a great variety of phenomena, depending on just how questions including the following are answered. Are pupils facing the front throughout and not talking? Are they allowed to turn and speak to each other? How often? What kind of dialogue is being encouraged? Why? What is the context? How old are the pupils? What subject is being taught? What degree of interaction takes place between teacher and pupils? Is the learning concerned part of long-term conceptual development, or is it knowledge or skills that can be acquired within a lesson or so? Are pupils used to 'sitting in rows' or is this a departure from the usual arrangements? Do they 'sit in rows' with this particular teacher, but not with others?

Could advocates of research-informed teaching support the utility for teachers of a positive 'sitting in rows' piece of research? It shows, they might say, that *whatever* teachers are doing, and *whatever* the context, it is better to do it with the students sitting in rows than in some other seating configuration. Yet once we carry the sitting in rows thought experiment this far, its potential absurdities begin to surface. For there are obvious exceptions in the sense that certain kinds of lessons are impossible within such a restriction. Sessions drawing on the performing arts such as drama and music come to mind.

Teachers might find research of this type helpful. It does nothing to undermine their autonomy and might provide broad and uncontroversial pointers to how matters might be organized in school. Nevertheless, by its very nature, it fails *and should fail* to imply any kind of *very* detailed guidance on teaching approaches.

So, at first sight, it is understandable why some might be especially interested in research focusing directly and in some detail on what the teacher might do in the classroom, rather than on the very general 'effects' of readily countable or measurable aspects of context such as sitting in rows. Nevertheless, it may never have occurred to many of those enthusiastic for research into the detail of teaching methods that government might use the results as justification for prescribing teaching methods for *all* pupils in state schools. Judging research about the detail of classroom actions to have value, need not and should not amount to supporting a rigid imposition of the teaching methods it concerns.

Earlier, we saw that interpretations of 'methods' such as Synthetic Phonics, Direct Instruction and Learning by Discovery involve grasping complex interrelated sets of constitutive rules and related intentions about what is to count as membership of these categories. I think that Alexander (2008) writes about these points in his reflections on pedagogy, though he would not use the Searle language that I did here. He refers to Brian Simon's *Why No Pedagogy in England?* where he points out that the continental 'science of teaching' has no place in England. Yet since New Labour, 'what works' and 'compliance' have become key features of government policy. He criticizes Millet's narrow concerns with 'competence, excellence and failure in teaching methods' (p. 45), and contends that her definition fails to embrace how 'pedagogy connects with culture, social structure and human agency, and thus acquires educational *meaning*' (p. 46). In this context, I interpret 'culture' as including the above-mentioned 'complex interrelated sets of constitutive rules and related intentions'.

Oancea and Pring (2009) also note New Labour's concern with 'what works', referring to the growth of what was held to be evidence-based and informed practice in medicine and nursing. As regards education, analogous developments included the EPPI-Centre (Evidence for Policy and Practice Information) at the Institute of Education, London University. They claim that initiatives of this kind favour 'commensurable standards of scientificity across the natural and social sciences' (p. 16). (In my treatment of 'scientism' above, I explore the very serious problems with such views.) They point up an opposition between those who wish to make 'a science of educational research, hypothesizing the causes of events … seeking to generalize…' and, by way of contrast, others who highlight 'the fact that human beings are not like purely physical matter and cannot be understood or explained within such a positivist framework' (p. 23).

Let us return to Cartwright and Hardie (2012) and their guide to evidence-based policy on a characteristic assertion and an equally characteristic question: 'It worked there': 'Will it work here?' They remind us that the policy concerned will almost certainly be just part of a set of 'causes that work together' (p. 25). They also seem to be grappling with the problem of the identity of 'It' when they observe that, when we wonder whether the 'same treatment' will work here as it did there: 'Using the same treatment can be fine-so long as you have identified the right description for the treatment' (p. 46). We rarely will be dealing with attempts to 'do exactly the same thing in exactly the same way' (p. 146), but we may well seek to 'do something that is faithful to the higher level principle that was instantiated by the previous success' (p. 146), but then it *really matters* what is to happen in detail in the new case.

I have argued that researching teaching interventions differs significantly from trialling fertilizers. Cartwright and Hardie provide some indirect support for this line when they include a drug programme example in their discussion. They doubt that 'it worked there' '… will provide a very good drug program that can play a positive causal role almost everywhere' (p. 146). Their reference to Babor et al. (2010, p. 253) makes the points that societies vary in their patterns of drug use and the control measures in force, while there are 'variations … between the sexes, across races, and age groups, at different stages of a drug epidemic. There is as a result no single globally homogenous drug problem'.

Their treatment of what they call 'fidelity' considers another well-intentioned strategy called 'Fight for Peace'. This programme is intended to help young people in communities afflicted by criminal behaviour and violence. It combines education with aspects of martial arts. At an abstract level, its aims are common to the locations in which it is implemented. Cartwright and Hardie compare its workings in Rio and East London. Unsurprisingly, they are able to identify a large number of significant differences because of the disparate characters of the two contexts. For instance, the programme involved contact with parents, yet family structures differ in the two countries concerned and hence it is likely that 'what is meant by contact with parents is quite different' (p. 149). Furthermore, the intervention was addressing homelessness in London, but not in Rio. The programme worked in Rio, so it seemed reasonable to hope that it would also work in London. Yet the features actually playing a causal role in any possible success look significantly different in London from those operating in Rio.

Reading Recovery – a case study

Some examples of empirical research purport to pit one teaching 'method' against another. Towards the end of the last century, some claimed to have evidence that 'Reading Recovery' was an effective approach. More recently, the opposite trend may be discerned (e.g. Tunmer et al. 2013). The results of studies still conflict with each other, however. For instance, Holliman and Hurry (2013) report positively about the long-term effects of RR programmes. Another piece of research (May, Sirinides and Gray 2015), describing itself as involving a large-scale Randomized Controlled Trial, is also very positive about RR.

These bewilderingly disparate results arise in part, I contend, because of the principled difficulties facing at least *some* attempts to categorize teaching approaches in a way that could command agreement between different observers. Another reason is that RR really should not be described as a 'method' at all. I will say more about this shortly. In any case, RR is designed to support struggling readers, so even if it were appropriately characterized as a 'method', its effectiveness would need to be compared with, for instance, Systematic Synthetic Phonics for struggling readers. (I am not saying that no research does this.)

Tunmer et al. (2013) describe RR as 'constructivist', as supporting multi-cuing and/or the Searchlights method and as playing down the role of phonics. We have seen that for a debate about the evidence for one method as opposed to another, a robust identity for each method needs to be established.

The first problem with Tunmer's characterization is the use of the term 'constructivist'. It can refer both to styles of pedagogy and to fundamental epistemological accounts of the growth of knowledge. At this point, we can only note the broad-brush character (or possibly caricature) of positions regarded as ineffective. The second problem is that it runs together (alleged) accounts of what reading 'is', descriptions of what readers need to know, and how reading should be taught. Tunmer et al. attribute to RR adherents the view that

> skilled reading is a process in which minimal word-level information is used to confirm predictions about the upcoming words of text based on multiple sources of information (Clay, 1991). Learning to read is seen largely as a process in which children learn to use multiple cues in identifying words in text. Text-based cues (i.e., picture cues, sentence context cues, preceding passage context, prior knowledge activated by the text) are used by students to predict the text yet to be encountered. Letter-sound information is generally used only to confirm word predictions. (p. iv)

This tells us Tunmer's version of what RR thinks reading actually *is,* but also, by implication, offers his account of how RR proponents think reading should be taught. Taking Tunmer's descriptions of RR on trust (which may not be a terribly good idea), it is far from clear that we have a clearly identifiable method, whether we are thinking in terms of teaching, or even about the strategies students are being encouraged to develop. The use of various cues is quite explicitly flexible. At a given time, one student might be encouraged to make strong use of phonics and rather less of semantic or grammatical context, while another is steered in the opposite direction. The teacher will make decisions based on careful observation of student responses. Moreover, over a period of time, a given student may well be supported in varying the kind of approach she brings to her encounters with text.

It is well worth attending to Marie Clay's own description (1991) of all this: 'Teachers … learned to take running records of text reading … observed and recorded exactly what the children were doing... . This ... guides the teacher in designing a program for that particular child' (p. 360). Given that RR can be found in many countries throughout the world, practices are likely to vary. Anecdotally, many current RR teachers tell me that they do indeed support the flexible use of cues.

Designing a programme for a particular child cannot readily be identified with a researchable 'method'. Yet some opponents of RR explicitly characterize it as a method, and indeed, a method that should have been subjected to rigorous Randomized Control Trials but has not. Note, for instance the title of this chapter, written by authors to whom we have already referred (Chapman, Greaney and Tunmer 2015): *Is Reading Recovery an Effective Early Literacy Intervention Programme for Children Who Most Need Literacy Supports?*

Tunmer et al. (2013) tell us that the 'scientific community' has pronounced that 'a large body of research shows that explicit, systematic attention to alphabetic coding skills in early reading instruction is more effective'. It should be noted that their phrase 'systematic attention' does not of itself obviously specify a teaching approach. Indeed, it could be interpreted as focusing more on knowledge than pedagogy.

Tunmer et al. (2013) also observe that research 'indicates that for progress to occur in learning to read, the beginning reader must acquire the ability to translate letters and letter patterns into phonological forms'. Assuming for a moment, just for the sake of argument, that they are right about this, it does not of itself settle the most appropriate ways in which pupils should be helped to acquire this 'ability' and it leaves open the possibility that there might be a range of good ways of doing just that.

In yet another revealing comment, Tunmer et al. say: 'The programme is beneficial for some struggling readers but not others.' A current paper reporting large-scale empirical research on RR seems to agree: 'While prior research on RR shows that the program's impacts on student achievement are often large, research also suggests that there is substantial variability in impacts, and that much of this can be attributed to variation in program implementation' (May, Sirinides and Gray 2015).

Since 'the programme' is not any kind of script written in great detail and followed by all teachers, this is not only unsurprising, but also needed no empirical research to discover it. Teachers will vary the extent to which they encourage one cue over another, depending on their judgements about the individuals or groups they are teaching. Pupil 'needs' and developmental journeys also vary one from another. 'Struggling readers' is a label tied to symptoms, giving no indication of the possibility that the cause of one reader's struggle might easily be quite different from the cause of another's.

Given that, as I say, we are not dealing with a script here, but with the results of teacher judgements, another possible explanation for empirical research providing conflicting messages about the effectiveness of RR is this: one of the factors being 'measured' (if any) by the relevant research is *the quality of teacher judgements* about how to approach each young reader. Teachers make decisions about the repertoire of cues to foster in any one pupil. Some teachers will do this 'better' than others. So, researchers seeking to compare teaching approaches may sometimes be tapping into teacher quality, rather than into the effectiveness of a teaching method. I am, of course, merely speculating here.

A different kind of educational debate may also be informing controversy over RR. We have already referred to it. On the one hand, we have those who seek provision to be 'good enough', this being established by empirical research and being unashamedly 'teacher proof'. Let us have, they will say, 'good enough' classroom delivery, and let us *not* leave any scope for teacher judgement. On the other hand, we have a group who would never countenance teacher autonomy being sidelined, and who would prefer schooling to be enhanced by concentrating on the education and professional development of teachers themselves.

A decision favouring the imposition of teacher-proof approaches reflects, among other things, a destructive pessimism about the quality of teachers and about the possibility of enhancing it with proper support and resources. I note in passing that some well-known synthetic phonics proponents are explicit about recommending that teachers should not be 'trusted' to make appropriate decisions. Our phonics enthusiasts sometimes distort the argument by implying that to trust would automatically be to trust *blindly*. Yet there is no incompatibility between trusting a professional, and exposing them to an appropriately rigorous form of accountability. It is beyond the scope of this book to discuss appropriate forms of accountability. The latter certainly should not involve high stakes tests, let alone the English Phonics 'Check'.

There is an assumption that those favouring RR are inclined to support 'whole language approaches'. This may or may not be true in all cases, and, in any case, is subject to the 'method identity' problem. A 'whole language' approach in the hands of an adult engaged in interactive teaching is no more of a tight script than synthetic phonics methods should be. Furthermore, even a 'whole language fundamentalist' will find it very difficult in practice when working with young readers to eschew all clues available from letter–sound links. For example, some pupils will notice onset-rhyme patterns by themselves, despite the 'best' efforts by their teachers.

Can RR approaches be said to amount to a *moral* perspective on how early reading should be tackled, rather than a 'method'? Is it, at least in part, about how we ought to treat struggling young readers? Of course, we now have to ask from whence the 'ought' here might derive. How would this 'ought' be justified?

Such a justification might be derived from the contribution of reading to human flourishing, and, arguably, cannot arise exclusively from any kind of empirical evidence base. Similarly, we cannot draw on empirical evidence alone to postulate that it is a good idea to show children that they are loved, and that cruelty to children is wrong.

The opposite of an ethical approach like RR would be the 'effective delivery' stance. Teachers could, as we have seen, adopt a teacher-proof script, and deliver it without regard for pupil responses that arise from varying levels of knowledge, understanding and motivation. When I talk of 'varying levels', I do not mean only that pupils vary one from another, but also that any one pupil's progress over time can be idiosyncratic. The mix of cues that are helpful at a given time for a given child can change over time. At time t, a strong emphasis on phonics may be effective for that child. At time t+1 a stronger focus on context and comprehension comes into play, while for another pupil the opposite may be the case (see, for example, Schwartz and Gallant 2011).

Reflections on the moral character of RR take us back to moral concerns about 'effective delivery'. Such practices, in their extreme forms, would overlook any one child as an individual person, with a unique value and specific levels of cognition and motivation that may not precisely resemble those possessed by any of her peers. When in receipt of a delivered package, children lose their status as individuals, and become something to be processed in the most effective manner.

'Proven' methods justifying universal imposition?

So could a justification for RR make reference to the idea of respecting persons, the intrinsic worth of each individual, and the associated thought that every person has a set of inalienable rights? In liberal theory such as that advanced by John Rawls, 'each person is to have an equal right to the most extensive basic liberty compatible with a similar liberty for others'. His list of 'basic liberties' includes the political liberty to vote and run for office, freedom of speech and assembly, liberty of conscience, freedom of personal property and freedom from arbitrary arrest. There are no explicit references to education here. Yet, in the modern world at least, several of these basic liberties cannot be exercised by an individual unless they learn to read. Hence, or so it might be argued, we can add to the list of basic liberties the right to learn to read, or perhaps, more cautiously, the right of each child to expect teachers and schools to do their very best to ensure that this happens.

I have to say that this line of argument has no prospect of an easy ride. For proponents of effective teaching methods *also* speak of a social justice agenda, whose aims would include maximizing the chances of *all* children to learn to read because 'every child matters'. Advocates of the 'methods that work' might claim that they were just as much on the moral high ground as RR specialists.

Over and above the idea that broadly speaking, RR approaches have a moral status, an additional justification could appeal to the point that new knowledge must, in principle, be properly linked and connected to existing knowledge for learning proper to occur. It is that existing knowledge of each child that RR concentrates on discovering in order to develop individually tailored programmes. The next chapter on constructivism explores the essential links between new and existing knowledge in some depth.

Early in the book, I made a comparison between being required to teach in a certain way and the meta-ethical doctrine known as rule-utilitarianism. The latter holds that an action is right if it conforms to a rule that performing actions of that kind would in general maximize preferences and/or minimize painful results. So a rule utilitarian may choose to act in a certain way, even where she holds that the *particular* action she is about to perform would not maximize preferences and/or minimize pain.

Those holding that there is clear evidence for the effectiveness of Systematic Synthetic Phonics might feel that Early Years teachers should approach their own teaching of reading as educational rule utilitarians, so to speak. On this rigid perspective, teachers should constantly have in mind the 'rule' that teaching reading according to the precepts of Systematic Synthetic Phonics maximizes good reading consequences for most pupils. These teachers should bypass their own reservations in particular cases. Examples of reservations might include a reception child who can already read on starting school or another child who does not seem to be responding to phonics but the teacher suspects might well be amenable to phonics in a year's time. Reservations of these kinds should be ignored and teachers should implement the 'first and fast' phonics programme for all their pupils, because following this rule maximizes reading progress for most pupils.

Davis (1999) recalled Hare's reflections about moral thinking, where Hare spoke of two contrasting views of morality. Hare called these the perspectives of the 'archangel' and of the 'prole'. The intuitive moral thinker is sensibly brought up to adhere to general maxims concerning what makes an action right or wrong. Hare thinks that these maxims will sometimes be in tension with each other, and can even conflict directly. So, in a second level of thinking, the role of the archangel is required. Here, critical moral thinking takes the agent beyond the level of general intuitive maxims. Sophisticated moral deliberations are informed by the complexities afforded by particular contexts, and enable the moral agent to make specific decisions about what should be done in these situations.

Teachers required to deliver first and fast Synthetic Phonics to all their pupils are being expected to limit their professional thinking and actions to those of the 'prole'. The trouble is that no one is being allowed to inhabit the 'archangel' perspective. Perhaps policymakers at the DfE or their equivalent have the opportunity to do so, but they have decided not to. The 'archangel' mode of thinking looks close to what some would feel must be a fundamental element in teachers' professional autonomy. Autonomous teachers will constantly have in mind precepts concerning what 'works' for the most part. Yet these maxims will be complex, hedged about with innumerable exceptions and will never be followed in a way that sidesteps the rich detail of particular pupils' cognitive and motivational states. Moreover, there will usually be a multitude of these precepts that might be applied in any one situation. It will often not be possible to follow them all, and the autonomous teacher has to weigh them against each other.

I suggest that there is an instability in the position of the 'prole' in Hare's discussion, though I acknowledge that my suggestion amounts to a piece of empirical speculation. Our 'prole' can only be counted on to continue occupying this restricted perspective so long as she is largely or wholly unaware of her position. Once she realizes what she is doing, or rather, what she is not doing, she may well be tempted to fall into the mindset of the archangel. Suppose a teacher to be trained into believing that there is an effective method for teaching reading and that she need trouble herself no further about it, over and above offering it in the classroom and using the best possible resources. She now may continue in this mode undisturbed for an indefinite period of time. However, if, for whatever reason, she comes to appreciate the limitations in her pedagogy, she may slip into the role of the archangel and seek to exercise some professional autonomy. If, when this occurs, she sees that the state is unwilling for her to adopt the archangel mode, she might well feel that her very integrity as a teacher is under threat.

In England, if you dial 111, you are connected to an arm of the National Health Service that deals with non-emergency medical problems. You describe your symptoms, and then your contact takes you through a long series of questions, most of which may well not seem relevant to your problem. You are required to answer all the questions. No flexibility is permitted. Presumably, research indicates that this approach is the most effective way of handling calls, in terms of its promotion of the health of the patients concerned. I also assume that this way of handling matters allows the employment of National Health Service personnel who do not need to be very highly qualified in medicine. Were flexibility permitted, these people would require a higher level of expertise to respond to patients. They cannot fall into the mindset of the archangel, since they lack the capacity. The role of a classroom teacher, at least up to the time of writing, is not and should not parallel that of those staffing 111 calls. The argument of this book is that there cannot and should not be a series of teaching recipes that would be equivalent to the 111 series of medical questions.

Suppose, just for the sake of argument, that we could identify a teaching intervention. Imagine that we could sidestep all those interpretation complexities and those formidable challenges involved in classifying the intervention appropriately and consistently. Finally, assume that we could offer robust empirical support for it.

This, taken alone would not justify imposing it. We have already addressed this point in the discussion about phonics as a method, and phonics as essential knowledge content. I just want to add a few more comments. Consider a parallel line of thinking. Imagine, in an entirely fictional thought experiment, that we had research showing that refusing to smile at the children when teaching them about multiplication improved their mastery of this important mathematical idea. Perhaps this intervention might be explored in a statistically rigorous fashion, preferably in a Scottish district. An alternative intervention might be devised for comparison purposes. One of these alternatives might be a combination of smiling, frowning and ignoring. It could be dubbed the 'Searchface' approach, and on the basis of some empirical research, shown to be less effective than the smile-refusal method.

This, of course, would not settle the case for refusing to smile. There would be moral considerations here. These would relate, in particular to the relative sensitivities of different pupils. Some would not mind, or even notice. Others would be upset.

Someone on social media compared implementing a synthetic phonics programme with using a vaccine against the Ebola virus. Suppose the latter was shown to be pretty effective, but that it turned out that there were at least a few cases where patients recovered without having the treatment. This would not, it was argued, mean that the vaccine should not be rolled out universally. Now, in the case of most medical treatments, patient choice should inform how and whether the treatment is administered, even if it is not the only factor to take into consideration. This is a moral point. The problem with Ebola is that neglecting the most effective treatment, if one is actually available, may endanger the lives of others. In such a situation, patient choice would be weighed against the importance of the treatment and obviously would be found wanting. The situation with an effective method for the teaching of reading, even if we could make sense of such a method's 'identity' and had incontrovertible evidence for its effectiveness is, of course, completely different. It is true that the standard to which any one individual is educated does have *some* effect on the well-being and education of others. Nevertheless, this is far from the life or death consequences for others associated with refusing an Ebola vaccine.

There are usually moral considerations relating to implementing any given teaching intervention. In the case of Synthetic Phonics, these especially concern that small number who can already read for meaning on arrival at school and may also be reading silently. Children could be disadvantaged by a teacher insisting that they look at a piece of text, sound out the letters and blend these sounds together when they see no reason to have to do this. If succumbing to such demands, they may perform poorly because their reading is already beyond this stage.

At this point in the argument I often feel I have reached an infuriating stand-off with those opponents who simply insist that these children do not exist, or that they 'need' the phonics intervention anyway, or that even if they do exist, what is right for the majority must be enforced and it will not be the end of the world for that tiny number of advanced readers. I can only say that there *are* children for whom it is 'the end of the world' for a time, and insist that this possibility is easily avoided with a little common sense about how national policies are worded and held to apply in detail to classroom practice.

Moral concerns should sometimes be to the fore when teachers make decisions 'on the hoof' about what to do, in the face of children's motivational states and emotions. It is open to schools and teachers to plough on with lessons regardless of children's interest levels. It may be thought that some pupils will be interested, others will not and this is inevitable. However, to suggest that children's motivation levels are simply not relevant when pedagogical decisions are being made would surely be an extreme position to adopt. If they *are* relevant, then sometimes they ought to influence teachers' decisions. If this is the case, it is another kind of explanation for the fact that lessons implementing 'Synthetic Phonics' should come in a variety of versions, rather than in the form of researchable Direct Instruction packages.

Moral considerations are classically sidelined in some uses made of educational research. For example, homework may be advocated on the grounds that research proves that it enhances learning (actually, relevant research is distinctly ambiguous on this point, but we will leave that to one side, just for the sake of this argument). If we had research showing that homework promoted achievements in mathematics, certainly that would be something we would want to take seriously. However, it is not, and should not be the only consideration. What about the moral arguments in favour of children, especially younger children having a proportion of their day making their own choices about how to spend their time? Parents might wish to spend time with their children in ways that are not always structured and defined by school imperatives. Weighing these against improving learning is challenging, and I am not for a moment implying that learning considerations are not important. I just want to emphasize the point that research cannot and should not assume that there is just one agenda at issue. Very similar points can be made about research on the length of the school day, what age children should start school, or the value of promoting competition in school. The danger comes from research allied to a simplistic value vision, or to the sidelining of value questions altogether.

The Phonics Check: Attempting to impose pure Synthetic Phonics

The Phonics Check is one of the tools employed by government in England at the time of writing to force teachers (with very mixed success!) to teach reading along synthetic phonics lines, on the grounds that it is a method that is supported by 'scientific' evidence. Its defenders also point to the fact that it is supposed to be a 'check' rather than one of those nasty tests. It allegedly enables teachers to discover which pupils are still experiencing problems in decoding. Such problems must be caught as soon as possible and dealt with. Or so this argument runs.

This will strike many Early Years teachers as completely bizarre. They deal with their pupils' reading all the time. If a teacher could glean information from a few minutes with the check materials that she would otherwise have missed, this suggests that she should seek a different profession. The check 'words' are out of context. Teachers regularly monitor decoding skills as and when necessary while the pupil is tackling text *in context*. That context might consist entirely of readily decodable words, but could include other words that the teacher knows the pupil already recognizes. These are *real* reading situations, as opposed to the highly artificial and limited examples afforded by the check.

The Phonics Check claims to measure whether children can associate certain sounds with letters, and blend them together to produce a plausible result. As a matter of fact, it only assesses decoding by means of the twenty pseudo-words it contains.

It is also claimed that the check contains twenty 'real words'. What this actually means is that twenty isolated letter sequences are presented, chosen so that such sequences could, in principle, be the text versions of real words. For example, 'blow' might feature. Suppose, just for the sake of argument, that none of these isolated letter sequences are familiar to the child. In this situation, such items also assess what vocabulary the child understands on hearing it spoken. This is because if she does not know that there is no word associated with the sound made by 'blow' to rhyme with 'cow', she may offer that pronunciation in the check, and be marked incorrect. (Although this example is cited in the sample materials, it looks as though steps are normally taken to exclude such cases in the 'real words' section.)

In addition, the check may also, in effect, assess whether the child already recognizes some words represented on paper unless, that is, a whole range of possible examples are excluded. Suppose, for instance, that 'bind' were included as a 'real word'. This could be blended to produce something either rhyming with 'lined' or with 'tinned'. Now, if 'bind' were offered as a pseudo-word, either pronunciation would be allowed. However, in our little thought experiment here, it is marked as a real word. So only the rhyme with 'lined' would, presumably, be marked correct.

But spare a thought for the child who blends it to rhyme with 'tinned', and thinks she remembers her mum saying that she has 'binned' some broken toys. The child does not know how you write the word 'binned', and so fails to realize that 'bind' is not how you spell her mother's action. Our pupil cannot work out from any kind of context that the very possibility of 'binned' is ruled out, because there is no context.

Similar points can be made about 'grind' (the train of thought goes through 'grinned'). 'Bear' ought not to be included as a real word, because the child might blend the letters to make a sound that rhymes with 'here'. The sound resulting from the blend does, after all, link to the real word 'beer', and even 'bier'. She needs to know that neither of those real words are spelt 'bear' in order to supply the right blended sound in the check. 'Mild' should be excluded as a real word, because the child might blend the letters to rhyme with 'killed'. After all, 'milled' is a real word, and uses the very sound our child might produce. Similarly, please do not use 'pear', since if the sound offered rhymes with 'here' the child might believe that 'pear' was the right spelling for 'peer' or 'pier'. 'Fear' should be banned, since if the child blended the letters to rhyme with 'hair' (she is thinking of 'pear', perhaps), she might believe that 'fear' was the appropriate spelling for 'fair' or 'fare'. There must be many other cases.

What these examples show is that, unless the check devisors are very careful in what they exclude, not only is the check doing an incompetent job of assessing the extent of the child's spoken vocabulary and confidence, but it also, in effect, identifies whether they already know how certain real words are spelt. For it is the child who does not know 'grinned' by sight who might 'read' the real word 'grind' to create the same sound as that associated with 'grinned'.

At the end of June 2014, an Open Letter was sent to the DfE urging that the phonics screening check be abolished. A DfE letter dated 13 July responded. Among other things, it said: 'We certainly do not encourage schools to spend time in excessive preparation for the screening check.' Yet when replying in this fashion they knew perfectly well that some schools, at least would do just this. So why have the check in the first place? They responded: 'The check provides reassurance that children have grasped the basics of decoding using phonics.'

Now who on earth did they think needed this 'reassurance'? Early Years teachers certainly did not, and do not. If the check discovers anything useful, teachers can find such things out more effectively, as we have seen, during their everyday interactions. The implication that 'reassurance' is needed at a particular moment is worrying, since it implies that all children need to show that they have these 'basics' at a particular time. Yet why would that be? Many have pointed out that there is a close link between the ages of the children and their scores in the check. This is absurd, predictable and very unhelpful to teachers, their parents, and the children themselves. The government justification for the check was further elaborated. They said that it 'enables schools to benchmark their pupils' performance against national standards'.

The government might, for some reason, want to check up on decoding standards. This could be achieved by sampling pupil performances. There would be no need for a universal check. But why, in heavens name, would schools want to benchmark their pupils' performance against national standards? If they were keen to do so, would they be assuming that all children's reading progress is linear, that they all ought to progress in the same way and reach specific learning targets at the same time? Such assumptions would be unwarranted and destructive.

The government said that 'the purpose of the phonics check is simply to confirm whether individual pupils have learnt phonic decoding to an appropriate standard'. But who needs this 'confirming'? Why? It really does look as though they are trying to make all teachers teach all pupils in a particular way, regardless of what those teachers know of individual differences and needs.

The government defended the pseudo-words in the following way: 'They are included because they will be new to all pupils. ... Pupils who can decode non-words should have the skills to read most unfamiliar regular words.'

The check guidelines make it clear that where more than one legitimate pronunciation of a non-word is possible, any of these will count as correct responses from pupils. However, the non-words are apparently selected so that they do not usually admit of more than one pronunciation. All the same, the contrast with the so-called real words in the check is startling, especially given that it is for five-year-olds. Barring considerations of accent, real words have only one pronunciation. So, half the test has text where, at least in theory, more than one pronunciation is allowed, while the other half has the opposite. This is really peculiar, because when pupils are reading 'properly', in situations where letter–sound correspondences admit of more than one pronunciation, the context informs the reader of which word is at issue, and this information guides the final decision about how to pronounce the letter sequence. However, with the pseudo-word task, the child must blend, and *then stop*.

The pseudo-words section of the check constitutes a highly artificial set of decoding tasks. A selective set of letter combinations is offered. For instance (and I do not even know that this is true, though I assume it must be), pseudo-words whose decoded sounds have homophones that happen to be real words should be excluded. (Homophones are different words that when heard in speech, sound the same, as with 'prince' and 'prints'.)

Why must pseudo-words that have homophones that are real words be excluded? We need examples to understand this. Suppose 'tind' was included as a pseudo-word. With one of its possible pronunciations, it has a homophone, namely, how 'tinned' is heard in speech. If the child would recognize and understand 'tinned' on hearing it in speech but has no idea how to spell it, she would be forgiven for thinking that she should not decode 'tind' to sound the same as 'tinned'. This is because the alien symbol will have alerted her to the fact that she is dealing with a pseudo-word. Accordingly, she may now fear that she is making a mistake if decoding 'tind' to produce the sound she hears when someone says 'tinned'. This could cause anxiety, and affect her responses to other parts of the check. Other examples include 'sind', where a pupil might recognize and understand 'signed' on hearing it said in an appropriate context, 'tand' (because of 'tanned'), 'mand' and 'manned', 'dind' and 'dined', and so on. The ingenious reader will readily produce other cases.

Even if these kinds of examples are excluded from the check, or only affect a few children, surely this still matters. We should be concerned about any child this might affect, and the whole surreal scenario points to the distance between what the check purports to measure, and reading proper. In Chapters 5 and 6, I explore the character of this gulf in detail.

There is much evidence of 'teaching to the test' directed towards the pseudo-word section, with young children spending hours practising with nonsense words. In any case, young children are especially prone to inconsistent performances – one day they will be reaching for the stars, while on the next they have regressed to the functioning of a toddler. Early Years teachers are very used to this, and automatically take it into account on a daily basis when arriving at an assessment of pupils' current achievements and difficulties.

Some defenders of the check are now appealing to empirical research that allegedly demonstrates that teacher assessment is likely to be 'biased' in comparison with standard tests devised by external agencies. They argue on these grounds that the check, after all may detect some problems with decoding that teachers may miss in their informal day to day assessments. Hence, because reading is so important, the check should be retained to 'help' teachers in their work.

Some may feel that it is absurd to award tests and teacher assessments similar status. Surely, they will urge, tests are 'objective' while teacher assessments are 'subjective'. It is just obvious, they may think, that the tests capture achievement accurately, and any kind of teacher assessment has to be evaluated in relation to the superior picture derived from tests.

I am afraid that the terms 'objective' and 'subjective' employed in that fashion are too confused to do any robust argumentative work. They may have superficial intuitive appeal, but this dissipates quickly on closer scrutiny. We make judgements about what others are thinking, what they know and what they are feeling many times every day. Needless to say, our verdicts are fallible, and *will* sometimes be coloured by the way we feel about the people concerned. In that sense, we are affected by our subjective states. Nevertheless, we are also often entirely correct. Our judgements are 'objectively' true. Teachers arrive at accurate beliefs about what reception children know and understand about the reading process all the time, whether they are dealing with a whole group or working one to one with a pupil. It is true that if they employ a test, whether written or orally delivered, and keep strictly to the guidelines both about how the test should be administered and how it should be marked, then any feelings they have about particular pupils, or particular *types* of pupils cannot colour the results. Yet this point does not take us very far forward.

Are defenders of the check seriously suggesting that, at least in theory, an Early Years teacher might judge a child to have poor decoding skills, having worked with them over several months, and then, when the child does well in the check, might revise her opinion? Is our teacher now supposed to think, 'Oh dear – I must have been biased against this child. He's a member of a minority group. That is probably why my verdict was so inaccurate. I now gather from the check results that he is much better than I previously thought, so I will alter my teaching accordingly!'

I referred earlier to the 'no validity without reliability' issue. Teacher assessments of any cognitive achievement, and of decoding in particular are almost certain to be less reliable (in the technical sense) than tests, including the Phonics Check. That is to say, if more than one teacher informally assesses a child's decoding on a particular occasion, there is a greater likelihood that their verdicts will not be wholly consistent with each other than would the strictly controlled conditions employed in the Phonics Check. It is also likely to be the case that a child's scores in a check will vary less from one occasion of assessing them to the next, in comparison with how teacher informal assessment of their decoding skills might vary from one episode with a pupil to the next one. Yet this type of potential inconsistency is not relevant to the way the check is actually scored or used by teachers. In any case, common sense points to the fact that teacher assessment of young children, especially if that assessment is gleaned from interactions with these pupils over a period of time, will be better at 'measuring' their real reading achievements than any check. Any claim that a check is 'scientific', 'objective', and therefore 'better' at capturing pupils' decoding skills than the normal classroom interactions between teachers and pupils, is implausible, to put it mildly. It is difficult to see how such a claim would be justified, or even to grasp what it actually means!

4

Teaching, Learning and Constructivism

Introduction: Overview of argument

Hurst (1980) argues that to teach, the teacher must ascertain what her pupils already know and understand. To teach 'requires the teacher to bring about some change in the pupil, so a claim to successful teaching involves, on the part of the teacher, a claim to knowledge of the relevant state of the pupil' (p. 216).

This outlines a key feature of the ground I intend to cover in this chapter. I will be concerned with the kind of learning that is understood at least to some degree. To explain this concern, the elusive notion of 'understanding' will need to be explored. I defend the insight that *understood*, learning requires an appropriate relationship between new knowledge and what the learner already knows. This is not, ultimately, an empirical point at all, but a conceptual insight about learning as such, or, at least, about learning that is not exclusively rote learning. I suggest that this is one way of understanding constructivism.

The need for an appropriate relationship between new knowledge and learners' resident knowledge means that the teacher must plan to be able to take account of learner responses when deciding what and how to teach. This is the case, as I will show, unless she is content to take the risk that the learning she engenders will not be understood to any significant extent by some or even all of her students. Her grasp of this crucial point must drive her to leading *interactive* teaching sessions, as opposed to delivering pupil-proof recipes or scripts. We cannot and need not codify the said interactions. It is not as if there must be no less than a given number of exchanges between teacher and pupils in a lesson lasting an hour. That will be a matter of degree, and will, of course vary, depending on the subject matter, the age and attainment of the pupils and many other factors. But *without* intended interactions of some kind, we are no longer talking about teaching, or so I will argue. The necessity for interactions is an additional reason for pessimism in principle about the possibility of identifying teaching methods in a fashion that affords scope for rigorous 'scientific' research.

The constructivism I will shortly elaborate has been a tacit assumption behind the attacks on teaching recipes in my earlier discussions. Yet it may strike some readers as startlingly unoriginal and, if true, only too obvious. They may wonder why any argument is needed for a well-worn and familiar idea. However, since it is a key component of my argument, I will devote some time to it.

Relevant conceptions of teaching

Surely, whatever else teaching may be, it is an activity designed to bring about learning that is not purely rote. (For ease of exposition, I will use the term 'learning' in much of this chapter to cover the kind of learning that is understood at least in some measure. This is nothing to do with any kind of opposition to *learning by heart*. Indeed, there is a case to be made that the move against learning by heart that accompanied more progressive trends in school education went too far. However, I *am* assuming that much of school learning must be more than rote. It must be understood at some level, since, otherwise, the learner will be unable to use and apply it.)

A question that has already come up in earlier discussion is the following: Should we count as teaching those activities merely *intended* to bring about learning, or only those that are *actually* responsible for it? For my purposes here, the former will be accepted and used. After all, if I had employed the stricter version, I would be unable to discuss the possibility of researching effectiveness, since I would have confined myself to methods that, by definition, *do* bring about learning. Indeed, a host of empirical research studies would also be ruled out.

However, the less strict condition is insufficiently strict. Surely, our teacher ought to have good reason to believe there is some chance that her activities will bring about learning. If she turned to the wall and started counting backwards, claiming on inquiry that she was teaching Synthetic Phonics, we would be forgiven for denying that she was teaching, whatever views we had about phonics. We would be unable to accept that she was justified in believing that counting backwards at the wall was a way of teaching the said content.

If an adult went into a Year 2 class and made the children sit on the carpet while she talked without stopping for half an hour on the topic of Fluid Dynamics, we could not be absolutely sure that no child would learn anything. Perhaps, present in that classroom, listening with all ears, there is a precocious infant with a senior meteorologist mother who has succeeded in sharing some of the joys of her profession with her daughter. Nevertheless, our courageous adult cannot have had any reason to think that the 6–7-year-olds held captive would learn much, if anything from her lecture. Accordingly, we refuse to say she is teaching, even if someone can come up with an argument that she was doing something valuable at the time, including support for the faint possibility that learning of some kind actually occurred.

Rote learning and 'understood' knowledge

Consider an imaginary and wholly artificial case of 'rote' learning. At time t, there is no sense in which a child has the fact 'Michael Faraday was a scientist' in her head. At time t+1 an adult 'tells' our child that Michael Faraday was a scientist. At time t+2, let us say, our student has learnt this fact by rote. She lacks, let us suppose, much understanding of what the claim means, and has no justification for believing what the adult has told her, except that the adult has proved to be a reliable source of knowledge on previous occasions. We perhaps could say of this rather strange example of learning, that the adult has caused our child to 'learn' a certain fact. However, given the way we have constructed this scenario, the fact is 'in' our child's head without being connected to other things that she knows. She could do little with it except produce it on demand, given a very simplistic kind of test.

A parallel example of the acquisition of a specific skill will now be rehearsed. At time t, our pupil cannot use a pair of compasses to draw a neat circle. The teacher demonstrates how to do this, the pupils are given some simple tasks with compasses and are afforded further direct support during the lesson. At the end of the lesson, at time t+1, our pupil can now use the compasses appropriately. A simple 'cause' narrative, namely, that the teacher brought about the pupil's acquisition of the compasses skill would seem appropriate and accurate. Again, because this is a self-contained skill, little role if any is played by the child's existing cognitive states in whatever changes are needed for the skill to be put in place.

These two examples are entirely untypical of school learning, especially in English primary schools. They represent thought experiments only, and fit a stereotypical 'transmission' view of teaching and learning, a position that can sometimes be helpful if we are trying to explain what constructivist approaches are *not*. Very crudely, on this perspective, the adult 'has' something that the pupil could learn – some facts or skills, and can do something to insert or transmit the something into the pupil. Familiar metaphors accompany the transmission narrative. The child's mind may be compared to an empty rucksack that can then be stuffed with knowledge by the teacher, or even likened to an empty vessel in to which knowledge can be poured. The mathematics educator Hilary Shuard famously remarked that children had proved to be very leaky vessels, at least in the context of mathematics.

'Constructivist' accounts of teaching and learning may concern themselves with pedagogy or even with 'radical' epistemological views about knowledge itself. The version I defend involves neither of those things. In what follows, I cannot avoid referring occasionally to empirical claims about how pupils learn. However, in the final analysis, the constructivism I support is not about how students actually learn, or about how teachers should teach. For instance, it does not recommend that students should be 'active' in some sense in order to learn, a claim sometimes associated with constructivist pedagogy. It does not advocate that teachers should never stand at the front of the class and 'tell' their pupils things. It does not fall into the trap of what Biesta in various places (for instance, Biesta 2012) calls 'learnification'. The latter mistakenly puts the learner in such a central place that the teacher falls out of the picture altogether – at best, she is a facilitator of learning. The learner has to do everything for herself. In the most extreme case, at least according to some narratives, Socrates taught nothing to his interlocutors, but rather drew everything from them, literally from what they already remembered. He is just acting as a midwife, helping his 'learners' to give birth to what they already have within them.

I am offering a *conceptual* account of what it means to acquire new knowledge that transcends rote learning. As we will see, this account draws on classic ideas from Piaget. Piaget probably thought of himself as offering empirical theories, but that is not how I am going to interpret him here.

Holism and rich knowledge

To develop a conceptual version of constructivism, I need to distinguish between what I call 'thin' and 'rich' knowledge. The first step here is to focus on the *content* of what is known – that $2 + 3 = 5$, that George III went mad or that, in Newtonian mechanics, Force = Mass × Acceleration. It appears to be straightforward to identify content items in this way using such noun clauses. Our facility with language can give rise to the illusion that we are picking out stand-alone items of content, just as we can use language to identify each of the chairs round the table in the dining room such as 'the chair with the small splash of red paint on the back'. Our chairs are independent of each other, in the sense that any one of them can remain in the room if we removed the others, and if we brought in some more, most of their individual characteristics would be unaffected.

Items of content do *not* resemble chairs in this respect. Content items do not exist in splendid isolation. There are few, if any 'stand-alone' content items. (I am inclined to think there are none, as a matter of fact, but I am using cautious language here, lest counterexamples are possible, and could distract from my main line of argument.) Any one content element has intimate relations with other elements. $2 + 3 = 5$ relates to the fact that 5 is both more than 2 and more than 3, that 5 without 2 is 3, and so on. By 'relates' I mean to include the thought that $2 + 3 = 5$ cannot 'be' the arithmetical statement that it is *without* its multiple relationships with the rest of arithmetic. That George III went mad is interconnected with facts about the British monarchy, what counted as 'madness' in the eighteenth century and an indefinite number of other aspects of social and cultural reality. As with the arithmetic example, what George III going mad amounts to cannot be separated from facts about the British monarchy, among multitudes of other things.

One example that makes this easy to grasp is the Newtonian proposition $P = MA$ (Force = Mass × Acceleration), since P, M and A are explicitly defined in relation to each other within the relevant theory of physics. The philosophical issue looming large here is that of holism, and we need to sketch some of its aspects in order to focus on what I take to be the most defensible variety or varieties. The vast literature in analytic philosophy distinguishes between belief holism, content holism, meaning holism, confirmation holism and many other varieties. I want to concentrate on belief holism and content holism, while acknowledging there are all kinds of links with other holisms too. I turn first to belief holism. When a pupil knows something, she at least believes it. Suppose, for instance, her knowledge that Durham Cathedral is over 900 years old is fairly 'rich'. If it is suitably connected in her mind with other aspects of Durham, the nature and purposes of Cathedrals, the calendar and so forth, then her corresponding beliefs will be similarly 'connected'. What would her knowledge be like without such links?

> What would it be like to believe that there's milk in the refrigerator, and nothing else? It seems as impossible as having money without the social and economic circumstances that give sense to something being money. To believe that there

is milk in the refrigerator, you have to have enough by way of belief to count as understanding what milk is, what a refrigerator is, and what it is for one thing to be inside another. It takes a lot of belief to be any amount of belief. (Braddon-Mitchell and Jackson 2007, p. 196)

The above quotation amounts to an orthodox statement of belief holism. Yet, it might be objected, there must be something wrong with it as just outlined. For it must be possible for a learner to hold one particular belief without others. If she says, for instance: 'Faraday discovered the dynamo', then that could be quite enough for us to attribute a relevant dynamo belief to her. Belief holism is being oversold. Hence, the objection concludes, the emphasis I have given to connectedness must be flawed.

One classic holist response to this runs as follows: What, precisely, *is* the belief that our learner is supposed to be holding? The answer to this question has to depend, in part, on what she thinks 'Faraday', 'dynamo', 'electricity' and so forth actually *mean*. If she holds, sensibly, that a dynamo is a device for generating electricity by moving magnets and coils in relation to each other, then we begin to have some idea of her belief, and to suspect that it may well be true. On the other hand, if she thinks that 'dynamo' means 'small solar-powered generator', then, again, we start to have a notion of what she believes, and to conclude that it is false. So the very identity of what she believes depends on, among other things, her ideas about the meaning of the words in the utterance used to express it. Moreover, she cannot have views about those key meanings without convictions about all kinds of other things.

An opponent of holism can return to the fray. 'We can tell what a learner knows (and so, believes) in other ways than by attending to what she says. We can observe what she does in various situations. So the insistence on connectedness cannot play the role in belief attribution being claimed by the holist.'

Far from helping our holism sceptic, however, this now draws attention to the dispositional character of belief, and hence provides support for belief holism. If a learner believes that Faraday discovered the dynamo (and has standard convictions about the nature of dynamos) she will be disposed to show this belief in all sorts of ways. If she is asked in a test who discovered the dynamo, and is motivated at the time of asking to come up with the right answer, she will manifest her Faraday belief by writing down an appropriate response. If the teacher asks her in a class science lesson who discovered the dynamo, and she is anxious not to appear to know too much in front of a learning-averse peer group, she might manifest her belief indirectly by answering that Prince Charles made the dynamo discovery. If she is asked by the teacher who discovered the dynamo, and misheard 'dynamo' as 'dynamite' she might respond 'Nobel'. We can easily multiply such possibilities indefinitely. Now, such indefinite possibilities depend on the Faraday content being embedded in an extensive network of other knowledge. We cannot say, of course, how many possibilities there should be, or even how 'possibilities' should be counted. It will always be a matter of degree.

If it is appropriate to refer to beliefs as 'dispositions', then they are not single track but multi-track dispositions. Examples of single track dispositions include being soluble in water. There is just one kind of thing that something with this disposition is disposed to do – namely, to dissolve in water. 'Being magnetic' looks as if it is 'multi-track', since attraction, repulsion, inducing a current in a coil and so forth all seem to be manifestations of this disposition. The distinction between single and multi-track dispositions is not marked by a clear borderline between the two, and whether we count a disposition as single or multi-track will depend in part on how we describe their manifestations. Be that as it may, beliefs manifest themselves in a great variety of ways.

One difficulty inherent in the holist position, it may be argued, is its inherent vagueness. If we try to pin it down, the task may prove impossible. Dynamos incorporate magnets. Hence, if you hold that Faraday discovered the dynamo it is fair to *report* you as believing that Faraday discovered a device incorporating magnets. However, you might not actually know that dynamos involve magnets. Hence, dynamos and magnets would not be linked in your mind. Yet surely this piece of ignorance on your part does not disbar you from believing that Faraday discovered the dynamo. However, if we extend this thought experiment a little, and add some more ignorance to our learner, matters become harder to settle. Suppose you think that dynamos generate gas to supply to households. This degree of cognitive incompetence might argue that you do *not* believe that Faraday discovered the dynamo, despite the fact that you might well use the sentence 'Faraday discovered the dynamo' to express your belief. There are no hard and fast rules here about the precise point at which misapprehensions concerning the meanings of the words in your utterance or about the nature of dynamos become so radical that it is no longer appropriate to say you believe that Faraday discovered the dynamo. We cannot pin down a precise number of hairs, fewer than which a man is bald, and more than which he is definitely not bald. This does not prevent us from being able to judge plenty of cases as either those of baldness or of not being bald. Similarly, a necessary condition for believing that Faraday discovered the dynamo is the existence of a degree of connectedness with other things you know, despite the fact that we cannot offer a precise point at which, in the absence of connectedness or in the event of the connections being plain wrong, the learner fails to hold the relevant belief.

As we saw earlier, rote learning that is *no more than rote* bypasses the connected character of most knowledge. You can 'know' something you have learnt by rote in such a way that it is insulated from the myriads of other elements that are needed for its full identity. Learning that is 'richer' than rote enables the learner's knowledge to begin to mirror the interconnected charter of knowledge illustrated in the previous paragraph.

To explore the 'connections' theme, I appeal to a familiar distinction coined many decades ago by the psychologist Richard Skemp. He popularized a broad division between what he called 'instrumental' and 'relational' understanding. He explained this by appealing to an analogy with two people, Smith and Jones, trying to find their way to a wedding in a town with which they are not familiar. Smith has been supplied by his host with a series of directions – turn right, under the railway bridge, past Sainsbury's, turn left by the War Memorial, etc. until he reaches the church. If Smith follows the directions he will arrive at the wedding on time. If he fails to follow that sequence of directions, he has no way of constructing a new route to the church. He is likely to be late. Jones has the same series of directions. He has a map of the town and can read it. If Jones loses his way he can look at the map and work out a new route to the church. He has a greater chance of being in church for the start of the wedding than has Smith.

A student whose understanding is modelled on Smith's position in the strange town is restricted to the instrumental variety. At best, she has knowledge and skills that are not interrelated – they are not, so to speak on her 'cognitive map'. They are isolated from each other. As with the rote learned items referred to above, she will only be able to do one thing with them – produce them on demand in a test or similar, and in a context very like that in which she acquired them in the first place. The fortunate student whose understanding echoes Jones's happy position in his attempts to reach the wedding possesses her knowledge as occupying 'positions' on her cognitive maps. She grasps connections between the things she knows. Her cognitive map enables her to travel in many different ways between one knowledge item and another. It enables her to 'transfer' her learning from contexts in which she originally acquired it to an indefinite variety of others. Having a cognitive map and the learning suitably located on the map is a necessary condition for being able to manifest the learning in a variety of contexts. So this, in turn, is a necessary condition for non-rote learning per se. It is important to note that the detail on the map, and the nature and number of the routes between the various locations is a matter of degree, and that, of course, this whole picture is deeply metaphorical.

I now turn to an argument from Lum (Davis, Winch and Lum 2015) that attempts to demonstrate that there is no such thing as rich knowledge. He characterizes the rich knowledge thesis as the claim that 'epistemologically vacuous components accrue meaningful content simply by virtue of being "connected" together' (Davis, Winch and Lum 2015, p. 114). I can appreciate why he is epistemologically cautious about the 'components', though I do not understand why his pessimism extends to characterizing them as 'vacuous'. Connectedness is certainly a matter of degree. Holists about knowledge and belief do not *have* to say that single beliefs and single items of knowledge lack *all* content or identity. Moreover, some content suffers especially from being isolated. Other content can do more in the way of surviving in an epistemically isolated state. That I feel warm is, arguably a piece of relatively primitive content that has a stand-alone identity making little appeal, if any to other content for its inherent character. That I can vote by going to a polling station and writing an X on a card differs markedly from this. To make any sense of the voting, content concerning democracies, parliament and social conventions of many kinds has to be taken into account.

Consider the Newtonian example of P = MA (Force = Mass × Acceleration). Taking 'P' on its own, it might well be viewed as 'epistemologically vacuous'. It seems to acquire its content entirely by virtue of its location within Newtonian mechanics. It acquires a rich epistemological life, as it were, by virtue of its relationships with Mass and Acceleration. However, no simplistic analysis is possible here, since some content for each of the three terms may be thought to be accessible from the folk employment of these ideas. For instance, the notion of force is understood to a degree in a bread and butter sense, independently of the technical meaning it acquires once it becomes part of a scientific theory. We all have everyday experiences of exerting force on things – for instance, pushing a car when we are trying to help a neighbour get it started, and of having force exerted on us – most days riding the tube afford unlovely instances.

Perhaps the apparent difficulties about whether components have any identity, as it were, stem from the metaphors being used. They do not survive too much pressure. The term 'connection' and even 'component' are metaphors. Knowledge components do not resemble physical objects. They lack a real position, in, say, the brain and cannot be connected by wires. I would urge caution about the very idea of a 'component' here. When we speak, for instance, about the notion of voting being inextricably tied to democracy, we should not think we refer to separable components. We are actually indicating aspects of a whole complex idea. Speaking of components may mislead us into thinking of discrete items that are connected in a network. The metaphor can seriously mislead us.

Another analogy that may be helpful is that of the position of a piece during a game of chess. I do not simply mean, for instance, where the Queen is on the board, speaking physically. I am referring to the situation of the game at a given time, in the light of where all the pieces are on the board, the facts about the pieces that have been taken, whose move it is, and so forth. Position is not a stand-alone feature of the Queen, but rather a matter of both where the piece is on the board, physically speaking, and then, more importantly, the interrelationships with other pieces, given the current rules of chess.

'Connections' can be semantic, conceptual, deductive, evidential, combinations of these and many other things besides. Here are some examples of connections that can exist between knowledge components: That Cicero lived in Ancient Rome is very closely connected to Tully living there, since Cicero was the same person as Tully. That $2 + 3 = 5$ is connected to the falsity of $2 + 3 = 6$. Michael Faraday being a scientist is connected to many claims about what it was to be a scientist at the time he lived. The move of a rook in a game of chess is interrelated in complex ways with the other pieces, the rules of chess and so on.

Of belief holism, Donald Davidson characteristically observed:

> It is impossible to take an atomistic approach, because it is impossible to make sense of the idea of having only one or two beliefs. Beliefs do not come one at a time: what identifies a belief and makes it the belief that it is is the relationship (among other things) to other beliefs … because of the fact that beliefs are individuated and identified by their relations to other beliefs, one must have a large number of beliefs if one is to have any. Beliefs support one another, and give each other content. (Davidson 2001, p. 124)

How does holism about belief content characterize claims about individual beliefs and about the possession of individual items of knowledge? It opposes any picture according to which someone can 'store' a *discrete* element of content, that is what it is regardless of anything else that individual knows. It contends that the content of any knowledge item is bound up with how it relates to other knowledge possessed by that individual. It notes the potential variety and extent of that other knowledge, and of the relevant connections and relationships.

Holists about belief need not commit themselves to a radically anti-realist view of individual beliefs, according to which there is no sense whatever to the idea that there are any such things and that talk of them should be abandoned. In the light of this point, what account can a belief holist provide about what it is for a 'single' belief to persist over time and to be held in a range of contexts? Suppose we wish to talk about Jones believing that Faraday discovered the dynamo. We want to speak of this belief today, and we assume that, other things being equal, he will continue to believe this tomorrow and the next day. Today a teacher asks Jones a relevant question, and he shows his Faraday belief by responding appropriately. Tomorrow he engages in a project on Victorian scientists and his Faraday belief informs how he pursues his project in several ways. How, then, should the idea of this belief be understood? Most philosophers broadly support a view about mental content dubbed 'social externalism', though inevitably there is endless debate about detail. On this view, the situations that belief attributions concern, involve not only the people themselves but also aspects of their social environments, and of their relationships with those environments. Earlier, we discussed the ideas of constitutive rules and collective intentionality. These ideas are crucial when we come to elaborate on what is actually meant by the phrase 'aspects of their social environments'.

When we attribute this Faraday belief to Jones, we invariably incorporate aspects of his sociocultural environment, and how he relates to these. Such attributions take in elements of social reality that extend beyond what, so to speak, is merely in Jones's head. As Davis 2006 explains, 'The variety of behavior and of conscious states that can manifest a belief stems from the links between that belief and others, and between that belief and the intentions, desires and motivations of the agent concerned' (p. 7). To repeat, this is not saying that we can make *no* sense of single belief attributions. It is rather to offer an account of what such attributions can possibly amount to.

The social reality referred to here includes institutions and conventions, especially those relating to the use of language, whether explicit or tacit. The very existence of these social phenomena is bound up with the maintenance of appropriate constitutive rules and collective intentionalities.

Piaget and that relationship between new and existing knowledge

The relationship between new and existing knowledge can now be elaborated in the light of the sketch of 'connected' understood knowledge. Piaget is held to be one of the fathers of constructivism. It is not at all clear to me that he is the true ancestor of all its instantiations, and if Phillips (1995) is right, many of them would hardly be to his credit. Piaget *does* succeed in offering ideas that help us to characterize the interface between what a learner already knows and understands, and *new* knowledge – or what is at the heart of learning. David Ausubel (1968) wrote in similar vein: 'If I had to reduce all of educational psychology to just one principle, I would say this: The most important single factor influencing learning is what the learner already knows.' Piaget's notions of *assimilation* and *accommodation* are designed to capture two aspects of learning. I now want to apply these ideas in ways of which he might not have approved, so apologies in passing to those interested in accurate Piagetian exegesis.

First, I sketch the idea of *assimilation.* The learner's existing knowledge must become related to new content if her grasp of the fresh material is to be richer than rote learning. To 'take it in' so as to transcend mere rote absorption, she must assimilate it. The fresh content must acquire a place on her existing cognitive map. In gaining a location, this content acquires all kinds of relationships with other content that is already on her map. Let us rehearse this important point by applying it to some examples (after Davis, Goulding and Suggate 2017). In my first draft of this, so to speak, I mix conceptual and empirical aspects of the Piagetian theory, before proceeding to distil the crucial conceptual components.

A learner already knows something of dogs. She has encountered them, so she knows that they eat, drink, bark and wag their tails. Now she meets a sheep, and attempts to place it, so to speak, on her existing cognitive map, where a range of dog elements are already comfortably situated and connected. The sheep eats and drinks. To this extent she can assimilate the sheep content.

Now, we move on to *accommodation.* Our learner has to digest the fact that the sheep is bigger than the dogs she has experienced, makes a different noise from dogs and lives in fields, unlike dogs. So she has to accommodate this new knowledge. That is to say, her existing knowledge and understanding has to undergo some changes in order to deal with the new content. The sheep must be placed on her cognitive map in a way that makes it clear that it is not a new kind of dog.

In a second example, we turn to primary mathematics. Nine-year-old Debbie already has some rich knowledge and understanding of number. For instance, she understands three digit numbers and why they are written conventionally as hundreds, tens and units. She is familiar with the representation of numbers on a number line. She grasps the basics of the four operations addition, subtraction, multiplication and division, and has a fair idea of how they are related to each other. She is now taught several lessons about fractions. The models she encounters include cakes and pizzas divided into halves, quarters or thirds and the idea of fractions of small groups such as a half of 12 and a quarter of 16. One day, the teacher demonstrates that fractions can be represented on a number line: they can be allocated positions between the whole numbers. So this new possibility must be added to Debbie's existing conceptions of what a number line can represent. That is to say, Debbie must assimilate it. However, her existing conceptions cannot embrace such a possibility without change. The new ideas challenge her existing grasp of arithmetic. From now on, numbers are not merely those whole numbers (positive integers) that can be used for counting. They are also ways of indicating measurements and quantities. We can have one and a half kilograms of flour or travel three quarters of a kilometre. These insights reverberate throughout her existing conceptions of number and arithmetic. The latter conceptions begin to undergo some fairly radical changes. That is to say, she begins to accommodate the new content. (At some point Debbie will be taught about negative numbers, and similar earthquakes should occur in the vicinity of her existing grasp of arithmetic.)

My problem with this outline of assimilation and accommodation is that it may appear to represent Piaget as making empirical claims about what actually happens during learning. I do not intend to offer evidence either for or against such claims. Nevertheless, I will need to continue to refer to them and to comment on them in order to achieve my ultimate objective. This is an account of the relationship between a learner's existing knowledge and new content that is necessarily true.

What are these empirical claims? He talks of young knowers being mentally and physically active. He holds that their cognitive development is driven by a process of *equilibration*. He explains the latter as follows: at a given point in time, children are satisfied with their thoughts. They are in equilibrium. With the impact of learning, they become aware of shortcomings in their existing knowledge and understanding. This is *disequilibration*, where they may experience cognitive conflict. With a move to more sophisticated thinking they achieve equilibrium once more. What is outlined here is an artificial and simplified snapshot of psychological processes that take place all the time during learning. They may occur on a small scale and almost instantaneously, or represent more substantial elements of cognition. So, complex as all this might be, it is open to observation and recording, at least in theory.

One example to illustrate this comes from the secondary science classroom. Pairs of students work together, each being armed with a spring balance. Their teacher informs them that they are about to conduct an experiment. Each student grasps their spring balances firmly, and the balances are hooked together. Each student in the first pair, on the word of command, will pull away from their partner. By way of contrast, when the second pair are given the word of command, one student does not pull at all but simply stands firm, while her partner does pull away. Before experimenting, the students are asked to predict the readings of the spring balances after the words of command have been given. This, we will say, is the stage where their thinking is in equilibrium. Usually, they will say that the readings will be the same for the pair where both are pulling. But they will normally have a different view of the second case. They are likely to think that where one pulls and one does not, the reading for the latter's spring balance will be less than that of her partner's, who is pulling. The prediction for this second pair is, of course incorrect, a fact familiar to all those who know their Newtonian mechanics. When the experiments are carried out, students are typically rather surprised, and even disconcerted, because their predictions have been overturned. This is the stage of *disequilibration,* where they experience a measure of cognitive conflict. The results are discussed with the teacher, reconciled with Newtonian mechanics and the students move to a more sophisticated level of thinking, achieving equilibrium once more.

In principle, it ought to be possible to explore the kind of 'learning' that might take place in the *absence* of what Piaget describes. Rote learning as characterized above might fit this, though it would have to be in extreme form. Imagine a four-year-old child repeatedly being told that hadrons are made of quarks. She might well come to 'know' it in a sense. If asked what her mother had told her several times earlier in the day, she could say that hadrons are made of quarks. In this situation there is virtually no scope for connections with other knowledge. Even the notion of something being made out of something else, a primitive idea that the child would probably already grasp, only applies to the subatomic world very indirectly. The child, of course would not realize that, and hence if any connections were made with her existing conceptions of 'being made out of', they might well be wrong, or at best very approximate.

Much of what has just been said about the child and the hadrons can be seen as necessarily true, the necessity arising from the concepts concerned. We need not indulge in empirical speculation about how 'active' the child might need to be and in what sense, whether she needs to be stimulated into cognitive conflict, or any contentions about equilibrium and its opposite. All that is needed is this: somehow or other, connections need to be established for the knowledge to become 'real'. The existence of connections will, of course, be a matter of degree.

I now turn to aspects of the recent history of mathematics teaching, especially at the primary stage in the UK. This will enable me to develop, elaborate and further defend a conceptual version of constructivism. To oversimplify the last few decades, sixty years ago, primary mathematics was dominated by whole class teaching from the front, rote learning of arithmetic facts such as multiplication tables, and traditional calculation algorithms such as subtraction with borrowing, long multiplication, and both 'long' and 'short' division. Eventually some teachers and maths education researchers began to react against this. It was noticed that many primary age children were spending countless hours being 'taught' these algorithms, yet they either never achieved competence in them, or they lost competence almost as soon as they had acquired it. The procedures included the extraordinary and meaningless patter that accompanied subtraction with 'borrowing' (no 'borrowing' was *ever* involved), division with 'Gzinta' (that technical term in mathematics involved when you say 3 gzinta 7?, which was often followed by 'bringing down zeros', and countless other semantic and mathematical outrages). Research into adult mathematics carried out around the time of the Cockcroft Report (1982) showed that many intelligent educated adults lacked competence in, for instance, the long division algorithm. They presumably had never understood it when it was taught to them at primary school. Hence it soon 'fell out of their heads'. They had been given 'rules without reason'.

Accordingly, alternative approaches gradually emerged, informed by a rationale that pupils should have at least some chance of 'understanding'. In England these approaches included government initiatives such as the National Numeracy Strategy. One of the ways in which understanding was centre stage in these developments was the explicit attention devoted to mental arithmetic. Pupils were encouraged to develop a flexible range of mental strategies on which they could draw when solving certain kinds of arithmetic problems. Within an increasingly high stakes accountability regime, mental arithmetic featured, for instance in the Natural Curriculum tests for eleven-year-olds. I mention mental arithmetic here because competence in this domain seems incompatible with minimal understanding. You cannot make an intelligent choice from an extensive repertoire of strategies unless such strategies are well-ensconced on your cognitive maps of arithmetical concepts. Confronted with a subtraction problem, the pupil decides whether to 'count on', 'count back', whether to do so in 'chunks' of tens, hundreds and so on. Such decisions are impossible without a 'connected' grasp of the number system, the relationship between addition and subtraction, and much else. The emphasis on mental arithmetic, then was thoroughly constructivist in the sense being supported in my treatment here.

Early on in the retreat from rules without reason, the subtraction method known as 'equal addition' was replaced by 'decomposition', since this could more readily be explained by appealing to pupils' existing grasp of place value. Incidentally, in the absence of the latter, decomposition could easily be a matter of following rules without grasping their rationale, just as equal addition always had been for many pupils.

Long and short division were also made less prominent in this retreat from narrowly procedural understanding. Older readers will remember the beginning of the extraordinary patter associated with long division '24 gzinta 2, you can't, 24 gzinta 21, you can't, 24 gzinta 215..8..' and so on.

These methods were still taught after the withdrawal from 'rules without reason', but there was no suggestion that *all* pupils should be taught them by the time they were 11. Instead, as many as possible were taught 'chunking' as an alternative to both short and long division. Chunking involved a focus on

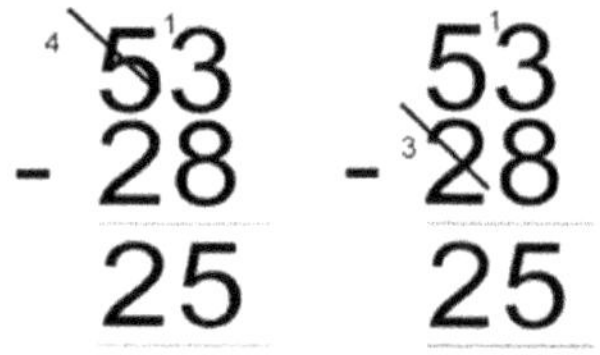

$$
\begin{array}{cc}
^{4}\cancel{5}^{1}3 & \cancel{5}3^{1} \\
-\ 28 & -\ ^{3}\cancel{2}8 \\
\hline
25 & 25
\end{array}
$$

Figure 4.1 Decomposition and equal addition

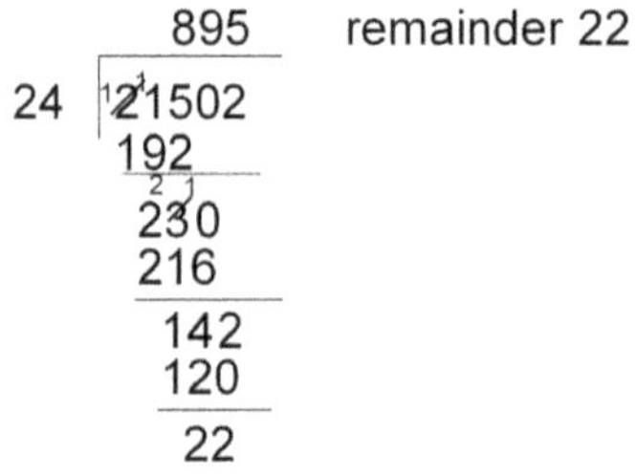

$$
\begin{array}{r}
895 \quad \text{remainder } 22 \\
24\ \overline{)\ ^{12}\cancel{2}^{1}1502} \\
192 \\
\overline{2\ }^{1} \\
2\cancel{3}0 \\
216 \\
\overline{142} \\
120 \\
\overline{22}
\end{array}
$$

Figure 4.2 Traditional long division

```
        31
24  744      10 x 24 = 240
   -240      10 x 24 = 240
    504      10 x 24 = 240
   -240
    264      31 sets of 24 in 744 altogether
   -240
     24
```

Figure 4.3 An example of chunking

one particular aspect of the concept of division – namely viewing it as repeated subtraction. This strategy was flexible, allowing students to deal with the subtractions a 'chunk' at a time, where they could choose the size of the chunk depending on their existing knowledge of numbers.

Suppose the division was 744 divided by 24. One interpretation of this problem is that it asks how many times 24 can be subtracted from 744. Some students would decide to subtract 10 lots of 24 at a time from the 744. They would proceed to subtract three of these 'chunks' – that is to say, three of the 10 lots of 24. By this point, then, they would have subtracted 30 lots of 24. Having taken 240 from 744 three times (so a total of 720), they then take account of the final 24. And so 30 lots of 24, plus just one more 24 gives the definitive answer to the division problem, namely 31. Other students will reach this answer more rapidly by handling 30×24 as one chunk.

Viewed through the lenses of assimilation, accommodation and Skemp's cognitive maps, the 'chunking' approach allows students to perform division calculations with the support of their existing knowledge and understanding. They can assimilate and accommodate chunking itself so that it acquires a coherent location on their cognitive map. The dangers inherent in the traditional long and short division algorithms are that some students can make few if any links between their skills with these specific procedures and their existing knowledge of arithmetic. Without such links, students cannot apply these procedures outside the limited context-free frameworks in which they are taught them. Needless to say, connections are always a matter of degree. For any kind of success with these calculation methods, they certainly must have some grasp of the number system.

The move in recent history away from traditional algorithms had little to do with claims that they were of no use to anyone. Nor did it relate to whether they were more, or less efficient than any of their more informal replacements. Those pupils who could readily acquire sufficient understanding of both short and long division were in possession of very useful tools. 'Sufficient understanding' in this connection implies that they could use and apply these tools flexibly and intelligently in a good range of contexts. The reason for placing less emphasis on these methods was, as I said above, that generations of pupils failed to understand them. Hence they were unable to access them and use them in their everyday lives.

It is worth noting that, in our experience, many Initial Teacher Training students feel that any opposition to rules without reason is misplaced. Typical comments include 'I learned the method at the time. I did not understand then, but I do now. I gradually filled in the gaps in my understanding. You cannot grasp all this stuff instantly. Teach children the rules – don't be obsessive about whether they understand at the time. It will sort itself out by the time they are grown up.'

Our response to such comments generally runs as follows:

> You are, broadly speaking, representatives of the most able in our society, or you would not be here as students in the first place. We are delighted that you were able to figure out the whys and wherefores of the calculation methods. Sadly, many other adults are never able to do that. Our point is supported by research on adult competence in traditional algorithms.

Having explored those essential marriages between new and existing knowledge through these mathematical excursions, I now return to the main theme of this chapter, namely the inextricable connection between teaching worthy of the name, the truth of constructivism, and the negative implications for the very possibility of pure teaching methods.

Didau (2015) claims that we do not need to teach children differently – at most we may need to vary the pace. Practice will sort out most of the problems, he tells us. Such an assertion denies the basic truth of the constructivism I am defending. (Didau is *not* engaged in research at the level of HE, and I only refer to him at all because his publications are widely read by teachers.) He is not alone in his opposition to differentiation. A popular contemporary narrative about teaching is that teachers have been urged to employ 'differentiation', but teachers now are coming to realize that this is both impossible and in any case unnecessary. As always in debates of this kind, participants talk past each other because of the great variety of ways in which 'differentiation' may be interpreted. Some oppose differentiation because they believe that it disposes teachers to have undemanding expectations of many students. This may be an important point in the context of some debates and some construals of differentiation, but it is not germane to my argument here.

Arguably, it would be quite impossible, even if desirable, to teach in such a way that all pupils at every moment of a lesson are able to assimilate, accommodate, and successfully take in new learning in such a way that it finds a firm and lasting location on each individual cognitive map. Some curriculum content, especially in mathematics is particularly resistant to treatment. For example, over the years I have worked very hard to generate models and analogies that will enable at least some primary pupils to grasp why $4 - (-6) = 10$. I cannot do the same with the meaning of $-2 \times -4 = 8$. I am not implying that I make no efforts of any kind with the latter. However, I believe that I am leaving 'gaps', and I cannot see that they could ever be filled in entirely.

There are also obvious and formidable bread and butter practical difficulties in 'matching' teaching actions to twenty or thirty individual cognitive maps. While these maps *sometimes* do not differ very much from one student to another in a particular group, at other times there can be significant variations.

So, if a teacher is working with a whole class, she cannot address each individual's existing knowledge at each and every moment in the lesson. Yet she ought to take account of it in the course of her interactions with them. In practical terms it is impossible not to in any case. This means that, as we saw earlier, any particular lesson is to a degree unpredictable, even if a detailed plan is being used, such as one informed by government stress on phonics. The teacher has to gauge minute by minute the level of her students' interest and motivation and the extent to which they seem to be gaining understanding. She continually modifies her style of explanation, tone, timing and organization. That is why one teacher's lesson on a particular topic may differ significantly from another's, even if the same content and similar age and attainment groupings of pupils are involved. We return to this crucial point later. Darling-Hammond 2006 speaks of teachers as 'adaptive experts' who 'restructure their knowledge and competencies to meet new challenges' (page unknown).

Surely I am overstating this point, or so it might be argued. Lectures are commonplace in HE. Although some are 'interactive' in various ways, students say that there are still plenty around where the tutor talks 'from the front' for just under the statutory hour, the torrent of words garnished with an implacable multitude of PowerPoint slides. The lecturer makes not the slightest attempt to gauge student interest or knowledge, and proceeds regardless. It is more than a mere urban myth that some academic tutors make use of yellowing pages of lecture notes that they first dreamed up twenty or thirty years previously. Such activity might be dubbed 'student-proof' academic delivery, or some such characterization. These deliveries arguably *do* amount to strategies or methods whose effectiveness could be subject to empirical research, whatever we may think of them.

(In a good learning culture that might be established in HE, students come to appreciate that they have to deal with lectures in a particular way. They know that module content vastly exceeds anything a lecture series can cover. Lectures highlight key ideas, questions and authorities in the subject. They enable students to go away and engage in the learning that *they* need to carry out in order to cover the content. Lectures assume a certain level of student knowledge and understanding. When students are working independently, they obviously start from where they are, cognitively speaking. For the most part, lectures cannot take account of varying student knowledge. In this sense, then, however wonderful a lecture might be, and however much students might learn from it, it is not, strictly speaking, teaching.)

Returning to the argument, suppose, for instance, that *school* teachers explained a concept in mathematics or science according to a specific recipe. Imagine that classroom events actually did mirror certain kinds of university lectures. Teachers might employ a blueprint devised by an expert. It could suggest tone of voice, body language, and even the chorus of response to be elicited from the pupils at key moments. This, as we saw earlier, is close to some of the versions of Direct Instruction that feature in recent empirical research.

It is very difficult to take such a suggestion seriously, especially in connection with primary age pupils. A teacher *ought* to note the reactions of her students after the first sentence or so. She might then take questions, amplify what she had just said, or even move very quickly to more challenging content if elements of the official explanation seemed excessively familiar and easy for her students. Young children are not expected to extract from their school teachers the tools that enable them to learn most of the curriculum for themselves. They do *not* resemble university students in this regard.

Am I stipulating a definition of 'teaching' so as to exclude adults' presentations that take place uncontaminated by pupil response? After all, most pupils would learn *something* from such presentations, even if they would have learnt *more* if the teacher attends to student reactions during the lesson. I concede this point, and that I am guilty of stipulation. We have seen in earlier discussion that the elusive 'it' in Cartwright and Hardie's 'It worked there. Will it work here?' can readily be identified if 'teaching' is allowed to cover classroom processes defined according to a closely specified and delivered recipe or script. However, I want to defend my stipulative definition. This book focuses in particular on method identity issues in connection with *interactive* teaching, or, as some would put it, teaching. If someone wishes to say that lectures as described above are also teaching, I would simply say that, if so, they are very different from the teaching that attends to the nature of and responses from the students being taught.

This is not to say that 'off the peg' good explanations of difficult ideas in, say mathematics or science are of no use to teachers. Presumably these explanations survive the test of time and of pupils' cognitive variations because they are peculiarly apt for the necessary assimilation and accommodation on the part of the pupils for whom they are intended. Nevertheless, professional use of such explanations does not encompass using them regardless of pupil responses in a particular lesson.

Have I invoked an extreme version of a rigid script that nobody would ever take seriously in the first place? I concede that for expository purposes only, I have simplified the prescription possibility, and that in schools where lesson plans are being devised by senior management for colleagues to follow there would be no question of individual teachers reading out a script. Recent controversy[1] about this issue has highlighted some of the complexities involved.

However, my basic point still holds. The lesson plan is supposed to be 'good' and 'effective' independently of the knowledge and understanding of any one group of pupils with whom it might be used. Frank Smith (1999) puts his objection to this vision in a powerful way:

> Teaching is a social activity. Pre-designed programs cannot take the place of teachers, even when the programs are administered by teachers. Teaching involves decisions made on the spot, not decisions to move from one instructional goal to the next, but decisions about the condition of the learner. Such conditions might include the learner's (and also the teacher's) physical, emotional, and psychological state at that particular time, together with interest, comprehension, past experience, self image, feelings about the task at hand, and feelings about the teacher (or about the student). All these considerations require teachers to interact with and be responsive to learners personally, as individuals, not as items on an instructional chart or data on an achievement. (p. 151)

Some readers may recall the 'experiment' of introducing Chinese teaching methods into an English Comprehensive school, broadcast on TV in the UK under the heading: 'Are our kids tough enough?' While even these Chinese teachers varied in their approaches, a particular lesson narrative was frequently to the fore. The teacher taught a large group of pupils 'from the front'. They employed a very rapid pace, writing and drawing on the whiteboard. The students were expected to write down what they were being told, and to do so in silence. They were not supposed to ask anything during the lesson, but to answer questions when posed by the teacher. One of the teachers decided to give the pupils a test at the end of a series of lessons in order to discover how much the pupils had learnt from the presentations. The teacher picked up little information about what the students were learning *during the teaching* and so deemed that a test at the end would be a sensible way of discovering this.

An important difference, or so it was claimed, between the English and the Chinese situations was that the former groups of students ranged in attainment and ability, whereas the latter did not. So the defence of the Chinese approach might be that there was no need to involve pupils actively during the teaching, since the teachers knew in advance that the whole group were 'ready' to assimilate and to accommodate the material about to be transmitted to them. (I am not for a moment implying that the Chinese would defend their position using Piagetian jargon!)

I am old enough to recall one defence of what was sometimes dubbed 'family grouping' or 'vertical grouping' in primary schools in England. Instead of groups of four-year-olds, five-year-olds and so on, the classes had a range of ages. The age range could be as big as four to eleven, something that happened in any case in 'dame schools' in Victorian times in Britain. One attempt to justify organizations of this kind was that it *forced* teachers to treat their learners as individuals. Groups of pupils in the same year group contained a great range of attainment. They could still differ in age by nearly a year. Yet some pedagogical practices appeared to ignore this point, or so it was maintained at that time, so approaches needed to be disrupted by radically different class organizations.

As I write, there is renewed concern about 'Summer Born' pupils in England, given the fact that in a typical Reception class, ages can vary between just over four (the child with an August birthday) to five (the child with a September birthday). There are various reasons for this concern. These may include the fear that the youngest children will be disadvantaged because teachers will fail to offer the kind of appropriate differentiation that affords appropriate support for them.

I conceded earlier that it is impossible for any teacher to 'match' what she offers to thirty different student minds. It is equally impossible, however, to arrange a teaching group in such a way that their minds are exactly similar. I will mention just two of the reasons. First, despite significant overlaps between the knowledge and understanding of, say, thirty school pupils, each student will have something of their own to bring to the classroom situation, including personal experience, motivation patterns and abilities to concentrate. Second, despite the fact that, as I said earlier, teachers do detect *during teaching interactions* hints of what their students are absorbing and understanding, this will never amount to a precise grasp of what they know, understand, and are interested in at any one time. This is partly an empirical and practical point, but matters do not rest there. Let me explain.

There are deeper philosophical doubts about the very idea of 'what someone knows and understands' at any given time. The implication of this idea is that the contents of a mind can be inspected and precisely delineated: such inspection might be compared to an aerial view of a landscape as seen from an aircraft. Yet judgements about an individual's beliefs, without which there can be no mental 'content', are matters of *interpretation* rather than verdicts arising from a direct scientific examination. Arguably, there is no one 'true' account of what someone believes. Wittgenstein famously remarked: 'If God had looked into our minds he would not have been able to see there whom we were speaking of.' Wittgenstein is talking here about our use of language to refer, but I would argue that we can apply his dictum more generally.

Enemies of differentiation in school classrooms might now be feeling rather pleased with the line of argument I have just presented. They could point out that I have just concluded that the very idea of an objective, definitive view of what any one student knows at a given time is radically suspect. Accordingly, they might continue, attempts to match teaching to pupils' current attainment are shown to be educationally bankrupt. Yet, those opposing differentiation might conclude, my argument against 'scientifically' researchable teaching approaches rests, or so I asserted, on the crucial element of interaction between teacher and students *during* the teaching!

My response to my imagined objector runs as follows: I maintain that a straw man has been created by overplaying my critique of an objective definitive view of what any one student knows. I developed that critique to question the viability of attainment groups that, were they to have been possible, would render differentiation otiose. Judgements about what a student knows and understands are interpretative and 'loose', rather than comparable to precise and rigorous measurements familiar to the natural sciences. Nevertheless, this still leaves open a situation familiar to most teachers. Quite simply, students vary in their understanding and motivation at any given moment. From the fact, if it is a fact, that as a teacher, I cannot ever make precise and robust judgements about the state of any one student's cognitive map, it does not follow that I should not bother to take account of the variation in such maps in a group during my teaching. That is just an example of letting the better be the enemy of the good. Even stalwart defenders of the efficacy of phonics approaches such as Tunmer (2014) broadly agree. Tunmer acknowledges that because reading 'involves a developmental progression from prereader to skilled reader in which different cognitive abilities are required at different points, consideration must be given to … existing knowledge, skills … that students have at the outset of learning something new' (p. 236). He argues explicitly against a 'one size fits all' approach – a fact that might well surprise some phonics adherents if they knew of it. This contention is repeated in Arrow, Chapman and Greaney (2015), proposing 'the use of differentiated instruction as an alternative to current literacy teaching practices' (p. 171).

Reading: A Philosophical Inquiry Into Some Nuts and Bolts

Introduction

The argument developed so far may be summarized as follows. The classifications of teaching methods, and, in particular, methods of teaching reading are part of the furniture of our social world. They are constructed and sustained in existence by our intentions that underpin prevailing constitutive rules. Judgements about the nature of complex social phenomena such as reading lessons involve matters of interpretation. Good interpretations are not necessarily wholly consistent with each other. To insist on the technical reliability of such judgements is to distance the verdicts from the true character of their subjects. Accordingly, confidence that observers can always achieve a reasonable level of agreement about the category to which a given teaching episode belongs ought to be modest, at best. Yet such confidence is surely required for truly solid empirical research into the effectiveness of the methods thus classified. Moreover, it just does not seem possible to combine a method with a clear identity with true teaching, that is to say, teaching that refrains from being 'pupil proof'. True teaching is interactive, because its opposite, a kind of recipe, fails to take account of the necessary truths in defensible constructivist accounts of the nature of learning. The essential virtues of interactive teaching imply the major thesis of this book: 'pure' teaching methods must at least approximate to recipes to be researchable using certain standard empirical tools. But these would be educationally unsound.

I now turn to a crucial component in any allegedly effective method for teaching reading, namely, the conception of reading itself. The assumption that synthetic phonics programmes are effective in the teaching of *reading* prompts an obvious question: What does 'reading' actually mean? What should it mean? Does it have more than one legitimate meaning? Associated debates rage in the continuing Reading Wars about 'guess' and 'decode'. Phonics adherents often accuse those departing from phonics orthodoxy of allowing or even encouraging pupils to guess words, rather than read them. I now offer a detailed investigation into the nature of reading itself, and many of the associated technical ideas that have been used to characterize it. The results of this investigation raise further questions about the very idea that we can sensibly conduct empirical research into effective ways of teaching reading.

Phones and phonemes

One of the points of dispute in the 'wars' is how some of those technical notions to which I have just referred are to be understood. At the very heart of the debates is the term 'phoneme', and how it has drifted from its role in its home discipline of theoretical linguistics, where it has a long history. We will see that this is not a simple and superficial terminological issue. It relates to just how we understand the difference between working with sounds, on the one hand and reading, on the other, where the latter is understood to be *reading for meaning*. It is fair to say that no one thinks that working with sounds is the same as true reading, and attributing to phonics adherents the view that decoding sounds and reading are the same is a tiresome straw man. Nevertheless, it also turns out that many do not properly grasp the gap between the two, and that this gives a spurious plausibility to rigid synthetic phonics approaches.

In my original investigations into this subject I wrongly assumed that a phoneme was, literally, a type of sound, a kind of 'auditory atom' into which the words we hear spoken can be segmented. Instances of this sound type would be physical events that could, at least in theory, be measured and recorded with scientific equipment. In the huge academic literature associated with research into learning to read, you can find writers who *do* use the term 'phoneme' in this way. Moreover, although this is *not* how it is conceived within contemporary theoretical linguistics, occasionally, even in this field, researchers express themselves in a fashion that leaves them open to the 'acoustic' interpretation of 'phoneme'.

There are ripe opportunities for 'misunderstanding' here, many of which have been exploited to the full in the Reading Wars. I will now try to explain why the 'acoustic' version of 'phoneme' is mistaken, and why that matters. Listen to someone saying the following three English words: 'farm', 'palm' and 'heart'. You should hear roughly the same kind of sound in the middle of each. If we had a piece of technology that could pick up these sounds and identify them in terms of physics, it should reveal the same middle component, acoustically speaking. Evidently there will always be very subtle variations between one speaker and another, but in these examples, identification of a sound type is arguably pretty straightforward. Using the same physical conception of sound, we can confidently say that when a northerner says the word 'grass', she is likely to employ a middle sound that differs from that used by a southerner – the former resembling the middle sound in 'cat', while the latter mirrors the middle sound in 'farm'. We are talking here about classes of sounds, where the membership of these classes can be defined in physical/acoustic terms.

So the words that we hear people say can share kinds of sounds. For instance, we can hear a common middle sound when a speaker says 'should', 'wool' and 'pull'. Hearing 'dog', 'death' and 'disaster', we encounter the same initial sound. The spoken versions of 'stop', 'lip' and 'map' have a final type of sound in common.

The idea of a sound type that I have just laboriously outlined is *not* the same as the notion of a phoneme as featured in linguistics. The theoretical notion of the phoneme is certainly *linked* to sounds heard when any given language is spoken. However, it is concerned in a very particular way with such sounds. It is an abstract approach to conceptualizing them. It has to do with *classes* of sounds that, when altered, may change one word into another. Membership of these sound sets that comprise phonemes is *not* established acoustically.

To say more about this, I need a little technical symbolism – I use it in standard ways that can be found in the academic literature. 'Phones' are kinds of sounds conceived of acoustically – those I have just outlined above. So the sound of the word 'nip' as heard in speech may be blended from three phones, [n], [ɪ] and [p]. The square brackets are used here in a conventional fashion to indicate phones. In what follows, I will sometimes speak of sounds rather than types of sound, in the hope of avoiding clumsy expressions. However, on other occasions I will have to maintain references to sound *types* to ensure that the argument is clear and robust.

Let us now attempt to pin down the idea of the phoneme. This is not straightforward. Suppose someone says 'hat'. The middle sound (or phone) may be represented by the symbol [æ]. Now, imagine that our speaker changes that middle sound from [æ] to [aː] and, in consequence, says 'hart'. In English, the relevant phones [æ] and [aː] are held to belong to distinct *phonemes* because of their roles in determining what word is being said. Exchanging a sound belonging to the set of sounds associated with one phoneme for a member of a set of sounds belonging to another phoneme *may* change the word we hear in speech, as it does in our example here. The two phonemes featured in the 'hat'– 'hart' example are represented as /æ/ and /a:/. It is really important to notice that the criterion for whether a sound belongs to a phoneme class of sounds has to do with *words*. Whether a sound belongs to a particular phoneme is not primarily determined acoustically.

Changing a sound may change the word we hear, but this does not always happen. A northerner says 'fast' and she is likely to use [æ] as the middle sound – that is, the middle sound we hear when someone says 'hat'. Her friend from the south, in contrast, will probably say 'fast' in a different way, using the same middle sound as the one we hear when someone says 'hart'. In this case, the fact that our second speaker uses a different middle sound from our first, does not change the word they are uttering. It just *sounds* different.

To sum up the points just made, the concept of a phoneme is abstract. Some of the ideas it embraces transcend the acoustic characteristics of the sounds we hear in speech. The notion of a phoneme has to draw on the distinction between different words for its very definition.

As we see later, once we are dealing with words, we should think of ourselves as operating in the realm of meaning. Once we do so, there is a key use of the term 'word', according to which a word is not a type of sound per se, though, of course, it can be expressed in sound.

Accent is not the only factor in how the sounds associated with phonemes may vary. The sound associated with the phoneme /t/ when the initial sound in the word 'top' is heard, is not exactly the same as that associated with the phoneme /t/ when someone says 'stop'. The possible sound variants for a phoneme are known as allophones. Accordingly, such variants do not have the power to change the word in which they occur. In any case, no two speakers will pronounce sounds linked to a specific phoneme in exactly the same way.

A rigorous purist may object to my exposition so far by complaining that 'phones' have variants too. One speaker's pronunciation of the phone [æ] will not precisely resemble that of another's. An exact acoustical characterization of one would reveal differences from that of another. Surely, my objector could conclude, talk of a 'phone', like talk of phonemes, is to talk of a *class* whose members vary. So I ought to concede that the conception of a phone is abstract. Yet, have I not attempted to draw a contrast between phones and phonemes by characterizing the former as physical – as concrete, so to speak, while insisting that phonemes are abstract?

It is true that I spoke of the abstract character of the phoneme, and have emphasized the acoustic nature of the phone. It is the *type* of abstraction afforded by phoneme discourse that marks it off from the phone. Phoneme identity is linked to the idea of a *word* – the latter taking us into the social realm of meaning. Phones and their identity conditions are basically outside that realm.

The notion of a phoneme is relative to a particular language in virtue of its conceptual tie with meaning. For instance, in English, the difference between the sounds associated with 's' and 'sh' is likely to be phonemic. I say the word 'sock'. I then proceed to alter the initial sound, so that I am now heard saying the word 'shock'. The change in sound has changed the word, and hence in English we are dealing with sounds associated with two phonemes here. Yet in Japanese, the two sounds that English speakers associate with 's' and 'sh' count as allophonic variants of the same phoneme. If I said a Japanese word using the sound linked to 's', and then said something similar where the 's' sound was changed to 'sh', I would still be saying the same Japanese word. Incidentally, it is even true that universal agreement about the number of phonemes in English is not to be had.

Robins 2014, discussing phonemic contrasts in different languages, comments:

> The ways in which sounds are distributed and contrast with one another may vary very considerably from one language to another. The degree of phonetic difference required to maintain a distinction is a matter for the language system ... [t] and [tʰ], non-contrastive in English, are contrastive, and so belong to different phonemes, in several varieties of Chinese and in a number of Indian languages. (p. 124)

Let us hear what some linguistics writers say about the conception of a phoneme, to support the account I have just given, and with which I intend to work from now on: 'By representing groupings of speech sounds – allophones – as being related to some single abstract notion – the phoneme – we start to gain an insight into the organization of speech sounds into systems.... . As an abstract representation (the phoneme) is *not* something that can be pronounced; it is not a speech sound itself, (Davenport 2010, p. 117).

Again, here is a very similar account from a different source: 'An allophone ... is a predictable variant of a phoneme. Allophones are the individual members of a class of sounds (a phoneme) or the pronounceable or concrete realizations of an abstraction (a phoneme)' (Brinton and Brinton 2010).

For belt and braces, so to speak, here are two last extracts from a third source:

> We must then conclude that our idea of the English r-sound is an abstract, mental category, rather than a phonetic fact. We call such a category a phoneme.... . A physical realisation of a speech sound like the voiceless or the voiced alveolar

approximant is a phone. Phones which function as alternant realisations of the same phoneme are called allophones of the phoneme. (Plag *et al.* 2015, p. 34)

Phonemes can distinguish words: allophones cannot… . Phonemes are distinctive in the sense that they enable speakers to distinguish between words (p. 37).

The phoneme has a history within linguistics and has evolved over a period of time. From the point of view of linguistics theory, Dresher (2011) comments: 'The phoneme is far from dead. However, it is not much talked about, and when it is, it is more often to dispute its existence than to affirm it' (p. 241).

Dresher (2011) notes that the term 'phoneme' existed before it acquired an exact definition, the latter process he describes as 'difficult'. The development of alphabetic writing systems began to embody the idea that symbols should not differ when they are associated with merely allophonic distinctions that do not serve to mark one word from another. Van Der Hulst (2013) draws attention to the existence of a twelfth-century anonymous Icelandic linguist who listed sound differences with phonemic properties.

Dresher (ibid.) points out that early in the last century there were two accounts, the physical and the psychological. According to the physical characterization, a phoneme was a family of sounds that, in a given language, counted as the same for practical purposes. This version was obviously incomplete because it omitted the crucial point. What unified any particular family of sounds? Why did they count as the 'same'? The psychological version fared little better. It cast the phoneme as a psychological reality – an auditory image, or some kind of mental representation. Given that such imagery needs to be able to represent not just one mental representation of a sound, but a range, we have still not been provided with the unifying principle.

How do synthetic phonics supporters use the term 'phoneme'? In the Rose Report it is a synonym for 'kind of sound'. The familiar phrase 'grapheme-phoneme correspondences', or GPCs for short, simply means, as far as I can understand it, 'letter(s)-sound correspondences'. We saw at the beginning of this book that UK government policies make liberal use of the word 'phoneme'.

Now, does it really matter whether this term is used with the technical purity expected of academic researchers in linguistics? Is it just that we fear that this pseudo-technical vocabulary lends a spurious air of scientific rigour to synthetic phonics advocacy, especially, of course if some liberties are being taken? Another story about all this is that the term 'phoneme' has undergone a kind of semantic drift, without any malign conspiracy behind this phenomenon. It had a place in classic theoretical linguistics, but now it is employed as a synonym for a sound heard in spoken words.

However, I would argue that there is a more serious issue at stake, and that there are very strong reasons for resisting any kind of semantic drift. In effect, the widespread use of the term 'phoneme' in synthetic phonics rhetoric blurs the difference between the sounds we hear when someone speaks, and words. We do, of course, hear the sounds as words, but the sounds per se are not words. Our synthetic phonics protagonists speak of blending phonemes to produce words, and will go on to say that the process is reversible, words being segmentable into their constituent phonemes. Rose says that pupils need 'to apply the skills of segmenting words into their constituent phonemes to spell', and to 'learn that blending and segmenting are reversible processes' (p. 20 para 51). Many synthetic phonics advocates also speak of reversibility.

I believe that the phone or sound versus phoneme confusion may already be at work here. Straightforward reversibility applies in many cases, of course, and makes sense at the level of sounds as acoustic items. Three phones or sounds can be blended to make the sound we hear when someone says 'cat', and, for sure, 'cat' can be segmented into those three sounds again. If, for some reason, this was a useful thing for children to learn, there seems no reason why they should not be able to do so. Blending and segmenting may need to be taught to most children, as it may not be a skill that comes naturally to them. Hence, up to this point at least, Rose is making reasonable claims. Only sounds can be combined, and then segmented. Nevertheless, the claim, apparently being made in the Rose Report, that *words* can be segmented into their constituent *phonemes* is incoherent nonsense. The idea that a *word* can be segmented embodies a deep and important category confusion. I will be explaining and justifying this claim in what follows.

Imagine a reader encounters the letter sequence 'wind'. In a thought experiment, let us artificially restrict her to the realm of sounds by denying her the opportunity to locate 'wind' within a sentence that has meaning. Neither 'Wind up the clock', nor 'The wind is strong', for example, are anywhere to be seen. Thus restricted, she then has a choice of either [aI] or [I] to be the sound linked to the letter i. That is to say, she can blend 'wind' to make a speech sound that rhymes with 'whined', or she can blend to make a different speech sound that rhymes with 'tinned'. Staying within the sound domain, either of these two speech sounds associated with 'wind' could then, at least in theory be segmented into constituent sounds. Reversibility in this limited situation seems uncontroversial. But it is only possible because our reader did not penetrate the realm of meaning and words at all. The reader *is not segmenting words here.*

The case shows that the blending and segmenting reversibility claim only makes sense and is true, *outside the realm of words proper.* The prevalence of the blending/segmenting content in synthetic phonics schemes and the language used to explain such content may make it very difficult for teachers and children to see this point clearly, as and when it becomes appropriate to do so.

Another example links spelling with the reversibility issue. Four sounds or phones can be blended to make the sound we hear when someone says 'wind' in the sentence 'Wind up the clock'. These are [w], [aɪ], [n] and [d]. Now suppose a child wants to write something about the fact that the family dog *whined* all night. Although 'whined' is in her spoken vocabulary and Listening Comprehension (LC), she has never knowingly encountered it as text, and does not know how to spell it. She now imagines that she can segment the speech representation of 'whined' into its four sounds. Her results are the constituent phones for what is heard for the word 'wind' in 'Wind up the clock'. Her sound segmenting is sensible, but it gives her the wrong answer. It works for 'wind' but not for 'whined'. Accordingly, the child proceeds to misspell 'whined'. (This example is not supposed to imply that children in the early stages of learning to blend and segment would encounter it, or similar cases. Evidently, teachers would avoid them. 'Whined' features here for illustrative purposes only.)

All of this is linked to the problems with that popular term, the 'phoneme'. It looks as though, as used in linguistics it faces in two directions. In one direction is the physical or auditory world of sounds that can be heard in speech. In the other direction is the realm of words proper and meaning.

An author of phonics teaching materials opposes the claim that the 'phoneme' is not literally identical to a kind of sound thought of acoustically:

> What does the writer of dozens of books (*The Cambridge Encyclopedia of Language*, for example) on all aspects of the English language have to say on this? David Crystal points out that the distinctive sounds in our language, by which we are able to differentiate one word from another – for example 'tip' from 'hip' or 'sip' – are called phonemes.

I concede that people do indeed talk like this. However, much more care is needed than is shown here, and, in particular, serious attention to what 'phoneme' actually means in theoretical linguistics. Even the reference to David Crystal fails to make the point my opponent intends. If we want to think about how to differentiate one word from another, *we have to deal with words as abstract carriers of meaning.* The next section discusses this in some depth. All that is needed at this point is the realization that in characterizing a phoneme we move a long way from 'mere' sounds.

Parents and other caregivers, when speaking to their young children may highlight those sounds that are 'contrastive' – that is, the sounds that are going to make a phonemic difference in the language concerned. 'Making a phonemic difference', remember, is *the potential to differentiate one word from another.* Cristia and Seidle (2014) observe: 'Talkers have an implicit goal of promoting language acquisition by highlighting phonemically contrastive categories.' It may well be that Japanese children learn not to hear such a difference between s and sh as English children do, just because that difference in Japanese is not phonemic.

Have I been distracted and confused by the fact that phonemes have allophones – sound variants that still count as the same phoneme? Surely, it will be urged, this is an obvious and familiar point, and does nothing to undermine the coherence and importance of the notion of a phoneme.

This misses the point. When we identify *phones* we are, of course, picking out a class of sounds. These sounds are not absolutely identical to each other. For example, no one speaker articulates the phone [a:] in precisely the same fashion as another. Yet we could lay down in physical and acoustic terms the range of physical features within which a sound would count as [a:], and outside of which it would not. No reference to words and meanings would be necessary. Such a manoeuvre would be impossible for phonemes. Their identities are inextricably tied to words as carriers of meaning. As such, words as abstract constructs in a realm far removed from the physical and the acoustic.

The concept of a word[1]

It would be convenient for synthetics phonics proponents if a 'word' could be appropriately thought of as a speech sound composed of component sounds and/or as a sequence of letters with spaces either side of it. In this section, I criticize such a conception of 'word'. I show that the force of this criticism threatens the purity of alleged synthetic phonics teaching methods.

A typical dictionary definition of 'word' is close to what Phonics supporters are likely to prefer (Modern Languages Association, 2016):

> A unit of language, *consisting* of one or more spoken sounds or their written representation, that functions as a principal carrier of meaning. Words are

composed of one or more morphemes and are either the smallest units susceptible of independent use or consist of two or three such units combined under certain linking conditions. … Words are usually separated by spaces in writing, and are distinguished phonologically (my italics).

In philosophical discussions, though dictionary definitions can be useful starting points, they are often contestable and make conceptual assumptions that are not always explicit or afforded justification. That is certainly true in this case. Furthermore, in linguistics, philosophical logic and philosophy of language, intense debate and study over decades has resulted in the realization that it is almost impossible to pin down criteria for word identity, and that in any case, 'word' is probably a family resemblance concept. There will certainly be differences between how the term is used in everyday speech in comparison with more specialist or academic contexts. My difficulty with the dictionary definition quoted above is the italicized 'consisting', and that, of course is exactly what synthetic phonics adherents need in their account of words.

The conception of word needed for an adequate account of reading is abstract and linked to meaning. The above dictionary definition ignores the distance between a word and its physical expressions. Understood as abstractions, words are not only represented in speech and text. Other possibilities include sign language, Morse and braille. The identity of a word can survive significant changes in its pronunciation (and, sometimes, mispronunciation!). For instance, across the world, 'schedule' has up to four different pronunciations. It is a familiar observation that the spelling of specific words has changed over time. For instance, 'maiestie' eventually became 'majesty' while 'raine' turned into 'rain'. Standard spelling is a relatively recent phenomenon, and contemporary English features both 'British' and 'American' spelling. The sound we hear when someone says a particular word in English may be identical to the sound heard when a non-English speaker utters a different word in another language. This possibility extends to complete sentences! [Ah 'key ess oon a 'may sah] means 'Here is a table' in Spanish and 'A cow eats without a knife' in Yiddish (Wetzel 2009, p. 66).

Accent is a familiar phenomenon in the UK. Northerners will pronounce 'grass' with a short a as in 'at', while Southerners will use the same middle sound as 'farm'. Someone from the northeast of England may well employ the same sound in the middle of 'book' as that you will hear in the first part of 'ooze'. Yet a southerner is likely to use the same sound in the middle as you can hear in the middle of 'should'. And, of course, there are the familiar divergences between received pronunciation in UK English and the range of American accents.

To support teachers using phonics approaches, alternative sound–letter schemes have been invented to suit local accents. These include Manchester English (Barry 2003), Newcastle upon Tyne English (Watt 2003) and Liverpool English (Honeybone and Watson 2006). They are offered as supports for teachers in England who are working with phonics-based elements in the teaching of reading and literacy.

There are multitudes of homophones in English – that is, different words that, when spoken, can sound the same or very similar. I am concerned here with those homophones that are spelt differently. This point alone drives a coach and horses through any claim that a word 'is' a speech sound. Consider 'prints' and 'prince', 'find' and 'fined', 'mind' and 'mined', 'pours', 'pores', 'paws' and 'pause', to name but a few.

In a primary classroom, suppose a child asks the teacher how to spell a word that the teacher hears as 'or'. Knowing the child, the teacher realizes that she can already spell the word that should be written as 'or'. Accordingly, she asks her pupil further questions about the context, to determine whether she needs the word denoting something made of wood used to move boats in water, rock from which metal might be extracted, or even the feeling her mother had when confronting her daughter's tidy bedroom.

Imagine that 'paws' is encountered in a list with no context. Our reader uses her knowledge of letter sounds to 'decode' – to blend sounds together to produce a sound – the sound, in fact that you would hear were an English speaker to say any of the four words 'pours', 'pores', 'paws' and 'pause'. She is unable, however, to identify *which* word she is dealing with (unless she already recognizes 'paws' as text and links it with a word that is part of her spoken vocabulary and of her LC.) Now, moving from a blended sound to full word recognition is quite a step. Our reader is likely to need a sentence, or even several sentences to provide a context. She must be able to discover at least some of the meanings of the words represented in these sentences, and she must know and understand a good stock of vocabulary in order to determine with which of 'pours', 'pores', 'paws' and 'pause' she is dealing.

Homophones are found in other languages too. Here is a French example: vert (green), verre (glass), ver (worm), vers (towards) and vaire (some kind of fur). This is not the place for an exhaustive list of the other places where homophones occur, but they certainly include Japanese, Chinese, Hindi, Russian and Korean. There are homophones in German, but not nearly as many as there are in English.

Consider the widespread phenomenon in English of the heteronym, where the same text can be pronounced in more than one way to say different words. This means, of course, that we not only cannot literally identify a word with something you hear when someone says it, but also we cannot literally identify a word with a piece of text, either.

'Does', for instance, might be several female deer, where it is pronounced to rhyme with 'toes', or, instead, a common verb where it rhymes with 'buzz'. When a letter sequence involves a heteronym, the reader must be able to identify which word it is representing before she is able to determine exactly how to pronounce the relevant text.

Let us rehearse the relevant processes in some detail. Our reader encounters a piece of printed text, written clearly as if to represent a particular word. She attempts to blend what she understands to be the associated sounds. This sometimes furnishes her with more than one possible result from the blending. She must now ascend, so to speak, to words in their semantic and abstract state, in order fully to understand which sounds to use when returning to the level of speech and pronunciation. Once she knows which word she is dealing with, she then links this to one or more speech sounds that she can hear and understand as the word in question. I now explain this process step by step by means of an example. The following explanation is artificial in the sense that readers will move through the processes almost instantaneously, and are unlikely to be conscious of what they are doing.

A reader encounters 'bass' as a piece of written text in a whole sentence. She attempts to blend the letter sounds in this text. She could, at least in theory, produce three possible blends as a result. The first shares a sound with 'farm', the second with 'gas' and the third with 'face'. She cannot match the first result with any of the words she knows, so she dismisses that one. ('Knowing' a word need not, of course, involve knowing how it would be written. It can cover an understanding of its meaning when heard in the speech of others, and possibly it can include being able to use it appropriately in an indefinite number of utterances.) She still has to choose between the second and the third blend. Imagine that the sentence with which she is dealing is: 'The double bass player sometimes wished she had learned the piccolo.' Her second result would have been a kind of fish, making no sense in this context. Hence she decides that her third blend is appropriate, since she can use it to talk about a musical instrument.

Here are some more examples of heteronyms, to delight the hearts of native English speakers, and probably to frustrate at least some of those learning English as an additional language:

- I don't want to live for a century. Live music is so much better than a mere recording.
- I want to tear the book. She shed a tear.
- Jones will wind his old watch tomorrow. Go saddle the wind.
- He is rowing with his wife. He is rowing with his wife.
- The leading philosopher insulted the vicar. The leading on the roof was damaged by the snowfall.
- The violin player complained that the piece was inappropriately bowed. After the performance she bowed to acknowledge the applause from the audience.
- She only had a minute to put on her minute brooch before going out.

Often the reader needs to know the context of a particular text item representing an individual word in order to determine its *grammatical* function. It is only when this is clear that she can then decide how to pronounce the word in question. The many common examples include 'use', which rhymes with 'loose' when a noun, but with 'yews' when a verb. Note also that which syllable is stressed in 'protest' can also depends on its grammatical role. There are innumerable other offences to be taken into consideration. Here are just a few: 'process', 'abstract', 'transfer', 'torment', 'pervert', 'digest', 'transport', 'fragment', 'contrast' and 'permit'. Each of these has two versions, depending on whether the first or the second syllable is stressed. Some of these are more complex than others, in the sense that the version that is a verb has a meaning that is only indirectly related, if at all, to noun instantiation. 'Digest' as a noun is to do with the summary of some content. As a verb it relates to what hopefully takes place in my stomach after a meal, and can, of course be used metaphorically to cover the situation in which someone is taking in some news. It is possible that the noun version is in some sense a metaphor based on the verb meaning, but that is by the way.

In any case, grammatical considerations aside, blending sounds does not produce a result telling the reader which syllable in multi-syllable words to emphasize. Consider what happens to the letter 'a' in azalea, alias, maniac, fatal, naval, banana, pyjama, drama, avocado and karate. As with heteronyms, the reader must ascend from sounds to the level of words and meaning. Operating at the latter level, she must consult her spoken vocabulary and the vocabulary she would understand if she heard it spoken in appropriate contexts. Only then can she make a decision about how to pronounce the text that she has, up to this point, 'decoded' incompletely. A reasonably advanced reader may encounter 'insight' and 'incite'. In addition to drawing on the meaning of the sentences in which these might feature, she must already 'know' these words to decide which syllable to stress. They must figure as elements in her LC. The letter representations of these words give her no clues as to appropriate syllable stress.

These are not just a few aberrations in a language where readers can otherwise calculate how to pronounce textual representations of words from recognizing and blending their constituent sounds, these clearly associated with the visual symbols for the letters used to spell the words in question. The linguistic phenomena concerned are very common.

It is of course true, and a point often made, that English spelling is exceptionally irregular when compared with most other languages. Yet its very irregularity is helpful in some ways, since it forces us to recognize the gulf between sounds and words. Incidentally, heteronyms occur in other languages too. I understand that all three letter words in Arabic are heteronyms, and that in Persian and Hebrew this phenomenon is fairly common. Examples of heteronyms are rarer in many European languages, though they are not unknown. Many Chinese characters are heteronyms, meaning each of the characters concerned can be pronounced in more than one way, each of which represents a different word.

Arguably, someone born deaf may well have a good concept of a word without any link to a sound. Admittedly it is not easy to explain just how this claim might be proved, but it seems plausible enough. Even readers who are not hearing impaired may still provide examples. I could read and understand some words before I had any idea how to pronounce them. I am certainly not alone in this. Goodman (1967) agrees: 'In some instances, of course, the reader may form a fairly accurate definition of the word, even if he never recognizes it (that is matches it with a known oral equivalent) or pronounces it correctly... . This phenomenon is familiar to any adult reader. Each of us has many well-defined words in our reading vocabulary which we either mispronounce or do not use orally' (p. 130). (I can imagine a synthetic phonics campaigner commenting that this just shows that Goodman himself never learnt to speak or to read properly.)

In connection with how words should be conceptualized, we must also consider the phenomenon of lexical ambiguity. Familiar examples include 'bank', 'will', 'light', 'volume' and 'arms'. Here, we are dealing with a particular letter sequence, linked to one specific speech sound, where this is associated with more than one meaning. There are many examples of this in English.

'The spoken word' is obviously a phrase we use happily and without complication all the time. However, by definition, the abstract notion of a word is not a physical one. It cannot literally be identical with a sequence of sounds. That would be a category mistake, like saying that my voting in the election last time consisted, physically, of pencil marks on a card. It is true, of course, that the voting necessarily involved the making of such marks, given our social conventions, institutions and so on. But the vote did not 'consist' of the mark. We can make any number of crosses in boxes on pieces of card where none of our actions count as voting. As we saw earlier in our exploration of collective intentionalities and constitutive rules, the physical properties of the crosses as such do not determine whether they are an element in the casting of votes. Hearing a word does indeed involve sound waves, events in your ear drum and associated neural events. Hearing sounds is a necessary condition for hearing spoken words. However, necessary conditions are not identity conditions.

Accordingly I now turn to some philosophical discussion of word conceptions, prompted by Kaplan (1990). His reflections on word identity have been widely discussed. His view is consistent with the one I have just been defending, opposing orthographic and/or phonetic shape or form as the criterion for word identity. In a more recent paper (Kaplan 2011) he discusses the identity conditions for *utterances* and *inscriptions* of words:

> What makes two utterances utterances of the same word is that they have the same phonetic form, or at least resemble one another closely enough in phonetic form, and what makes two inscriptions inscriptions of the same word is that they have the same orthographic form, or at least resemble one another closely enough in orthographic form. Sounds and shapes are kinds that have instances which must resemble one another in critical ways. (p. 508)

So the situation in respect of utterances and inscriptions, though far from straightforward, can be pinned down in the way Kaplan suggests. However, the status of utterance and inscription identity differs sharply from that of words in their abstract-meaning senses, which, as we have seen, are such that their identity can survive orthographical and inscriptional changes, among other things. On this account, words are not concrete empirical entities. Any one word can be written, uttered or otherwise employed an unlimited number of times. Yet words are not typical 'universals' either. Universals are that which particulars can have in common, such as redness or being a father.

Words are not typical abstract objects either. This point needs some further development. Kaplan was interested in the nature of non-empirical entities such as words and how they exist over time. He compared them with stories, songs and ballets. The story of *Sleeping Beauty* can certainly survive changes of wording, and to a degree, changes of plot detail. It can be told in different languages. It is not, in any sense, a straightforward empirical object with a continuity over time, but neither is it exactly like an abstraction such as beauty or justice. It does exist in time, and there was a time when it did not exist, and there may be a future in which it no longer exists. Whereas beauty and justice just are, so to speak. They do not come into, or go out of existence. They may have vague or fuzzy boundaries, but that is a different issue.

There is no precise point, beyond which changes in wording and plot detail mean that we are dealing with a different story. Of course, given very substantial changes, such as the sleeping princess regaining consciousness and taking up cannabis cultivation instead of the prince waking her with a kiss, we would say that we no longer are dealing with the story of *Sleeping Beauty*. However, there is nothing absolute about the criteria for story identity and change: small children are known to apply such criteria in a different way from adults, but we cannot legislate here about the correctness of any of these applications.

Words are created by people and their existence has a continuity over time, though not, of course, an unchanging continuity. We have seen that their representations on paper and in speech can alter. They exist *in* time, unlike the abstract idea of 2, for example, of which it makes little sense to say that it exists in time. Its existence is timeless. It could not have a beginning and an end in time, whereas words might have just that, for all the practical difficulties there might be in establishing a very precise point at which a word sprang into existence, or died. In that respect, words resemble stories. Our criteria for word identity do not provide us with a clear dividing line between word life and death, and there does not seem to be any particular reason why they should.

How are words created by people? I have no simple answer to that, but suggest that they are *sustained* in existence by the phenomena of collective intentionality and constitutive rules over time, ideas explored in an earlier chapter. Here I draw on Searle (1969), who writes, in Wittgensteinian tones: 'Speaking a language is engaging in a rule-governed form of behaviour' (p. 41). He goes on to note that 'sometimes, in order to explain adequately a piece of human behavior we have to suppose that it was done in accordance with a rule, even though the agent himself may not be able to state the rule and may not even be conscious of the fact that he is acting in accordance with the rule' (p. 42).

The word 'tear' (referring to what comes from the eyes when someone is sad, or laughing uncontrollably) exists so long as English speakers intend that it should, intend that it can be written using a particular set of four letters and that it should be pronounced in a certain way (with all the qualifications and flexibility already rehearsed in earlier examples). Intentions are expressed and evidenced by utterances and inscriptions. They can undergo changes.

An obvious objection to this account relates to the obscurities inherent in the claim that words exist as long as English speakers intend this to be so. We cannot expect to be able to interrogate a 'typical' English speaker and discover that they have suitable intentions about 'tear'. Even if a word is not spoken for many years, it may occur as text in dusty archives. It may be out of sight and out of mind in respect of a whole generation of speakers. Yet I would claim that there *is* a sense in which English speakers intend, and pass on their intentions to fresh generations, and that these inscriptions are embodiments of the word in question. The individual intentions contributing to collective intentions do not involve psychological processes of which the agent is conscious all or even any of the time. Moreover, such intentions could not possibly involve conscious thoughts about every specific word in English. That would be quite beyond the cognitive powers of any human being. The notion of collective intentionality in this context is a subtle one, and it certainly does not comprise an aggregate of individual conscious intentions.

One way of thinking about all this is that there is a social division of labour here, along the lines proposed by Hilary Putnam for natural kind terms, though it is far more complex than Putnam's semantics. First, I briefly rehearse an example of Putnam's thinking: 'Gold' is a term for a natural kind. It has been recognized as a special kind of substance for millennia, as have its properties of ductility, heaviness and resistance to corrosion. However, it was as recently as the eighteenth century that the idea of a chemical element with specific underlying properties began to be conceptualized by scientists. In all that time, of course, speakers made perfectly sensible use of 'gold' or the equivalent in their own language.

Putnam recognized that English speakers who speak of 'gold' might lack detailed knowledge of the periodic table, and the science according to which anything that is gold has certain underlying atomic features. According to Putnam, it is now the case that English speakers tacitly defer their use of 'gold' to the experts – they intend to mean by 'gold' what the experts mean, though they lack the experts' knowledge and understanding. They can make full and coherent use of the term in the light of the existence of scientific experts and because they employ it in their utterances and writings with the intention that the experts play an important and distinctive role in how 'gold' functions in a public language.

I suggest that, analogously, a word continues in existence in part because ordinary speakers intend it to be so. The latter could not, of course be a mere moment, but would have to be a period of time. Little purpose would be served in any attempt to be precise about this. That might reflect all kinds of cultural and communication factors making an impact on the stability of the language concerned. There will be times when a putative word is undergoing birth pangs, so to speak, but has not yet been sufficiently accepted by a community of language speakers to be credited with full-blooded existence. And, as I indicated above, the speaker intentions are largely tacit and could be quite indirect. The specific conventions for a word might be delegated to a subgroup of speakers with particular purposes and/or expertise.

However, it may be argued that the crucial intentions would need to extend much further than this. Depending on the point in historical time, they might need to include allocating responsibility to the compilers of dictionaries, to the intentions of the originators of the written and electronic locations where the word may be found, to the myriads of speakers who will use the word in question even if other speakers of that language never make use of it, and so forth. Needless to say, these intentions are relatively recent in the history of mankind. The intentions required to sustain a word's existence in ancient Greece would be different.

The intentions concerning spelling and pronunciation are, as we have seen, subject to change over time, and as regards the latter may also be relative to accent. If I mention a word that has 'died' I may seem to have contradicted myself. For the very mention of it may appear to give it continuing life. However, 'brokking', to be found in Middle English and used by Chaucer, meaning 'throbbing, quivering', looks as if it is just one of a multitude of words that used to exist and now exist no longer. If someone wishes to object that since I have actually mentioned an allegedly obsolete word, it cannot actually be obsolete, I might concede the point since little seems to hang on this point for the purposes of my arguments.

Kaplan claims that what makes two utterances to be of the same word is that they have a common ancestor. On such a view, there are no implications for degrees of resemblance or replication. Ancestry would, in theory at least, be captured by means of a narrative that dealt with historical chains of events of various kinds. Now I have a nasty feeling that ingenious counterexamples could be devised by philosophers who enjoy engaging in moves of that kind. Perhaps there are instances of what we would now count as two or more words that turn out to have a common ancestor. However, difficulties in providing precise criteria for word identity that might be traced back to challenges in providing criteria for common ancestry do not undermine the plausibility of Kaplan's broader claims about the nature of words.

The 'Simple' View of Reading

Confusions about notions of phoneme and word also relate to the widespread and erroneous idea of the 'Simple View of Reading', or SVR, often beloved of synthetic phonics enthusiasts. Gough and Tunmer (1986) described this as the view that reading comprehension is, in some sense, the 'product' of decoding and LC. I outline each of these two elements in turn, before showing that they are not separable from each other in the way that SVR seems to assume. Moreover, neither decoding nor LC is readily defined and codified. Finally, the notion of a 'product' is deeply obscure in this context.

First thoughts about LC point to the understanding someone has when she hears examples of her own language. For instance, a parent says to a toddler, 'Put your coat on', as he holds it up. Let us suppose that the child has already seen the parent don their own coat and knows that it is pouring with rain. In such a situation, 'coat' may well be an element in the child's LC. She understands the meaning and role of 'coat' in her parent's speech. Of course, if such understanding were restricted to that specific parental request, we would hesitate to credit the child with a 'full' LC of 'coat'. Arguably, for full inclusion, the child would need to be capable of a similar grasp of an indefinite number of possible utterances that featured 'coat'.

LC needs further elaboration. It extends beyond a grasp of the meaning of individual words and must incorporate an appreciation of relevant syntactical rules and conventions. This will be a matter of degree. 'Coat', for instance, can function as a noun, a verb and an adjective. Consider, 'I'll get my coat', 'You've broken the coat hanger', and 'You need to coat that wood with varnish.'

If a child's LC included 'back', there would be even more to take in. 'Back' can feature as verb, noun, adjective or adverb, but we can readily imagine a toddler having 'back' in her LC at a rudimentary level. At this stage its grammatical role might be restricted to noun function. Only later would her LC extend to cover a broader range of syntactical functioning. Other examples have more restricted syntactical potential. 'Of' cannot feature as a verb, adverb or adjective, and only appears as a noun when used to name itself, as in '"Of" is a two-letter word'.

Our toddler's encounters with auditory versions of words in the speech of others in the absence of a context may not take her very far. If she only hears a speaker say single words, she may be unable to identify them. The context will often be supplied by the rest of an utterance, though a vivid non-verbal context can also facilitate single word identification.

The idea that every word heard in speech has a specific meaning, and that it is the understanding of this gleaned from hearing the relevant speech that earns the word a place in someone's LC, is open to challenges familiar to first year undergraduate students of philosophy of language. For instance, what is the meaning of 'it' in the utterance, 'It is raining'? Does 'Tuesday' mean something in particular? What about 'bucket' in the sentence, 'She has kicked the bucket'? Hence, we need to take great care with any attempt to characterize what it is for a word to be part of LC, and to avoid the assumption that this is an all or nothing affair.

Suppose a child hears: 'There came a white hart running into the hall with a white brachet next to him and thirty couples of black hounds came running after them' (Rapaport and Kibby 2007, quoting from Malory's *Morte D'Arthur*). On the assumption that our child has never heard 'brachet' before, she may nevertheless understand that it is an animal of some kind, especially if she knows the word 'hart' already. In any case the black hounds reference strongly point to this conclusion. So, she has some comprehension of 'brachet', but it will be severely limited. It will fail to measure up with the comprehension she is likely to have of many of the other words here, such as 'running', 'white' and so on. In the case of the latter examples, she is likely to grasp their meaning without much help from context, and they will already be in her speech vocabulary.

Incidentally, if asked whether she knows what 'running' means, she would give a positive answer. Yet, if told that a temperature graph showed a five-year running mean, she may not have the slightest idea of the meaning of 'running' in this context, even if she can uncover the meaning of the rest of the sentence.

To sum up here, the SVR is most easily pinned down if it assumes that LC is itself a simple, straightforward idea that is not open to interpretation and that it has no shades of meaning. Yet this assumption is damagingly false.

I now turn to decoding. In support of an explication of the SVR, Gough, Hoover and Peterson (1990) note: 'In his dotage, Milton wished to reread the Greek and Latin classics, but he was going blind. So he taught his daughters to decode Greek and Latin. They read the classics aloud while he listened to them. Between them, there was reading comprehension' (p. 3). 'Decoding' is thought by some to be testable with 'non-words' such as 'ect', 'osk' and 'han' (examples from the English Phonics Check sample materials). However, the use of the term 'decoding' seems to vary a little. It can be restricted to the process of using letter–sound associations and blending, but sometimes is used more broadly to cover any kind of recognition of how to say a word by means of attending to the written text – hence whole word recognition may be included. (That broader use would not, of course be favoured by synthetic phonics adherents.)

It is worth noting in passing Gough and Tunmer's (1986) perspective on 'decoding', as they seem to be responsible for the familiarity and popularity of the 'SVR'.

> The term (decoding) means different things to different people: Some equate it with 'sounding out', others with (context-free) word recognition. Our position is closer to the latter, for we believe that sounding out is (at most) only a primitive form of decoding ... we believe that the skilled decoder is exactly the reader who can read isolated words quickly, accurately, and silently. Yet ... the term decoding surely connotes, if not denotes, the use of letter-sound correspondence rules.

While they strongly emphasize letter–sound correspondence rules, their understanding of decoding extends to the 'recognition', without blending, of words as represented by sequences of letters flanked by spaces. We will see shortly that talk of 'reading' isolated words can be very misleading, but, nevertheless, it is interesting to reflect on the breadth of their notion of decoding. Many synthetic phonics adherents are deeply attached to the SVR, but their version of its 'decoding' component is invariably construed narrowly as blending sounds using letter–sound correspondences. They eschew any notion of recognizing text items as wholes, because they link this idea to 'whole word, 'look and say' and related approaches that they regard as misguided.

Tunmer and Chapman (1998) report research showing that early readers who are competent at decoding are superior to other readers with lesser skills because they are better at recognizing what they call words, in isolation. Such readers have a lower reliance on context.

On the face of it, this is an extraordinary piece of research, at the heart of which is a flawed conception of the very idea of a word. To repeat, text in isolation merely exemplifies a way of representing a word, and words only attain a full existence *in a context*. Since attention context is often required before a reader can 'read' a word, it is difficult to make sense of what was going on here.

Note, in passing, the bizarre phenomenon of a huge number of empirical studies seeking to confirm the SVR, when in fact its limitations are readily demonstrated by simple counterexamples. Here is an illustration of the said phenomenon. Savage *et al.* (2015) observe, 'There is also evidence that the successful derivation of a word pronunciation for exception words after a partly successful attempt using only decoding strategies requires additional vocabulary knowledge of that word' (p. 4). Unless I am misunderstanding something here, this simply is not something for which evidence could possibly be relevant. There is no other way that the pronunciation of a piece of text with 'exception' letter–sound relationships could be firmed up *except* by drawing on 'additional vocabulary knowledge' (and, presumably, aspects of the context in which the item of text is situated).

Closely related empirical research pursues some equally odd lines of inquiry. Ouellette and Shaw 2014 report, 'There is now a sizable body of empirical research that reports moderate to strong relations between measures of oral vocabulary and reading comprehension' (p. 623). This assertion provokes us to ask how on earth there could *fail* to be a link between oral vocabulary and reading comprehension. The association is surely conceptual in origin. Let me follow up this question for a moment or two: Suppose an early reader encounters a sequence of letters flanked by spaces, and, for the sake of the example, uses the constituent letters and letter combinations to blend the associated sounds into a putative speech representation of a word. Imagine further that this result matched nothing in our reader's oral vocabulary (and to avoid confusion, this matching failure includes the absence of any homophones of that result in the reader's oral vocabulary). The only way our reader might now have to read that text for meaning and understand it is by looking at the rest of the sentence or sentences in which it is embedded, and using semantic and grammatical clues (in a psycholinguistic guessing game?).

There are many examples of empirical research into early reading that speak of decoding and LC as two distinct abilities (see, for example, Hjetland *et al.* 2014). Enough has been said here already to cast doubt on the very coherence of this kind of discourse. What counts as 'one' ability, and when one ability is 'different' from another are questions that lack definitive answers. This is not because we need better empirical research than we currently possess, but rather because the problems here are conceptual, not empirical.

SVR is explicitly a 'simple' view rather than a definitive and comprehensive characterization. Nevertheless, as baldly stated it seems to be seriously misleading. It implies that 'decoding' can be thought of independently from words with meaning and then as 'combined' with LC to supply reading. The arguments above suggest that the relationship between decoding and meaning is more complex and interactive than this. We saw that the widespread occurrence of heteronyms in English implies that the reader sometimes needs context and meaning *before* she can decide how to pronounce a piece of text. The prevalence of homophones means that the context in which a letter sequence occurs, whether it consists of other words, environmental factors or both can be essential for the reader to uncover which word that letter sequence represents.

It has been pointed out that much of the research into reading, and indeed of the application of the SVR, has been restricted to English (Share 2008). Florit and Cain (2011) claimed that their meta-analysis showed that 'the relative influence of decoding and linguistic comprehension on reading comprehension is different for readers of different types of orthography during the course of early reading development' (p. 553). This is an important issue, of course, but it fails to undermine the fundamental point that decoding and LC must *interact* in order for reading for meaning to take place.

At this point I pause to consider an objection to my use of 'word'. I am, it may be protested, engaged in a stipulative definition of 'word' for my particular purposes in this book. It is perfectly reasonable, it could be maintained, to use 'word' in a different way. For example, when the word 'bank' is said to have more than one meaning, we understand that claim perfectly. In this kind of usage, 'bank' is a piece of written text. Not only is this a common use of 'word', my objector will conclude triumphantly, but it also is a use that I myself have employed in my earlier discussions.

Hanks (2000) goes to the opposite extreme. He asserts: 'It seems obvious that the noun bank has at least two senses: "slope of land alongside a river" and "financial institution". But this line of argument is a honey trap. In the first place, these are not, in fact, two senses of a single word. They are two different words that happen to be spelt the same. They have different etymologies, different uses, and the only thing that they have in common is their spelling' (p. 205–6).

Admittedly, my earlier uses of the term 'word' included a 'lexical' version – that is, the use of it to identify *types* of text, identified visually. In the latter usage, 'bank' and 'bank' count as two tokens of one word type, and more than one meaning is associated with that type. Yet proponents of Synthetic Phonics cannot afford to favour *this* particular restricted conception of 'word' since it fails to fit the SVR that many of them regard as sacred doctrine. The latter is sometimes expressed as LC × Decoding. If 'LC' is, as we saw above, about words that someone understands on hearing them, then it already points to a notion of word that is *not* identical with text and types of text.

So SVR proponents, by implication, are already working with an abstract notion of a word. That is, their conception of word is something that has both textual and speech versions. It is independent from any particular pronunciation or spelling. And when readers ascend to the level of meaning, they extend the abstraction even further. Readers vary in how they say words and must, for instance, detach words as such from speech in order to deal with homophones, among other challenges. Of course, those who already grasp the flaws of SVR have no reason to favour a 'lexical' notion of 'word' since they do not accept that 'decoding' and comprehension can be kept apart conceptually in the first place. Be that as it may, I conclude that words as carriers of meaning cannot be as pure synthetic teaching methods might like to envisage them.

So What is Reading?

Having explored some of the components of reading and associated specialist terms, we are now ready to focus on the question at the heart of our discussions. What *is* reading? Government-led policies on how reading should be taught are based in part on a favoured conception of reading itself. I argued earlier that there is no simple route from the nature of *what* is to be taught, to how it should be taught. The situation is even more problematic if claims to identify the nature of what is to be taught are themselves open to objection. Savage et al. (2015) point out that the recommendations of the Rose Report depend on construing reading along SVR lines. If the SVR is unsound, this weakness will surely infect (already contestable) claims about how reading should be taught that depend on SVR.

Reading and guessing

A strong light can be shone on the conception of reading favoured by synthetic phonics adherents by focusing on something they emphatically *deny* is reading, namely, what they are determined to call 'guessing'. A familiar meme in the Reading Wars is an endless controversy over the use of this term. Now no one would want to advocate encouraging young children to 'guess' while they are learning to read. At least, no one would favour such a state of affairs if 'guess' implies that pupils should be happy to stab around blindly and irrationally in search of the word they are trying to read, and not mind very much if they come up with the wrong answer. Some synthetic phonics proponents deliberately employ 'guess' in an emotive way, accusing their opponents of advocating approaches that allow early readers to 'guess' in precisely that sense of the word I have just sketched. Lurking behind the fury may be some sensible but modest empirical points about children needing to acquire a habit of making intelligent use of letter–sound correspondences and the possibility in some cases that they may acquire bad habits if they make random and thoughtless use of context. However, such points are, as I say, quite modest.

It took me a long time to appreciate (if I am right), that there is a history both to the antipathy and to the distorted use of 'guessing'. It relates, of course to so-called whole language approaches to the teaching of reading, and it is highlighted by the following quotation from Kenneth Goodman: 'Reading is a psycholinguistic *guessing* game. It involves an interaction between thought and language. Efficient reading does not result from precise perception and identification of all elements, but from skill in selecting the fewest, most productive cues necessary to produce guesses which are right the first time' (Goodman 1967, p. 127: my italics). It looks as though Goodman is making both empirical claims about effective ways of reading, and indirectly implying a definition of reading itself. Be that as it may, it looks as if Goodman may be at least one of the major sources of current debates and disagreements about this term 'guess' when used in connection with early reading.

Language changes constantly, and the world sometimes seems to be divided between those who take that for granted, and those who resist it fiercely. History suggests that resistance is futile. If those favouring phonics are trying to change the meaning of 'reading', so that a necessary condition for its application is that the individual concerned 'decodes', how should we respond? It is perhaps worth putting the same question in another way too, so that the focus is not merely on phonics. If 'whole language' adherents sought to change the meaning of 'reading' so that a necessary condition for its application was that the reader recognized at least some pieces of text as representing words *without* blending the sounds of letters and groups of letters, how should we respond?

What kinds of arguments are sound in connection with debates about changes in language use? The interface between informal 'folk' ways of speaking and more scientific uses is an interesting place to look. The outcomes of such disputes sometimes give science the authority over language use, but quite often they fail to do that, and with every justification. We still speak of the sun rising and setting, centuries after discovering that the earth goes round the sun. This happy habit of language does not, of course, mean that most of the population still believe that the sun goes round the earth.

Some phrases hang uneasily and incorrectly between ordinary language and scientific language, such as 'centrifugal force'. The latter is hardly ordinary language, but we may be told that it is not correct scientific language either.

Physicists may deny there is any such thing as centrifugal force, and that we should speak rather of centripetal force, since 'centrifugal' force wrongly implies that there is an outward force bearing on objects in circular motion.

In yet another example, many would hold that the argument has gone against a scientific adjustment of 'ordinary language'. Darwin, and later on his follower Paul Ekman (1972) researched what they thought to be universal, culture independent emotion phenomena. These so-called basic emotions were, according to this research, expressed in similar ways across the world.

Some were disposed to draw from such scientific investigations, the thesis that we now know what emotions 'really are'. The implication seemed to be that our current 'folk' use of emotion language might well need significant amendment. Yet others would argue that this conclusion gives science an inappropriate authority. They would urge that science cannot ignore the fact that the psychological phenomena labelled 'emotion' do not form a natural class. Some kinds of primitive fear are very different, for instance, from grief, pride or contempt. Some emotions incorporate significant sociocultural elements while others do not. The neo-Darwinian Ekman research was world-class, but, according to its critics, this quality could not justify hijacking the term 'emotion' in the direction of its results.

A different type of case is afforded by the semantic 'drift' of the word 'refute'. For a long time, its meaning was as follows: To 'refute' a claim or an argument was to provide objectively compelling evidence, analysis or argument demonstrating that the claim was false or the argument unsound. For instance, Copernicus refuted the claim that the earth is at the centre of the universe. That is, he provided compelling considerations for giving up such an assertion.

While this meaning retains something of a foothold, it is much more frequently used now quite crudely to mean 'object'. 'The politician refuted the newspaper's claims about his expenses' means no more and no less than that she asserted that the newspaper's claims were wrong. It no longer means that the politician produced solid evidence to demonstrate objectively the falsity of the newspaper's claims. We can accept the point that resistance to change is futile, as far as language is concerned. Yet here, frustration may well set in, since we *need* a word to perform the semantic task formerly carried out by 'refute', yet there is no obvious candidate waiting in the wings.

The crisis over the word 'refute' is not unlike that in which phonics enthusiasts have placed the term 'phoneme', discussed earlier. We will set to one side for a moment the theoretical issues attached to the idea within linguistics, and the possibility that, if we follow the thinking of the linguistics researcher Robert Port, its demise may be overdue. So, assuming that the term 'phoneme' is coherent, for the sake of argument, if people start to use it to mean a *physical* sound, we lose the possibly important idea of a concept that relates to how sounds help speakers to distinguish one word from another.

Can reading be defined? Different kinds of reading?

Which of the foregoing examples does the dispute over the word 'read' resemble most closely? There are some affinities with the case of 'emotion', since emotions do not form a natural class. Analysis of psychological phenomena classed as emotions shows them to be not too unlike Wittgenstein's games, where there is nothing in common to all of them, but rather a series of family resemblances. 'Read', in the everyday use of this term may be linked to a class with similar properties. This would be in part because there are, genuinely, a number of different kinds of reading. We are familiar with at least some of these, such as skim reading, reading aloud or even 'reading' without meaning. It is possible to 'read down the middle of the page', where the reader acquires a gestalt of whole paragraphs and absorbs the broad meaning very quickly. Grabe and Stoller 2011 (p. 7) discuss the range of legitimate reading *purposes*. These include reading to search for simple information and reading to skim, reading to learn from texts, reading to integrate information, write and critique tests, and reading for general comprehension. Different purposes need not imply wholly distinct reading processes. Indeed, any such implication would be pretty implausible. Nevertheless, a range of reading purposes at least hint at some variety in the reading processes concerned.

Opinions differ over whether reading takes different forms at different stages of *learning* to read. For instance 'whole language' protagonists such as Kenneth Goodman (1982) and Frank Smith (1985) believed that learning to read should resemble learning to speak. Christopher Winch (1989) takes' whole language' adherents to hold that reading is qualitatively the same from the earliest stages through to maturity, varying only in complexity. However, others insist that early reading differs qualitatively from mature reading, and that the initial phase involves a significant element of phonetic decoding. Beck and Beck (2013), who clearly belong in the phonics camp, agree with Winch, commenting: 'Proponents of various code-emphasis approaches … find it appropriate to engage beginning readers in behaviours that are not comparable to skilled performance, such as systematic analysis of the relationship between written letters and their sounds in speech' (p. 3).

So are Goodman and Smith on the one hand, and Beck and Beck on the other, representatives of opposing parties in an empirical dispute? Suppose we investigate a reasonable-sized sample of readers, and discover what they are doing. We might learn that early readers are engaged in different processes from mature readers and that early readers were doing the 'right' kinds of decoding. Would such discoveries support phonics advocates and count against whole language adherents?

Inevitably, matters are going to turn out to be rather more complicated than this. If any early readers prove to be performing Goodman's 'psycho-linguistic guessing', then our phonics supporters will throw up their hands in horror. They will urge that early readers 'should not' be doing that kind of thing. They 'should' be decoding *and they should only be decoding. Mixed methods or multi-cuing approaches are anathema.* If I am accurately capturing the character of the debate at this point, it becomes clear that we are not dealing with a straightforward empirical disagreement that could be settled definitively by appealing to relevant evidence.

What is going on here? Undoubtedly, phonics adherents will defend their claims by appealing to evidence for teaching methods involving pupils being taught to decode, and being required to decode. However, they will also *define* reading as necessarily involving decoding. Processes lacking decoding are called (in intentionally scathing tones) 'guessing', after Goodman. Processes *including* the use of cues other than letter–sound associations are felt to have incorporated elements of guessing. I am not sure at this stage of the argument, however, whether we have arguments for how the term 'reading' should be used, arguments for how reading should be taught, arguments for what readers should be doing, or some combination.

One way of moving forward here is to establish that something like 'psycho-linguistic guessing' will often be *essential* to the reading process, if, that is, we now define reading as involving uncovering the *meaning* of the text. If we allowed decoding text without meaning to count as reading, then this move would, of course, be impossible. (I am not suggesting that defenders of phonics methods equate decoding with uncovering meaning – that well-worn move was never plausible, and opposing the rigid prescription of phonics needs to employ much better argument than such a crude straw man.)

The necessity for psycholinguistic guessing can be established quite easily though, of course, the negative loading of 'guess' provided for it by some phonics supporters is rejected here. We need to return to the discussion of the SVR above. When our early reader successfully decodes 'paws' and seeks to identify with which of 'pours', 'pores', 'paws' and 'pause' she is dealing, she examines, as we noted, the rest of the sentence or sentences in which 'paws' occurs. She may well attend to other aspects of the context too, if any are available. She will make precisely the kinds of moves recommended in the National Literacy Strategy 'Searchlights' approach, so despised by some phonics proponents. She will scan the surrounding text for semantic and grammatical clues. These will allow her to *make an intelligent guess.* Yes, guesses can be intelligent, rather than simply random stabs in the dark. Her 'scanning' will almost certainly involve her looking at the letters in other pieces of text in the relevant sentences, and using her knowledge of letter sounds to help her read them too. The 'guessing' process will be interactive and dynamic. Detailing this may well make the process seem artificial and scarcely plausible. Needless to say, it happens very quickly, even with many early readers. The so-called guessing will allow her to home in on her word, and finally reach a conclusion about which one it is. She *cannot* read 'paws' for meaning without something like the above process taking place.

If the very word 'guess', as used by Goodman, has proved so problematic for some people, we could, of course find alternative vocabulary. Some RR teachers would be happy to speak of a 'Psycho-linguistic Deduction game'. I fear, however, that this would not really solve the problem, since I suspect that the attack on 'guess' is rarely a rational move, but rather, part of a non-rational attempt to discredit anyone who opposes 'pure' Synthetic Phonics.

Researchers into Artificial Intelligence have developed related lines of thought. Rappaport and Kibby (2007) discuss what they call 'Contextual Vocabulary Acquisition' (CVA). They define this as 'the active, deliberate acquisition (or learning) of a meaning for a word in a text by reasoning from "context"' (p. 2). As they describe it, this process is, arguably, more demanding for a machine than for a reader, since readers have a store of vocabulary – their 'LC'. These authors' notion of 'context' extends beyond mere surrounding text, and includes background knowledge. As we have repeatedly seen in earlier discussions, human readers also make use of context in this broad sense when engaged in their 'psycho-linguistic guessing game'. Rappaport and Kibby claim that CVA is 'algorithmic' and can be taught to students. It is beyond the scope of this book to assess such a claim definitively. Given the range of background knowledge and vocabulary that students are likely to bring to bear, any simple set of rules for context reasoning seem very unlikely, but I will leave matters there.

Psycholinguistic guessing accompanies what can lead to reading 'tricky' or 'difficult' words, by which I mean words with orthography of a kind that is not easily decoded. (I note in passing the insane controversy that such claims may provoke, in which phonics adherents insist that *all* words are decodable. I can only suggest that they can *have* the terms 'decode' and 'decodable' to keep, if they must, and use them how they like. While they go away and do that, some of us *still* need a way of talking about, on the one hand, text that is readily turned into sounds using conventional knowledge of the sounds made by the letters and letter combinations concerned, and, on the other hand, text that is less easily dealt with in that way. Examples of the latter might include 'colonel' and 'lieutenant'. To talk of text being 'less easily dealt with' is not, of course, to say that the letters and letter combinations concerned afford no clues for the reader as to which word might be represented. Nor is it to imply that the letter(s)-sound associations in such text can be found in no other words. The 'irregularity' of a spelling is, then, a matter of degree, and there may be very few examples where the text-sound representation is *completely* idiosyncratic.)

A well-known phonics scheme says of 'irregular' text: 'The only way these words can be read and spelt correctly is by learning them and having plenty of practise' (*sic*). This claim would be plausible, perhaps, if we replaced 'The only' with 'One'. For such words *can* sometimes be identified by means of processes akin to psycholinguistic guessing games, though even here, attention may be given during that process at least to one or more of the letters that are featured in the text.

One of the arguments for readers needing letter–sound correspondence rules (and for the refusal to count any process other than the use of such correspondences as reading) is that, without memorizing these rules, readers will have to learn many thousands of individual words. Among other things this is, of course, a false dichotomy. Nobody actually fitted the extreme caricature of a whole language enthusiast teacher who literally prevented pupils from using clues in the form of letters and letter combinations to be discerned in the text with which they were wrestling.

If there is an argument here, it is an argument for the *efficiency* of learning to read by means of learning letter–sound correspondence rules. It is not obviously an argument for the claim that *inefficient* decoding is not reading at all. Memorizing is required in all cases, use of context in some and as we have noted, irregularity is a matter of degree, with some words placing more demands on the memory than others. I also think it is a mistake to portray memorizing whole words as if the standard situation in which that is done is learning the appearance of a piece of text in isolation, and learning to link a word in one's spoken vocabulary with it. When a young reader encounters one of the more 'irregular' pieces of text for the first time, and succeeds in reading it by employing a complex combination of attending to at least some of its letters, its context, syntax (and possibly even adjacent illustrations) she registers the shape of the text as a whole, making a link with a real word that is part of her spoken vocabulary. This may be all she requires to remember the shape of the text as a whole as linked to a real word, though it is possible that she will need more than one encounter with the text for this process to be completed. As described, this way of fitting a piece of text into memory and associating it with a known real word is very different from learning pieces of text in isolation.

Reading for meaning

Up to this point we have relied on an intuitive grasp of how 'meaning' functions in the idea of 'reading for meaning'. Unsurprisingly, however, there are complexities here, and it is important to appreciate at least some of these. I have unguardedly spoken of words as carriers of meaning. This may seem to imply that there is a specific meaning that accompanies each word. Whatever may be going for this idea, it must not be taken to invoke the crude and long abandoned 'Fido'-'Fido' theory of meaning, according to which each word has a meaning in a fashion that resembles the way 'Fido' might be thought to 'mean' a dog. Evidently, vast numbers of words including those functioning as verbs, adverbs, adjectives or conjunctions fail to fit this model.

Moreover, insights into the fundamental character of meaning stem from thinkers at least as far back as Frege, whose perspectives on meaning were taken up by Wittgenstein in the *Tractatus* and maintained, albeit in a transformed version in his later work to be found in the *Investigations* and elsewhere. Drawing on these insights, we can say that a word only has its full meaning in context. Contexts are often sentences, sometimes a bigger extract from the relevant language, and on other occasions are actually non-linguistic. 'Gate 32', seen on an airport sign, has no surrounding language to give it meaning.

Instead, the whole function of an airport provides the setting within which the sign has meaning. Wittgenstein significantly extended the idea of context to encompass aspects of language-independent reality. In his account of meaning as use, to characterize use is often to describe the non-linguistic circumstances in which an utterance is performed. Incidentally, it is quite often impossible to assign meaning to a sentence as a whole unless we appeal to the context, including the speaker or writer's intention. Consider the sentence: 'The tourist saw the astronomer with the telescope.' This can mean either that, with the aid of a telescope, the tourist was able to see the astronomer, or that the tourist saw the astronomer and the astronomer had a telescope with her. You may feel that such ambiguous sentences are flawed and should not be used. Yet many perfectly acceptable sentences *considered outside a context* have more than one meaning. All this must be taken into account when we try to understand what reading for meaning really amounts to.

A more radical version of this thinking is that the very idea of word meaning conceptualized as independent of context is fundamentally problematic. Yet, as against this, there is also the thought that without some notion of individual word meaning, we cannot explain a speaker's capacity to use a given word that she knows in a limitless variety of sentences.

It is common in the literature to meet the view that words have a context-independent 'lexical' meaning, and that, according to that same view, this is perfectly compatible with the fact that, *in* context, additional meaning is conveyed. So the word associated with the text 'cut', for instance, would have such a context-independent meaning. Searle (1995) writing in the shadow of Wittgenstein, asks us to ponder uses of 'cut' in 'Sam cut the grass', 'Sam cut the cake', 'Bill cut the cloth' and 'I just cut my skin'. Our knowledge of the meanings of other words in these sentences, and, crucially, our grasp of all sorts of aspects of empirical reality, enable us to assign additional specific meaning to each use of 'cut'. The grass may be cut in various ways, but almost certainly not with a knife, while the cake will not be sliced with a lawn mower. It should be noted in passing, that knowledge of the meanings of other words together with an insufficient grasp of reality may also *prevent* us from assigning additional specific meanings. We saw this in the earlier example of a temperature graph that showed a five-year running mean.

In order to make proper sense of our references to *'additional meaning'* here, should we be able to specify the core meaning of 'cut'? What would such a specification amount to? A set of criteria that must be satisfied if the word 'cut' is to be appropriately employed? A few moments thought tells us that such criteria are not available.

If meanings were thought of as discrete abstract entities, it was never going to be possible to explain them. Suppose, then, we give up on that idea. Yet imagine that, for the sake of argument we *do* accept the idea that individual words can be thought of as possessing context-independent meaning of some kind or other. Now we hear the word 'cut' spoken. We announce that we know what it means. There is no context, so we must be claiming that we grasp its context-independent meaning. To repeat, whatever such grasp amounts to, it cannot be an encounter with an abstract entity.

What, then, *do* we mean when we speak of words as carriers of meaning? Let us return to the example of 'does', referred to earlier. When an early reader employs context to determine that 'does' is not about several female deer but a form of the verb 'to do', she is not thereby encountering an abstract 'thing'. Nevertheless, she is moving around in an interconnected realm of abstract ideas in which 'does' features. Context is often a relevant sentence or several sentences, but single text items can have an extralinguistic context. At a little country zoo, a cage might be labelled 'Does'. The reader uses her environment to decide that the text is representing the word for female deer, and consults the vocabulary she understands when she hears it spoken, to determine that it should be pronounced to rhyme with 'rose', rather than a form of the verb 'to do' that would be pronounced to rhyme with 'buzz'.

Hank (2000) prefers to think of meaning as a word's potential to contribute to sentences of which it may be part, and such potential is, of course vast. The familiar phenomenon of Wittgensteinian family resemblances affects attempts to 'pin down' the meaning of many words, as does the equally familiar degree of vagueness between the 'meaning' boundaries of one word and the boundaries of another. Innumerable examples of such problematic boundaries include colour words, 'cup', 'vase' and 'bowl'. Labov (1973), for instance, reported that subjects were unable to offer clear verdicts about examples that tested the borders between what, for instance, counts as a cup and as a vase. The closest language comes to specific meanings is in its use by some sciences.

I have frequently spoken of readers employing 'context' to determine meaning, and hence which word they are encountering. 'Context' comes in a variety of guises, some of them rudimentary, while others are complex and rich, as Searle's 'cut' example vividly demonstrates. Early readers are hardly likely to meet Chomsky's famous 'Colourless green ideas sleep furiously'. Nevertheless, it is interesting to reflect on how the context afforded by this sentence can still help a reader to determine meaning of a kind. There are important syntactical clues. These help the reader to appreciate that Chomsky's sentence has a degree of syntactical coherence, and, partly in virtue of this, they then realize that it could not be used to make any kind of coherent claim. When we read 'Twas brillig, and the slithy toves' we attach rudimentary meanings even to what are basically meaningless pieces of text, and we are able to do so because we are aided by important syntactical clues, and, of course, the presence of a few perfectly decent textual versions of words such as 'and' and 'the'.

Readers may grapple with text that could be used to express self-contradictory claims. Again, the latter need sufficient meaning, so to speak, for it to be clear that in the final analysis they are meaningless – but they are not meaningless in quite the same way as Lear or Lewis Carroll. 'I have made a round square', or 'An omnipotent being has created a stone too heavy for Him to lift' each contain a logical contradiction, and so might reasonably be considered to be meaningless. Yet there is plenty of meaning, without which the contradictions could not be judged. There is real content here. So the slogan 'reading for meaning' does not entail that everything that can be read has, in the final analysis, a definitive coherent sense.

Hirsch reminds us that in reading for meaning, the meaning is a matter of degree. For a rich version of meaning and understanding, the reader's pre-existing knowledge of the content of what she is reading plays a crucial role. We saw this earlier when exploring Searle's treatment of the 'cut' example. Hirsch (2015) observes:

> In '83 Walter Kintsch and Teun van Dijk published a book ... which extended insights from ... psycho linguistics and this was the key insight.

One of the major contributions of psychology is the recognition that much of the information needed to understand a text is not provided by the information expressed in the text, but must be drawn from the language user's knowledge of the person, object, state of affairs or events the discourse is about... . If students lack the domain knowledge required by the topic ... they can't comprehend what's written down. (No page number in this lecture text)

The most important distinction for the purposes of my argument is that between operating 'merely' at the level of sounds, characterized physically, and operating at the level of meaning even at the most rudimentary level. The fact that reading embraces both acoustic and semantic domains together with the interactions between these domains, does not sit easily with the possibility of 'pure' methods of teaching reading.

Physical sounds and abstract meaning: John McDowell

I have argued that words are at a different level of conceptual abstraction from both of (a) types of speech sounds and (b) letter sequences as represented on paper. Nevertheless, it should be noted that both words on the one hand, *and* speech sound types and kinds of inscription on paper on the other, are also, of course, abstractions. If a child utters a physical sound at a particular time, this is a specific datable event in the empirical world. Yet as soon as we think of classifying that sound in any way, we are invoking kinds or types that are immediately in the realm of the abstract. I now explore these abstract realms further, showing the radical differences between the kinds of abstractions that feature in our characterization of kinds of acoustic events or inscriptions on paper, and the abstractions that belong in the realm of meaning inhabited by words. To repeat, inadequate grasp of the gulf between the two levels of abstraction informs some flawed conceptions of reading itself.

To support my explorations, I draw on the thought of Wilfred Sellars (1956) as developed by John McDowell(1994). These philosophers are exploring a fundamental and all-embracing question. How is our thinking answerable to how things are in the empirical world? McDowell characterizes what he calls the 'logical space of nature' (the empirical world itself) as the realm in which the natural sciences function. Relations in the latter realm 'do not include relations such as one thing's being warranted, or … correct, in the light of another' (xv). In contrast, the concept of *knowledge* belongs 'in the normative framework constituted by the logical space of reasons' (xiv). McDowell summarizes Sellars as follows. On an empiricist account of our knowledge, it is 'based' or 'founded' on experiences given to us via our five senses, these putting us in touch with the empirical world. This is sometimes referred to as a 'foundationalist' approach. Sellars asks how empiricism as a theory of knowledge is possible. How is our thinking answerable to the empirical world? McDowell develops a response to Sellars' question. The foundationalist holds that unconceptualized experiential states can provide the foundation for perceptual beliefs. For instance, on such foundationalist thinking, you can experience a yellow sensation, and on the basis of this conclude that you are actually seeing something yellow. Or you can experience a 'ffff' sound (the sound that a good phonics session might feature when children are focusing on the first sound in 'fun'), and on the basis of this conclude that you are actually hearing a 'ffff' sound.

Such thinking, however, constitutes the 'myth of the given', according to Sellars. 'The Given' in his writings refers to what is given to us in sense experience. Sense impressions are in a 'logical space' where things are not 'connected by relations such as one thing's being warranted or correct in the light of another' (xv). The 'myth' is, in short, that the given *is* encountered unconceptualized. On his view, it cannot be. For if sensations or experiences were 'given' unconceptualized, they could not play any kind of role in justifying an individual's belief about them. Raw experiences would be in the wrong category to support beliefs. Only conceptualized material can feature in beliefs, beliefs that can be involved in our knowledge. So, experiences must come to us already conceptualized. When we characterize someone's state as one of knowing, we are talking of something that is subject to justification. Justification involves reasons. Hence, when we speak of knowledge, we are speaking of something that belongs in the logical space of reasons.

Knowledge is at least true belief. Only beliefs can support (or count against) other beliefs. If we are good empiricists to the extent that we believe our knowledge is 'based' on our experience, the latter cannot come to us unconceptualized. We must operate in the 'space of reasons', where we deal in justifications for what we claim. McDowell argues that *all* experience is conceptual, falling within the space of reasons. Experience makes an impact on our knowledge and beliefs because it is already conceptual – it already belongs in the space of reasons. Some philosophers object that we can still undergo some experiences that are not conceptually embedded. I will not assume the impossibility of experiences that are outside the space of reasons, but I do want to apply an analogy of the 'myth of the given' to ideas about words and about what these could be 'made' from.

Within this space of reasons there are 'subspaces'. These house reasons that are related to each other more closely than they are to reasons within other subspaces. It is difficult to talk about this clearly, partly because the notion of a 'space' is heavily metaphorical in the first place. Examples may help to clarify the idea. Reasons for claims in physics are more closely related to each other than to reasons for claims about Western Art Music, or so it may be argued. Reasons for claims in politics have more affinities with each other than they have with reasons that feature in linguistics. Nevertheless, total isolation of one subspace from another is, of course, inconceivable. For instance, a reason within physics may turn up in some reasoning within music about harmony and well-tempered scales. The Enlightenment French composer Rameau seems to have thought so. A reason relating to the chemical constitution of paint pigment several centuries ago might feature in an examination of the aesthetic qualities of a Vermeer painting.

Bakhurst (2011) toys with the possibility that there might be more than 'one' space of reasons. He immediately rejects a radically relativistic reading of this idea. Following McDowell and Davidson, he dismisses the very strong relativist idea that 'inhabitants of different spaces of reasons are taken to live in different worlds' (p. 96 Note 20). Along Davidsonian lines, he argues that if we can interact with another individual as if they are someone capable of thinking, then the way they see the world must be open to us. Bakhurst proceeds to reflect on how we might conceive of more than one space of reasons. These might be thought of as 'different domains of enquiry *within* a world view' (ibid.). However, he warns us not to get carried away by this metaphor.

I will work with the possibility of 'sub-spaces' for a while, though it mostly helps to tell a conceptual story about different levels of abstraction. It will not bear too much argumentative weight.

Pursuing the analogy with the Sellars-McDowell claim that unconceptualized 'raw feels' cannot enter into justificatory relationships with beliefs, types of speech sound must be conceptualized. Hence, they must belong in the space of reasons in some overall sense. The sound 'fff' is conceptualized in such a way that it can play a role in the hearer having reasons for believing that she is not hearing the sound 'mmm', for instance. However, the conceptualization is insufficiently rich for these sounds to have reason-bearing relationships with claims within the subspace of reasons involving meaning. Examples of claims within the latter space include the following: that 'tear' and 'tear' can have different meanings, depending on context, that the meaning of 'bachelor' is the same as the meaning of 'unmarried man' in English, that 'bank' can be used to refer to the side of a river and to a financial institution, and that the meaning of a Proper Name is not that to which it refers. Also within this realm of meaning are assertions about grammatical or syntactical role. In the sentence 'Twas brillig, and the slithy toves', we can remark that 'toves' plays the role of a plural noun, even if little else can be said about them, other than that they just might be creatures of some kind given that we are shortly told that they did 'gyre and gimble in the wabe'.

We saw earlier that relations between speech sounds and inscriptions on the one hand and meaning on the other in all languages is conventional, with the possible exception of examples of onomatopoeia together with those early words in various languages for 'mum' and 'dad'. Hence we cannot 'reason' from the physical character of a speech sound or an inscription to anything to do with meaning.

In contrast, words viewed as being in the realm of meaning are embedded in a complex web of interrelationships. These belong to the semantic and syntactic realms. Types of speech sounds or inscriptions merely characterized in physical terms cannot possess these kinds of interrelationships. One speech sound may be physically close to some examples and physically distant from others: [e] resembles [I] more closely than [p], with concomitant relationships in terms of reasons in the subspace of reasons concerning speech sounds. No corresponding claims can be made about, say [e] and meanings.

I have repeatedly emphasized the gulf between physical sounds/inscriptions and meaning. The discussion in this section has elaborated on the detail of this gulf, and why it exists. The synthetic phonics meme of 'reversibility' has the effect of covering the gap with a blanket of deceptively clear and simple discourse. It represents matters as though there can be an almost seamless transition in both directions between acoustic sounds, on the one hand and meaning carriers (what I am calling words) on the other.

The last few paragraphs appeal to some difficult and arcane areas of philosophical thought. The most sophisticated and research-informed teachers may well think they have priorities other than grasping ideas of this kind. It is also true, in general terms at least, that treatments and interventions in a whole variety of areas may prove 'effective' even where neither those administering the treatments nor those on the receiving end have a full grasp of what is taking place. This may even be the case when a significant proportion of the beliefs held by the relevant practitioners are actually false or confused. The history of science contains plenty of examples, and the history of medicine is a particularly rich source of cases. Doctors drew on their experiences to treat patients, and sometimes their treatments worked well even when their own theories about *why* the treatments worked were completely mistaken. Generally, later developments uncover the problematic and false conceptions, and can explain how the interventions were effective despite the confusions of those offering them.

However, the clouded perceptions of the relationship between sounds, and the realm of words and phonemes go to the heart of the reading process. Such flawed perceptions, if informing putative methods for teaching reading, seem likely to threaten their integrity and the very possibility of appropriate research.

How the brain learns to read

Given the burgeoning research in neuroscience, I will briefly explore the question whether scientific investigation of the brain's involvement in learning to read might help synthetic phonics supporters to escape my critique of 'methods' research. Surely, it may be urged, this kind of science is the future, and my complaints about taxonomies must now give way to these exciting scientific advances.

Writing about neuroscience and learning sometimes features talk of the brain 'learning'. Is this simply a *facon de parler*? After all, we also encounter phrases like 'the social brain' and the 'emotional brain'. But a hostile reading of such discourse will accuse neuroscientists of committing category mistakes. According to criticism of this kind, neuroscientists are overlooking the fact that *persons* rather than brains learn. It is *persons* who are emotional and are social. To speak of brains learning resembles talking of square roots being red or justice being in the key of A major.

Earlier in the book I contended that detecting the presence of a teaching approach did not resemble detecting the presence of an element such as gold because of the contrasting characters of the categories concerned. I was able to flesh out the argument in considerable detail, demonstrating just how these categories differed from each other. Related arguments have been used by Bennett and Hacker (2003), for instance, to combat discourse featuring the idea that brains can be said to either 'know' or 'believe'. If brains cannot know or believe, then they cannot learn.

When you learn something new you usually acquire beliefs of some kind. When I learnt that Octavian became the first Roman emperor Augustus, I acquired a belief to that effect, though as we saw in the discussions of constructivism, this process is complex and cannot be 'reduced' to the crude claim that at time t I lacked the relevant belief while at time t+1 I acquired it. If it *were* appropriate to think and speak of brains knowing and believing, it might also be legitimate to refer to brains learning.

Bennett and Hacker (2003) observe: 'We know what it is for human beings to experience things, to see things, to know or believe things.' They go on to ask: 'But do we know what it is for a *brain* to see or hear, for a *brain* to have experiences, to know or believe something?' (p. 70). They urge that psychological predicates apply to human beings, and not to their parts. They label the contrary view, which they attribute to some neuroscientists, the 'mereological fallacy', mereology being the logic of whole/part relations. However, the alleged fallacy to which they refer looks similar to Ryle's original example of a category mistake that involved confusing a university with its parts, so I will continue to talk of category mistakes rather than venturing into mereology.

Hruby (2012), a psychologist reviewing the recent credentials of educational neuroscience follows Bennett and Hacker, claiming: 'Research from the neurosciences on the brain cannot support theories from other domains on other phenomena so simply. Interdisciplinary synergy is not the same thing as categorical conflation of fields and their discrete phenomenal foci' (p. 5).

I have some reservations about the category mistake meme, since the debates about this sometimes seem to be reducible to a situation where some opponents of the relevance of neuroscience to education assert the existence of such mistakes, while some neuroscientists cannot see this problem at all, and proceed with their research regardless. It is hard to see how we can proceed to *argue* either for or against category mistake claims, if our opponents simply 'don't see it'.

When it comes to matters of *detail*, however, I believe we can take the argument for category mistake assertions further. As I have also shown earlier in this book, learners cannot learn with understanding unless connections obtain between new content and their existing knowledge. For instance, a reader cannot in principle understand quantum physics unless some links obtain with her relevant existing knowledge of physics. This is a conceptual point. Hence it cannot be deduced from any empirical discoveries about neural processes. In particular, connections made at the level of brain biology *do* differ categorically from connections between new content and existing knowledge. Now this point is independent of any opinions held by neuroscientists, or, indeed by those who think neuroscience has little or nothing to offer teachers and learners. An unsympathetic reader will be quick to point out that, despite my earlier cautions about category mistake accusations, I am now confidently asserting the existence of a category mistake! I have to admit the fault, and can only say that some prima facie category mistakes are more equal than others.

In the face of the category mistake criticism, some neuroscientists may simply sidestep it by urging that they are merely finding convenient ways of speaking, and mean nothing radical by it. With this in mind, we turn to some recent research on the brain's role in learning to read.

Phonics supporters have been known to appeal to educational neuroscience to further their aims, claiming that it can support teachers in their choice of methods to teach reading. In one recent example of research cited for this purpose, Yoncheva, Wise and McCandliss (2015) report that 'alphabetic training generalizes to decoding novel words'. They claim that learning grapheme-phoneme mappings can have an impact on the brain 'circuitry that supports later word recognition'. Their opening assumption is that success in early reading acquisition depends on a learner's ability to master the association between spoken words and their corresponding visual word forms' (24). The authors claim that beginning readers need to focus on 'grain size'. This refers to whether they are looking at letters or combinations of letters on the one hand, or whole sequences of letters that might represent a whole word on the other. When early readers view a word, a range of grain sizes is available, and they need to be able to switch between grain sizes as and when appropriate. Our researchers say this in the light of what they regard as 'exception words' that cannot be decoded. (We saw earlier how some phonics supporters would strongly contest the latter claim.)

The subjects of this particular study were adults, and they were presented with lists of what the study calls words, rather than being asked to address text in context. I will refer to what they deem to be 'words' as 'letter sequences'. Hence, the processes being studied were highly artificial. The researchers compared the brain activity of people who learnt to 'recognize' letter sequences by means of letter–sound instruction with others who were taught to recognize those sequences as wholes. They found that the 'phonics' approach involved neural activity focused in the left side of the brain. They describe this as a location where visual and language processing occurs. (The meaning of that seems profoundly unclear, but let us continue.) The whole-letter sequence recognition group manifested neural activity concentrated in the right hemisphere.

This study restricts its investigations to the level of decoding at the physical or acoustical level. The realm of meaning is not reached. The reference to circuitry supporting later word recognition has to be accepted, but may almost be too true to be good. No one denies that brain functioning is a necessary condition for learning, and, indeed, a necessary condition for all psychological functioning. Yet there is a crucial ambiguity in the phrase 'word recognition'. This could merely mean decoding, or it could embrace reading words for meaning. If the latter, we have seen that meaning is bound up with knowledge. If someone is reading for meaning, brain areas other than those apt for decoding are bound to be involved. This may be yet another case where the SVR's assumption of the independence of decoding and LC causes trouble.

Another recent study not only restricts its focus to 'physical' decoding but also employs a stipulative and mistaken conception of reading itself: 'Reading is fundamentally audio-visual, entailing mapping between visual orthographic representations and auditory phonological representations' (McNorgan and Booth 2015). This is an extraordinary proposition. At best, what they describe is a necessary condition for reading. Earlier, I mentioned the possibility that some children born deaf read without the aforesaid mapping. Moreover, I have already referred to Andrews and Lo (2011), who report that some proficient readers are not in possession of fully comprehensive or accurate mappings. Furthermore, to sustain McNorgan and Booth's conception of reading, the SVR yet again is required to be a defensible account, in the sense that letter–sound mappings need to be separable from meaning and comprehension. Yet we have repeatedly seen that SVR fails to appreciate that, for reading to take place, complex interactions must often take place between the physical level of sounds and the abstract realm of meaning.

There is a deeper problem about investigating learning to read by discovering neural concomitants. It sometimes appears to resemble the hopeless task of researching how my computer handles Windows 8.1 by opening it up and scanning which silicon chips are active. It might be objected that I have overstated this point. After all, if I spill coffee on my machine and some circuits are damaged, this might be a pretty good explanation of why Windows 8.1 now no longer functions. (In fact, it is likely to explain why the machine is, to all intents and purposes, dead.)

So, an approach to grasping the importance and role of neural concomitants through a deficit situation may seem to be promising, at least in the initial stages. If someone suffers brain damage – as a result of an accident, or a stroke, for example, then she may be unable to function in certain ways. If areas of the brain broadly associated with language are affected, then her language processing may be severely impaired. Similarly, perhaps, if certain parts of my computer are damaged, then it will be unable to function. Thomas Szasz, a leading proponent of 'anti-psychiatry' in the middle of the last century, argued that the major mental health conditions could not properly be thought of as illnesses because no specific brain 'lesions' could be identified that were associated with these conditions. Szasz's contestable assumption here was that a condition was only an illness if it had a biological foundation.

However, Papineau (1994), in a move that will prove important for my argument here, suggests that the neural concomitants of at least some psychiatric disorders should be thought of along the lines of a software malfunction. If Windows 8.1 suffers a malfunction, it is possible, I suppose, that this is due to a hardware failure inside my machine. Yet much of the time, computer failures are linked to software difficulties, and no inspection of the components and their interconnections will reveal what has gone wrong.

It follows from this that the notion of a neural 'malfunction' cannot by itself aid us in pinning down what brain processes are necessary conditions for effective routes into reading. If the software analogy is appropriate, we cannot read off from the fact that certain parts of the brain are 'involved' in decoding, the conclusion that reading should be taught by means of letter–sound correspondences. For such neural involvement is compatible with both constructive and unhelpful learning, just as good software functioning *and* software failure are compatible with healthy circuit conditions inside my computer.

Furthermore, returning to McNorgan and Booth's mistaken conception of reading itself, we need to focus on the realm of meaning. As was discussed extensively in earlier sections, this realm incorporates aspects of social reality that in turn require the existence of constitutive rules and collective intentionality. So, when someone reads, rather than merely decoding, they must access their knowledge and beliefs about these aspects of social reality. This means, surely, that the relevant neural activity required must extend beyond those brain areas designated by McNorgan and Booth as relevant for decoding.

Proponents of so-called effective methods for teaching reading, and, in particular, adherents of Systematic Synthetic Phonics cannot resort to the authority of neuroscience to support their views.

Reading, Narratives, Families and Selves

Children who can read before they start school

One particular aspect of the objectionable imposition of Synthetic Phonics on all teachers and pupils relates to a small minority of children who begin schooling as readers. In this chapter, I explore the distinctive challenge to pure synthetic phonics teaching approaches that these pupils pose. They are, as I say, only a tiny percentage of those starting school in England at the age of four, but that still means that we are talking about quite a number of children. (I would like to be able to offer the figures of preschool readers, but have been unable to find a source of such data. However, most readers will know informally of one or two cases.)

They can do more than merely decode simple texts. They can read for meaning, succeeding at least at one of the earlier levels of meaning richness discussed above. They grasp that written text can, in principle, be transmuted into language that they can understand if they heard it, language that they could use coherently in speech, and language that they will eventually be able to write down for others to read. These achievements sometimes flower early because they have a history of sharing books with their parents.[1] Some of this small minority of children can even read silently. They are well beyond the stage of 'sounding out' words, if, indeed they ever went through such a stage in the first place.

A larger number are not quite so advanced, but, nevertheless, have made significant progress. Not all of them can recognize many textual representations of words, whether as distinctive shapes or by sound blending of some kind. Yet they are already familiar with some letter sequences as wholes. They grasp the idea of employing letter–sound associations to move towards determining the word linked to the text they can see. They are beginning to be able to make intelligent use of context. In short, they have begun to grasp that written text can be transformed into meaning and that it can host some wonderful stories.

Teachers and parents close to pupils who come early to reading know what a privilege and joy personal involvement in this process can be. Some preschool children (certainly not all), may be very interested in the text on the page before they can read. They are fascinated by the idea that these marks are somehow the source of the magical stories that they are enjoying. There should be relaxed and natural interactions between parents and children about such text. It would be very sad if adults began to abide by 'rules of engagement', gleaned from what they think either will be, or actually is taking place at school. No parent should be afflicted by anxieties over whether they are 'allowing' these emergent readers to do the 'wrong' thing about the text they encounter. Left unchecked, the child may make use of the opportunities of using pictures to aid identification of the text, or scan other text in the relevant sentences that they can already recognize to help them read. Sometimes she learns the story off by heart as a result of repeated sessions with parents. She may then begin to map her knowledge of the exact words back onto the groups of letters she can see on the page. She knows that the letters encapsulate the story. This is a powerful and exciting insight for her.

The ultimate logic of the 'rules of engagement' that might be determined by attempts to exclude multiple cueing, would be to hide the words from these young readers altogether while the book is being shared and the story read by the adult. This is a vile possibility, and immediately tells us something very important about the destructive potential of rigid approaches to decoding. Needless to say, many parents and carers would neither be prone to such anxieties, nor would they show such 'deference' to schools pursuing certain kinds of phonics policies. Nevertheless, others would be less robust, wanting desperately to do the very best for their offspring and believing that they should model their behaviour on what they take to be school practice.

As I say, some children are already passionately engaged with this wonderful aspect of our culture, and reading can play a crucial role in the development of parent–child relationships. Some families attach great importance to sharing books with their children, particularly when this involves delight in stories.

Rigid phonics diets, stories and the development of selves

In this final chapter, I explore one particular reason for concern about the impact of rigid phonics programmes on children who can already read. There are a number of reasons for worrying about this, some of which have already been mentioned earlier in passing. Here, however, I look in some depth at one particular issue. I want to suggest that to subject either the full-fledged readers, or those who are well on their way, to a rigid diet of intensive phonics could make a destructive impact on their emerging identities as persons. Michael Oakeshott once wrote:

> As civilized human beings, we are the inheritors, neither of an inquiry about ourselves and the world, nor of an accumulating body of information, but of a conversation, begun in the primeval forests and extended and made more articulate in the course of centuries. It is a conversation which goes on both in public and within each of ourselves. (Oakeshott 1962, p. 196)

Even quite young children, if already reading for meaning, are entering into this conversation, and into the exciting worlds of story and poetry. The vast majority of teachers, if allowed, take account of this and will exercise appropriate flexibility to cater for the presence of one or two 'real readers' in their classes.

Some of that minority who have already been immersed in stories at home are the most likely to be reading for meaning at the age of four or even earlier. Here, they begin to appreciate the possibility of extracting meaning from text and, in particular, that text can be the vehicle for story.

Brighouse and Swift (2009) comment, 'The parent reading the bedtime story is ... intimately sharing physical space with his child; sharing with her the content of a story selected by one of them; providing the background for future discussions ... reinforcing the mutual sense of identification one with another. He is giving her exclusive attention ... at a particularly important time of her day' (p. 57).

Ideas about story, narrative and links with the self and identity have become fashionable in the last couple of decades or so. I will draw on some of these, without attempting any kind of comprehensive critical review of the vast and multifaceted literature concerned. I will suggest that where young children are immersed in story at home before they start school, they are already experiencing a distinctive contribution to their selfhood.

I believe that a rigid phonics programme has the potential for making a destructive impact on a wonderful synergy that can obtain between the development of story reading and the development of the self. This will not necessarily happen, but teachers should have the professional freedom to act flexibly in relation to any pupils who they fear may be victims of this negative effect.

Am I finally venturing into territory where I have vowed I would not go? Davis (2013) was criticized for making claims without supporting evidence. The response to these critics was that at least 90 per cent of that short book did not consist of empirical claims at all, and hence evidence would not have been relevant. Yet now, or so it may seem, I am outlining what may appear to be an empirical assertion about the role of story in young children's constructions of their identities. So, I should either abandon this project, or be prepared to offer evidence. Furthermore, perhaps I should not even do the latter, since the search for evidence, or the lack of it, would be best left in the hands of an empirical researcher.

There is at least a grain of truth in this. I cannot provide a robust and definitive argument for what follows. However, I hope to show that my offerings comprise a complex mixture of the normative, conceptual and empirical and that there is plenty of philosophical meat here even though the issues could not be settled definitively without evidence. Moreover, it would be very challenging indeed to design any kind of empirical research into phenomena such as 'constructing a self'. How on earth would that be measured? How could we possibly know, if we came up with some kind of diagnostic or assessment device, that it was 'measuring' this, rather than something else? Evidently, much philosophical work would be required to elucidate the notion of 'constructing the self' before we could even begin to think about relevant measuring devices.

How is it possible that immersion in narratives can be implicated in a child's developing sense of self? If we are to take seriously a possible threat to advanced young readers posed by the experience of rigid phonics early in their school reading lessons, the potential for links between prior narrative experiences and the development of the self needs elaboration and defence. In order to do this, we must first touch on some basic philosophical ideas about personal identity and selves.

Personal identity and selves

Do *numerical* identity verdicts make sense when applied to selves? It is easiest to see how numerical identity works in the context of what philosophers have referred to as medium-sized dry goods. Is the chair on which I am now sitting *numerically identical* with the one that was temporarily put in the dining room yesterday? We have two chairs that look exactly the same as each other. We purchased them at the same time from a Department Store that stocked these goods from a particular manufacturer. I want an answer to my question about the chair, since the dog had a sleep on the one in the dining room, and although I cannot see any dog hairs, there might still be some, and I do not want them on my jacket. The two chairs are qualitatively identical (well, almost, if there are dog hairs on one of them), but numerically distinct. A superb forger might make an exact copy of a famous work of art, and, for a profit, pass it off as the original. Those interested in art works for their monetary value are very concerned indeed that they get hold of the originals, and not copies, however superb the latter might be. Numerical identity is the key to market value.

When we move on from medium-sized dry goods, numerical identity questions become much more difficult. Is the cumulus cloud I am now looking at numerically identical with a cloud I saw half an hour ago? Does it even make sense to ask whether the Berlin Philharmonic Orchestra to which I am currently listening is numerically identical to the Berlin Phil that existed in 1962? None of the current players were there in 1962. The orchestra certainly has an identity over time, but an application of numerical identity to this seems to be a kind of category mistake. Yet there are indirect uses of numerical identity in connection with physical phenomena such as hurricanes. These are named, and can be tracked over time. A storm born in the Caribbean may end up dying out near New York.

Descartes held that each individual is a mental substance, a 'thinking thing'. On his dualist account of reality, there are physical things and mental things. He did not employ the terminology of numerical identity, but it is clear that, according to his dualist view of reality, a self can continue through time as a mental thing, that a later self can be numerically identical with an earlier self, that at any one time there are many human beings and hence that there are multitudes of numerically distinct selves at that time. Identical twins may be qualitatively identical, at least at birth, but are always numerically distinct. David Hume argued that there was no such thing as a self, so there were, in his view, no items associated with the idea of a self to which judgements of numerical identity could be applied. In a more recent version of a 'no self' view, Fay (1996) observes, giving his remarks the status of speculations: 'The self is not a given thing which has experiences; it is the activity of owning certain experiences … the self would not be a fixed entity with definite boundaries but a process whose nature was fluid and changeable … the self is not a noun but a verb' (p. 39). Those who believe in reincarnation must think that, if they 'come back' as someone else or as an animal at some future time, the future person or animal has some kind of numerical identity relationship with the believer's present self.

We think of ourselves, Strawson (1997) reminds us, as 'things' that continue through time, as owners of experiences and as agents. Of course, as they stand, these thoughts are mere intuitions. They may be philosophically flawed. If they, in effect, embody beliefs that require notions of numerical identity to be applicable to selves, these beliefs may be false and confused. Nevertheless, such fundamental ways in which we see ourselves seem impossible to discard. They comprise necessary conditions for the possibility in principle that we can envisage a future, in which we can undergo changes, achieve changes and, in particular, imagine actions that we might or might not carry out. The changes we can contemplate include the acquisition of character traits and the transformation or even death of some habits and ways of being that we regard as undesirable. These imaginings are, to repeat, to do with *qualitative change* and *qualitative identity.*

This brief excursion into the kinds of identity claims that might or might not be made about the self enables me to set the scene for what follows. Whatever view is taken about the application of notions of numerical identity to the self, the aspects of the developing self with which I am concerned in this chapter relate to *qualitative identity* and *qualitative change.*

I think that Rudd (2012) would support my approach here, holding that we can think constructively and effectively about 'what it is to be a self', while, as he puts it: 'Setting aside-the traditional metaphysical disputes between dualism, materialism, dual-aspect theory... We can experience ourselves as selves (self-conscious subjects with characters) without having any clear views about the ultimate ontological nature or status of those selves' (p. 24).

Story, narrative and selves

In this spirit, I now explore certain aspects of story and narrative that can contribute to how children experience themselves as selves, and imagine their futures. Gergen and Gergen (1986) claimed that the rules of narrative creation within a culture offer a set of ready-made intelligibilities, or a range of possibilities for the social construction of the self. This sounds as if it is significant in relation to my argument, but is enigmatic as it stands. I will try to take it further.

MacIntyre (1981) observes, 'Narrative history of a certain kind turns out to be the basic and essential genre for the characterisation of human actions' (p. 194).

Since I rest much in this chapter on notions of story and narrative, it seems sensible to set out by outlining some key characteristics of narrative. Bruner (1991), in his outline of 'narrative diachronicity' makes the point that narratives offer an account of events over time. Compare this feature with a description of a house in an estate agent's brochure, a manual or guide for using an electronic device or the text used in a piece of legislation. While all such textual material will be accessed by people *while time passes*, their structure and sequencing itself is not time related. Narratives concern people acting in a setting, and involve their intentional states such as beliefs, intentions, theories and values.

Our actions become intelligible to us as ingredients of stories. We are at least partly responsible for constructing these stories. Isolated actions outside narrative contexts, examples of which are often favoured in the action theories of analytical philosophy, are rarely explicable when considered on their own, in terms of a human agent's intentions, motivations and beliefs.

Of course, at any time, I can stop to think about an action, seemingly in isolation from a context. As a result of doing this I can, for example, then choose to wiggle my finger or raise my arm as a 'stand-alone' act. Yet, even here, that act has already become part of a small narrative where I ponder philosophically about the possibility of stand-alone acts, and carry out one or more of them.

For the most part, actions need embedding in a coherent sequence over time. MacIntyre offers the example of a man gardening. In theory, we could analyse his activity into components. Just one of these might be a downward thrust of the spade. Imagine him to contemplate a mere aggregate of such possible components as a way of thinking about his immediate future and what he might do if he goes out into the garden. In this small thought experiment, have we not failed to envisage a human agent whose behaviour is capable of appropriate interpretation? Here is an example of just one of these components: Once in the garden he stabs downward with that spade, lifts it at an angle with some soil, moves the spade round approximately 50 degrees, turns it, the soil sliding off the spade to the ground. But why is he doing this? There is likely to be a good reason. Yet this description, at the level of characterizing a stand-alone action, make little sense. We really do need to locate his activity in a broader 'story' in order to achieve some kind of understanding of the man as a human agent, a self that exists over time. Is he taking exercise, or preparing for winter, or even pleasing his wife? Could his activity even be an element in 'the narrative history of a marriage'?

Bruner (1987) and Ricoeur (2010) argued that the only way we have of describing 'lived time' is to employ a story mode. Bruner held that the forces informing the stories we tell about our lives have a significant impact on our perceptual experiences, on how we organize our memories and even on our lived and experienced life events. Ultimately, we 'become' the autobiographical narratives that we use about our lives.

Our journey through time as continuing selves becomes intelligible to each of us as a story or series of stories. These may overlap, and sometimes more than one story fits our journey. That is not to say that every aspect of our journey possesses total coherence or rationality. Indeed, it is often only within the context of a narrative self that we can begin to grasp degrees of senselessness and irrationality that are sometimes present.

There has been controversy about whether we live a narrative that is already, so to speak, laid out before us, or whether we create the story that we live. Williams (2007) argues that we can have a basic sense of a self through time without narrative, and that it is when we are social beings, interacting with others, that narrative acquires a fundamental role. So he disagrees with the strongest claims about the links between narrative and the self that are advocated by MacIntyre and Bruner. I will not attempt to settle that particular debate here. Williams's line of argument may well be compatible with Galen Strawson's (2004) widely discussed sceptical treatment of narrative theorizing over recent decades. Strawson denies that human beings 'typically' live or experience their lives as a story or collection of stories. This, he contends is an empirical thesis and it is not true of everyone. It is linked to a self-experience that he characterizes as 'Diachronic'. That is to say, a sense of oneself as something that was there in the past and will be there in the future (p. 430). He offers by way of contrast, an 'episodic' self-experience, where those in this category have no tendency to see their lives in narrative terms, and lack a sense 'that the self that one is was there in the … past and will be there in the future' (430).

Rudd (2012) comments that I may think of myself in more than one fashion. In the first, I cast myself as that which I 'consciously will to be'. If I am overwhelmed in some way, for instance, by a desire to hurt someone who has betrayed me, I may regret this, and hold 'that my true self has been pushed to one side'. In another example, we may say of a bereaved friend that they are 'beside themselves with grief', or simply that 'they are not themselves just now'. In a second contrasting attitude to the self, an individual may take her true self to be 'a set of dispositions or characteristics that are just there, irrespective of … consciously willed attitudes or … values' (Rudd 2012, p. 11).

I have no wish to resolve the tension between these two attitudes to our selves, and indeed, am unable to do so even if I wanted to. I draw from Rudd's comments the idea that we live with both ways of thinking about ourselves. They relate to the complexities of our identity *in the qualitative sense*. Finding my 'true self', if that were a coherent idea, let alone if it were possible, would not be departing from my numerical identity, even if such an idea *were* applicable to selves.

I take from Williams and Strawson the point that any very strong claim about necessary links between selves and narrativity is open to question. All I need for my argument is the plausibility of the claim that for at least some of us, the development of the self can become inextricably linked with narrative, and I will now proceed to explore the nature of such a link in some depth.

When encountering story, especially within the loving security of a family who love sharing books, the child's imagination is engaged and developed. 'Imagination' can be employed by writers to capture all sorts of creative and exotic faculties of the mind. Stevenson (2003) offers *twelve* conceptions of imagination. These include the ability to think of something that is not presently perceived, but is, or was or will be spatio-temporally real, the ability to think about what I hold to be possible in the empirical world, to entertain mental images, and to conceive of or represent anything at all. He also covers aspects of the aesthetic dimension, but for the purpose of my argument I will set these to one side. What I intend to mean by imagination here runs together several of Stevenson's strands: the ability we all possess to entertain thoughts about what is and what might be but is not and may never be. We may do this with the help of words, visions, even auditory, kinaesthetic or olfactory sequences, and usually in complex combinations of these.

Nearly every waking moment in a human life involves decisions; many of these are made in but a fraction of a second, and are scarcely, if at all present to the conscious mind. Nevertheless, to make a decision you need the capacity to 'have in mind' one or more action possibilities. The latter could concern things you might do that involve using your body, or topics that you might want to think about, or some combination of these. As characterized so far, we could be dealing with an isolated action. Yet, as we have seen, for a potential action to be yours and for you to have reasons for performing it, surely you need to locate it in your imagination within a larger canvas; in fact a narrative that gives it coherence and links your putative action to who you are. Often enough, the formation of your intentions involve considering other people who are part of the context in which you may act. You remember their past behaviour, you contemplate their personality traits and you *imagine* how they might react if you were to do this thing rather than that.

Jones wonders whether to go and apologize to his aunt for the impatient way he answered her question about his health this morning. To carry out his project, he would need to leave work early and take the car to see his aunt today. The previous night, he had slept badly after hearing some bad news during a hospital appointment and was feeling anxious about the future. Yet he knows that he should not take out his worries on his aunt, who meant well, and is likely to have been hurt by his impatient and aggressive manner. In this example, we are sketching a human intention that might, or might not be realized. It is complex, and takes the form of a brief narrative sketch. It is, of course, broader and richer than specific immediate intentions such as the intention to raise my arm.

So what role might encounters with narratives play here? Narratives sometimes embrace the third party perspective; stories about people 'from the outside', so to speak. Here, readers and characters *in the stories* infer the nature of the actions of others in those stories from what they do and say. Narratives also can offer a view of agency 'from the inside'. They can portray the inner world of a person, in which they hope, doubt, are confused and think about what to do (Bruner 1987).

Other stories portray characters as seen through the eyes of one individual, who may well be the one with whom the reader will identify, whether or not the author intends it. Let us call this individual the hero or heroine, for expository convenience, even though, needless to say, not all stories offer any characters playing such a role. This heroine is sometimes shown as imagining what is going on in the heads of other characters, so to speak. She may speculate on why they are acting as they are, on how they are feeling about events and what they think about other characters. A child reader is exposed to these processes. The child is likely to bring to the book their own experience of imagining the thoughts and feelings of family members, friends and enemies. There will be interactions between such experience and the related phenomena portrayed in the narrative they are encountering. So the fortunes of a crucial aspect of their developing identities, namely their capacities for empathy and sympathy, will become linked in various ways to their journeys in story. If the story is told from an 'omniscient' point of view, that is to say, in such a way that the reader can 'see' into the heads of all the characters and grasp all their thoughts, then less attention may be paid to the heroine's (fictional) imagination about other characters' inner psychology.

However, sometimes the reader will be offered both 'what is really going on' in the head of a particular character, *and* the heroine's own speculations about just that. So the reader can compare and contrast a particular perspective with the omniscient view. Again, the child reader will bring to this their own imaginings about the thoughts and feelings of others, and there may well be a potent chemical reaction as the reader's and the author's imaginations interact with each other.

It may be objected that the picture I am painting here not only is speculative (which indeed it is) but seems to be about sophisticated stories of a kind that children arriving at school will certainly not have enjoyed by then. I would respond that it is unwise to underestimate what some advanced four-year-old readers can achieve, even though we are speaking of just a small percentage of those starting school. Furthermore, some parents of advanced readers will share books that are still well beyond their children's reading abilities. This gives the young readers the anticipation of riches to come, that their simple readable texts are only divided by gradual degrees from the richer and more complex stories that they are confident they will be able to read when a little older.

The other point here is that even quite simple stories can embody at least some of the potentially imagination enhancing elements discussed in the previous paragraph. A child reader may 'become' Goldilocks in that familiar tale, yet can 'overhear' the bears' comments when, as is usually the case, the narrator offers an omniscient perspective. In Sendak's *Where the Wild Things Are*, Max becomes King of the Wild Things towards the end of the story. Nevertheless, he begins to feel lonely and to want to be where someone loved him best of all. So again, we have a character with whom a child reader will identify, imagining a situation not present to him, and the imagining extends to the feelings of his mother (?), who 'loves him best of all'. The narrator in the classic *Not Now, Bernard* does not tell the reader directly how things are in the heads of Bernard's parents when Bernard (and, later on, the Monster) address remarks to them. However, the reader is prompted to imagine that neither parent is thinking about Bernard at all. They refuse to listen, and continue their own thoughts and activities. The reader can readily imagine this, which, of course, provides the story with its pace and tension.

Stories need not always offer even indirect textual catalysts for imagination of the kind I am illustrating. Instead, it is sometimes a matter of what the child brings to the text. My youngest daughter was passionately fond of a version of the *Three Little Pigs*. At the beginning, a picture shows Mother Pig waving goodbye to her children, accompanied by some appropriate simple text. My daughter often wept at this point because she thought Mother Pig would be so sad at her children's departure or, possibly that the little pigs would be so upset at leaving their mother. So the child was stimulated by the story into bringing her own imaginings to the text, and, in particular, speculating on what might be going on in Mother Pig's head or the heads of the little pigs.

This example brings to our attention the place of reader emotion in story immersion, and the extent to which such emotions make any kind of constructive contribution to the child's own developing emotional life. For the latter is a crucial aspect of the development of her sense of and control over her emerging character and personality. Some children's stories are written to invite the reader to identify with the hero or heroine: to be joyful when their favoured characters are joyful, to be unhappy when their actors are sad, and to fear for them when they are in danger. It is easier to illustrate these points with examples of books suitable for older readers, but the same points apply to many of the very simple stories that some advanced four-year-old readers may be tackling.

The reader probably roots for all of the goats in *The Billy Goats Gruff*, a combination of fear that they will be eaten by the troll, and delight in their victory. In *Charlotte's Web*, young readers have great anxiety about the threat to the life of the piglet Wilbur, and hope desperately that Spider Charlotte will succeed in saving him. They grieve at Charlotte's death, and rejoice at the end of the story when the three spiderlings Joy, Nellie and Aranea remain to keep Wilbur company.

Of course, all this is unreal, and some might argue that it is wrong for children to feel strong emotions in relation to pure fiction. Indeed, it might be thought that they should be taught to reserve their reactions for real people's happiness and grief. It is perfectly possible for children to be strongly moved by stories, feeling compassion for the downtrodden, for instance, and for those same children to behave atrociously in the playground, joining in with bullying victims who are *really* downtrodden. However, this objection, though making factual claims that are only too plausible, misses the point I am trying to make about the role of emotion in story. I am not for a moment suggesting that children's reading of stories will necessarily contribute to their moral education, if by that we mean, an education that helps them to be morally better than they otherwise might have been. Nor am I ruling out the possibility that it might happen sometimes. I am suggesting that stories can help to awaken the possibility of emotion focused on people, or animals that are anthropomorphized in the tale. Such emotions are essential for the child to develop an identity in terms of personality and character. Part of the development of a self as understood in this way is the formation of the capacity to *empathize* with another. This returns us to the theme of imagination, discussed earlier in the chapter. I am taking empathy in the standard way to mean imagining what it is like to be another person. This includes entertaining the holding of certain beliefs imagined to be possessed by others, of seeing the world from a particular point of view (both metaphorically and literally), and of imagining having feelings and emotions about people and situations. I may, or may not have any of these beliefs myself, and I may or may not have similar emotions to those of the person with whom I empathize.

Narrative thinking of this kind hints at the possibility that a child's acquaintance with rich narratives could play a deep role in the development of her sense of identity. Must the narratives be fictional? Given their contribution to the narrative self explored above, the answer has to be that the extent to which they mirror reality does not seem crucial. Must the narratives be found in books? Again, the answer is no, not necessarily. Children can encounter narratives in a range of media. Film, TV, audiobooks and even computer games offer plenty of opportunities for story. Some parents tell their children stories directly, with no books in the vicinity. Some families make up stories with their children together. All I am arguing in this chapter is that stories found in books provide one important stimulus for the imagination and emotion for *some* children, and that in *some* cases this can begin when they are very young, well before they start school.

This, at best, would be a claim belonging to psychology, and since many children apparently develop perfectly adequate conceptions of their identity without narrative in their cultural capital, the claim would be true of only a limited minority. Nevertheless, any child for whom narratives have come to play an important part in their developing selves could be especially vulnerable early in their school lives.

I end with a moral point. Such children begin school, some of them only just four years old. Certain kinds of rigid phonics programmes tell them, whether explicitly and intentionally or otherwise, that silent reading is not 'proper' reading. They must read aloud, and not only that. They must manifest the fact that they are sounding and blending. Pictures, such as those in *Where the Wild Things Are* have been intimately associated with their experiences of reading for meaning. In the phonics reading aloud situation, pictures will not be present, or, if they are, the children will be told emphatically that they are *not* to take account of them, for to do so is not 'real' reading, but only 'guessing'. I do not think that we should ever treat young children like this.

Conclusion

Phonics supporters worldwide are *still* repeating over and over again the claim that 'scientific' research indicates that Synthetic Phonics is clearly *the* effective way of teaching reading. They want it implemented everywhere. At the time of writing, evidence of this can be found in their efforts to influence the Australian Government to implement a Phonics Check similar to that in force in England, and discussed earlier. I predict that if any of my opponents read this work, they will once again cast me in the role of a 'phonics denialist': that is to say, someone who opposes the use of phonics, and of Systematic Synthetic Phonics in particular. Let me now try to summarize what I have really done in this book, and what my true position is in reality.

I began the main discussion by distinguishing between the knowledge pupils need, and the teaching methods employed to enable them to acquire it, arguing that the knowledge does not itself determine appropriate teaching methods. Of course, while logic alone might not implicate particular approaches, it might be thought that empirical evidence could fill the gap. How evidence might support social science claims depends in part on how the relevant social phenomena are categorized, and some attention was devoted to the logical and conceptual status of such classification. The focus then shifted to the classification of teaching methods themselves, from the very broad-brush categories such as 'Direct Instruction' and 'Discovery Learning' to the specific 'Synthetic Phonics'. Research often seems to proceed as if such categories resemble those of the Natural Sciences. Yet it emerged that there are some important differences between Natural Science and at least some social science categories, and that the latter include classifications of classroom teaching. Efforts to trap teacher actions within an identifiable method turned out to be incompatible with teachers exercising autonomy within interactive teaching, as opposed to delivering extreme forms of Direct Instruction on the lines of a recipe or script. Even without the fundamental 'method identity' problems, it would not necessarily be morally appropriate to impose these putative approaches on all teachers and children. I showed in some detail why this is so. RR is often portrayed by phonics enthusiasts as a method that they wish to oppose and replace. I consider this as a case study, and conclude that RR is as much an ethical approach as anything else, and cannot properly be referred to as a 'method'. The Phonics Check in England is one way in which a government attempts to impose a pure teaching method, and I show many of its flaws in some detail.

An important challenge to method identity springs from the truth in constructivism, and I devoted a whole chapter to exploring this particular issue. The constructivism with which I was concerned is not a teaching style, but, rather, a conceptual account of what it is to learn. I argued that recipe implementation is incompatible with teachers giving proper space for learning that is understood. This in turn implies that teaching must be interactive, which undermines the putative 'purity' achieved in any attempts to specify teaching methods closely. From this, I moved to the nature of reading itself, since inappropriately stipulative definitions of reading are sometimes implied by conceptions of 'pure' phonics teaching methods. To develop a reasonably comprehensive account of reading, I looked extensively at some of its 'nuts and bolts', including the notion of phoneme, and of word itself. Reading for meaning was a key element in the argument. In consequence, much attention was devoted to meaning itself, and the variety of levels of meaning that reading might involve.

Finally, I explored a topic that is independent of the main argument. I reflected on the fate of children who may arrive at school already reading, having experienced a story-enriched home environment. In these intimate and loving encounters with narratives, they may be supported in developing their sense of self. If they are subjected to a first and fast phonics regime early in their time at school, they may, as a result of their previous experiences at home, prove to be distinctively vulnerable.

Appendix: A Brief History of Events Leading to This Book

Much of my academic life has been dedicated to Mathematics Education, the Philosophy of Education and in particular, philosophical issues linked to educational assessment. Some years ago, I presented a paper at the annual conference of the Philosophy of Education Society of Great Britain, called *A Monstrous Regimen of Synthetic Phonics: Fantasies of Research-Based Teaching 'Methods' Versus Real Teaching*. Was the title a little provocative? Perhaps. Yet the audience was likely to be (and was), modest in number, and to comprise, for the most part, academic philosophers of education from various parts of the world. In addition there would probably be one or two practising teachers, conference regulars, with a penchant for philosophy of education. My talk was just one of at least six parallel sessions. I enjoyed creating an eye-catching title for my paper but expected few to take the slightest notice. An improved version of the paper was eventually published (2012) in *Education Policy: Philosophical Critique*, a collection of academic articles edited by Richard Smith.

So, whatever possessed me to write in this way? I began my career as a primary teacher, concentrating on Early Years, and in consequence spent much time teaching children to read. Primary teachers in England are often general class teachers, and have to do everything. Inevitably reading always has a high priority. After a number of years in primary schools I moved into Higher Education. I worked first at Cambridge and then at Durham University, visiting numerous primary schools in several local education authorities. Inevitably I saw a great variety of reading and literacy lessons. I had the privilege of discussing these in detail with very many teachers and students.

I was dimly aware of the ongoing 'Reading Wars', but paid them little attention. Nevertheless, even from the mid-1990s onwards, I was aware of an increasing emphasis on phonics for early reading. This did not seem particularly disturbing or objectionable. After all, I reflected, as a teacher, I had made extensive use of phonics in the broadest sense. By this, I mean that I had taught children directly about letter sounds, the sounds linked to letter combinations, how words are often 'built up' from them, about families of rhyming words with common patterns and the relationships with writing and spelling. This aspect of supporting early readers seemed like basic common sense. Discerning the importance of phonics hardly seemed worth making a song and dance about, and my primary teacher colleagues had similar views. I do not remember any extreme 'whole language' or 'whole word' enthusiasts, but of course, my memories are, at best, mere anecdote.

However, around five years ago, I began to hear odd stories from parents about children bringing home tins of letters to learn the sounds, and of books being deliberately created *without pictures*. These anecdotes provoked me into investigating further, and then into writing that conference paper, *A Monstrous Regimen*. At that time, I knew nothing of the commercial interests in phonics schemes and the very large sums of money at stake. To my utter astonishment I discovered, quite by accident, that the said paper had been 'noticed' by people linked to a group calling itself the 'Reading Reform Foundation' (RRF). Some of its members were subjecting my reflections to some peculiar online attacks. Their hostility extended to the Philosophy of Education Society of Great Britain (PESGB) itself, as a body who had hosted my modest and obscure conference paper. The PESGB is a reasonably respectable academic organization that has existed since 1964 and would have been mildly surprised at featuring in any kind of RRF commentary, had they known of it. At the time, I had absolutely no idea why the 'RRF' had taken any notice of what I had written. I was compared to the poet and children's author Michael Rosen, and it took me a while to discover just what an insult *that* was in these people's minds. I came to appreciate later on that in fact this amounted to a great (but unintended) compliment. The theme of 'Monstrous Regimen' was then taken up by posters to an online thread hosted by the Times Educational Supplement (TES). This continued for a year or more, and featured many thousands of contributions.

The short book *To Read or Not to Read: Decoding Synthetic Phonics* (Davis 2013), published in late 2013 was the twentieth in PESGB's IMPACT series. These publications are designed to apply philosophy of education to aspects of educational practice. They are meant to be written in an accessible style, for an audience that includes policymakers and teachers, and readers need not be versed in any way in academic philosophy. It provoked a brief but quite extensive outbreak of national publicity early in 2014. I suddenly found myself in the middle of fierce and abusive exchanges between opposing parties, the existence of which I had been ignorant up to the time of writing 'A Monstrous Regimen'. I was held to belong, ideologically speaking, to one of the parties.

I was accused of lying. I was never entirely sure what this was about. One possibility was that I had said that I was not against phonics, when, according to my opponents, I really was. Yet I used phonics in all shapes and sizes when a primary teacher, and supported students along the same lines in hundreds of schools, several local authorities and when working in two Higher Education institutions. This may be where a kind of fundamentalism is at work. Apparently, unless you actually support Synthetic Phonics in a way that means teaching Synthetic Phonics *and nothing else* for a period of time for early readers, you are in fact deemed to be against it. If you allow pupils to use *any* cues other than letter–sound correspondences, you are hostile to phonics. So, if you countenance other ways of identifying words than Synthetic Phonics during this crucial period, then you are not a phonics supporter, but a 'denialist'.

('Fundamentalism' does seem the appropriate term to use in this connection, which is why I wrote a short newspaper article in early 2014 entitled *A Plague on the Fundamentalism of Synthetic Phonics*.) The hallmark of religious fundamentalism is the belief that your faith is correct, the only one that is correct, and that its truth directly implies the falsity of all other faiths. The 'purity' of Synthetic Phonics is central in my discussion of teaching methods. At the beginning of this book, I rehearsed a number of policy sources that are very explicit about this purity. I did this in order to combat accusations that I have constructed a straw man as an element in my arguments against imposing a 'pure' phonics teaching method.

I was also said to have compared phonics teaching to child abuse, the latter almost equated by some commentators to sex abuse. The relevant passage from *To Read or Not to Read* was this:

> To require this (making them subject to an intensive and exclusive diet of synthetic phonics) of students who have already gained some maturity in the rich and nourishing human activity of reading is almost a form of abuse. Is this overstated? I can only appeal to teachers and parents close to pupils who come early to reading. Some of the latter are already passionately engaged with this wonderful aspect of our culture, and reading can play a crucial role in the development of parent-child relationships.

This passage was written about the *possibility* that children who arrived at school at the age of four already reading would be subjected to the full programme of 'first and fast' phonics. I immediately go on to ask whether I am overstating the position, and proceed to explain just why I used the word 'abuse'. Incidentally, in everyday language, we use phrases such as 'emotional abuse', 'abuse of power', 'abuse of language' and many others that have nothing whatever to do with child sex abuse.

Some critics of *To Read or Not to Read* accused me of making claims without evidence. As a matter of fact, most of what I wrote did not consist of empirical assertion. The nearest to *any* kind of empirical claim in *To Read or Not to Read* was the point that a few children who could read on arriving at school might be damaged by rigid phonics programmes. Stuart (2014) complained that government policy was perfectly compatible with a flexible approach for advanced readers and that I had offered no 'evidence' for the damage suggestion.

Many were in touch with me personally in the months immediately following the publication of *To Read or Not to Read*, including parents and teachers dealing with young advanced readers. Some of these people told me very sad stories about what had happened to the children concerned when subjected to a first and fast phonics regime that ignored the fact that they could already read. There were even cases where children had become school refusers. Hence, I now do have at least anecdotal evidence for that tiny quasi-empirical element in *To Read or Not to Read* (I certainly would not assume from these stories that all children who can read on arriving at school will be in some way 'damaged' by first and fast Synthetic Phonics. I have never said this, and do not think it. I speculated that *some* could be, and I have since been told that *some* are.)

As I have already noted, three long-running threads on the TES Opinion Forum, resulting from someone posting extracts from my 2012 PESGB conference paper *A Monstrous Regimen of Synthetic Phonics* accumulated many thousands of responses. I would have supplied the weblinks, but the TES has either got rid of these now, or buried them somewhere and I can't find them. Some other websites, blogs and posts on social media continued the coverage. See, for instance, the 'Reading Reform Foundation' coverage at http://rrf.org.uk/messageforum/viewtopic.php?f=1&t=5887&hilit=Davis entitled 'Outstanding overview addresses nonsense in Davis's paper'.

A fresh wave of social media activity in the summer of 2014 followed the publication of an Open Letter in the Times Educational Supplement that urged Michael Gove, the then Secretary of State for Education, to abolish the Phonics Check (https://www.tes.com/news/school-news/breaking-views/open-letter-michael-gove-why-year-1-phonics-check-must-go). Of course, I say quite a lot about the 'Check' at the end of Chapter 3. Anyhow, I was one of the signatories to the Open Letter, alongside major teacher unions and a range of significant academic figures.

None of the social media commentary would be worthy of much attention, if it were not the case that some of its heroes are actually listened to by UK government ministers and other influential education policymakers. This is a profoundly depressing phenomenon. The educational policies of a liberal democratic state should *never*, in any circumstances be influenced by material of this kind. I can only hope that this book plays some role in taking the discussion back where it belongs, namely to civilized, rational and rigorous debate about these important issues.

Notes

Chapter 3

1 The next few paragraphs follow Davis, Goulding and Suggate (2017) fairly closely.

Chapter 4

1 There has been fierce controversy in the UK about the possibility of teachers 'not needing' to plan, working instead from lesson plans devised by school senior management teams. In a brief article by a young teacher at Michaela community school (https://www.tes.com/news/school-news/breaking-views/why-new-teachers-should-not-have-plan-lessons-they-should-just-get), she argued that she could concentrate on her subject knowledge because she had no need to spend time on plans; these were already in place, being created by senior staff. As always in disputes of this kind, confusion creeps into the debates because protagonists mean different things by the key terms. In these discussions, 'plan' can mean a number of different things. These include (a) an outline of key concepts and information to be taught, (b) similar to (a) but with more detail about the form of words to be used in explanations, and (c) something more like a script that all teachers follow, taking little or no account of the responses of pupils in any one lesson. There have been examples on this extreme end of the dimension where the required pupil responses are actually built into the script. Evidently the plausibility of any claim of the 'teachers not needing to plan' family depends fundamentally on that meaning of 'plan'.

Chapter 5

1 In my discussions of 'phoneme', 'word', and other language components, I have drawn on Wetzel (2009). I have not referenced her text in detail. This is because there are some points about which I differ from her, but elaborating on these would

take me too far from the main aims of this book. Nevertheless, I am greatly indebted to her treatment of word and phoneme identity.

Chapter 7

1   To avoid clumsy exposition, I will restrict my language to 'parents' and 'family' throughout this chapter. Needless to say, carers other than parents share books with young children, and 'family' may include extended families such as grandparents.

References

Aitken, S. and Beardmore, K. (2015), 'Accent, Dialect and Phonics', in Kathy Brodie and Keith Savage (eds), *Inclusion and Early Years Practice*, 56–73, London: Routledge.

Alexander, R. (1992), *Policy and Practice in Primary Education*, London: Routledge.

Alexander, R. (2001), *Culture and Pedagogy*, Oxford: Blackwell Publishing.

Alexander, R. (2008), *Essays on Pedagogy*, London: Routledge.

Allor, J., Mathes, P., Roberts, J., Cheatham, J. and Otaiba, S. (2014), 'Is Scientifically Based Reading Instruction Effective for Students With Below-Average IQs?' *Exceptional Children*, 80 (3): 289–308.

Andrews, S. and Lo, S. (2011), 'Not All Skilled Readers Have Cracked the Code', *Journal of Experimental Psychology*, 38 (1): 152–63.

Arrow, Chapman and Greaney (2015), 'Meeting the Needs of Beginning Readers through Differentiated Instruction', in W. Tunmer et al. (eds), *Excellence and Equity in Literacy Education*, 171–93, Basingstoke: Palgrave-Macmillan.

Ausubel, D. (1968), *Educational Psychology: A Cognitive View*, New York and Toronto: Holt, Rinehart and Winston.

Bakhurst, D. (2011), *The Formation of Reason*, London: Wiley.

Barry, S. (2003), 'Phoneme-grapheme Correspondences and a Manchester Accent', *Education Committee of the Linguistics Association of Great Britain*, www.phon.ucl. ac.uk/home/dick/ec/accents.htm (accessed 3 November 2013).

Bastian, B. and Haslam, N. (2006), 'Psychological Essentialism and Stereotype Endorsement', *Journal of Experimental Social Psychology*, 42 (2): 228–35.

Beck, I. and Beck, M. (2013), *Making Sense of Phonics*, New York: Guilford Publications.

Biesta, G. (2007), 'Why "What Works" Won't Work: Evidence-Based Practice and the Democratic Deficit in Educational Research', *Educational Theory*, 37 (1): 1–22.

Biesta, G. (2012), 'Giving Teaching Back to Education: Responding to the Disappearance of the Teacher', *Phenomenology & Practice*, 6 (2): 35–49.

Biesta, G. (2015), 'On the Two Cultures of Educational Research, and how we Might Move Ahead: Reconsidering the Ontology, Axiology and Praxeology of Education', *European Educational Research Journal*, 14 (1): 11–22.

Bodman, S., Taylor, S. and Morris, H. (2012), 'Politics, Policy and Professional Identity', *English Teaching: Practice and Critique*, 11 (3): 14–25.

Braddon-Mitchell, D. and Jackson, F. (2007), *Philosophy of Mind and Cognition: An Introduction*, Malden, MA: Blackwell.

Brighouse, H. and Swift, A. (2009), 'Parental Partiality', *Philosophy & Public Affairs*, 37 (1): 43–80.

Brinton, J. and Brinton, D. (2010), *The Linguistic Structure of Modern English*, Amsterdam: John Benjamin Publishing.

Bruner, J. (1987), 'Life as Narrative', *Social Research*, 54 (1): 11–32.

Bruner, J. (1991), 'The Narrative Construction of Reality', *Critical Inquiry*, 18 (1): 1–21.

Buckingham, J., Wheldall, K. and Beaman-Wheldall, R. (2013) 'Why Jaydon can't Read: The Triumph of Ideology over Evidence in Teaching Reading', *Policy: A Journal of Public Policy and Ideas*, 29 (3): 21–32.

Cartwright, N. and Hardie, J. (2012), *Evidence-Based Policy: A Practical Guide to Doing it Better*, Oxford: Oxford University Press.

Chapman, J., Greaney, K. and Tunmer, W. (2015), 'Is Reading Recovery an Effective Early Literacy Intervention Programme for Children Who Most Need Literacy Supports?' in W. Tunmer and J. Chapman (eds), *Excellence and Equity in Literacy Education: The Case of New Zealand*, 41–70, London: Palgrave-Macmillan.

Clay, M. (1991), 'Why Is An Inservice Programme For Reading Recovery Teachers Necessary?' *Reading Horizons*, 31: 355–72.

Cockcroft, W. (1982), *Mathematics Counts (The Cockcroft Report)*, London: HMSO.

Cook, B., Smith, G. and Tankersley, M. (2012), 'Evidence-Based Practices in Education', Chapter 17 in K. Harris, S. Graham and T. Urdan (eds), *APA Educational Psychology Handbook: Vol 1 Theories, Constructs and Critical Issues*, Washington: American Psychological Association.

Cook, C., Holland, E. and Slemrod, T. (2014), 'Evidence-Based Reading Decoding Instruction', in Steven Little and Angeleque Akin-Little (eds), *Academic Assessment and Intervention*, 199–218, London: Routledge.

Cowen, N. and Cartwright, N. (2015), 'Making the Most of the Evidence: Evidence-based Policy in the Classroom', CHESS Working Paper No. 2015-03 Durham University, http://dro.dur.ac.uk/16441/1/16441.pdf (accessed 14 January 2017).

Cristia, A. and Seidle, A. (2014), 'The Hyperarticulation Hypothesis of Infant-Directed Speech', *Journal of Child Language*, 41: 913–34.

Dancy, J. (2000), 'The Particularist's Progress', in Brad Hooker and Margaret Little (eds), *Moral Particularism*, 136–56, Oxford: Oxford University Press.

Darling-Hammond, L. (2006), *Powerful Teacher Education: Lessons from Exemplary Programmes*, San Francisco: John Wiley and Sons.

Davenport, M. (2010), *Introducing Phonetics and Phonology*, London: Routledge.

Davis, A. (1999), 'Prescribing Teaching Methods', *Journal of Philosophy of Education*, 33 (3): 387–401.

Davis, A. (2004), 'The Credentials of Brain-Based Learning', *Journal of Philosophy of Education*, 38 (1): 21–35.

Davis, A. (2006), 'High Stakes Testing and the Structure of the Mind: A Reply to Randall Curren', *Journal of Philosophy of Education*, 40 (1): 1–16.

Davis, A. (2012), 'A Monstrous Regimen of Synthetic Phonics: Fantasies of Research-based Teaching "methods" versus Real Teaching', *Journal of Philosophy of Education*, 46 (4): 560–73.

Davis, A. (2013), *To Read or Not to Read: Decoding Synthetic Phonics*, Oxford: Wiley-Blackwell.

Davis, A., Winch, C. and Lum, G. (2015), *Educational Assessment on Trial*, London: Bloomsbury.

Davis, A., Goulding, M. and Suggate, J. (2017), *Mathematical Knowledge for Primary Teachers*, 5th edn, London: Routledge.

Department for Education (2011), *Criteria for Assuring High-Quality Phonic Work*, www.education.gov.uk/schools/teachingandlearning/ pedagogy/phonics/a0010240/criteriafor-assuring-high-quality-phonic- work (accessed 3 November 2013).

Department for Education (2012a), Teachers' Standards, www.gov.uk/ government/publications/teachers-standards (accessed 3 November 2013).

Department For Education (2013), *English Programmes of Study* https://www.gov.uk/government/uploads/system/uploads/attachment_data/file/335186/PRIMARY_national_curriculum_-_English_220714.pdf (accessed 3 November 2013).

Dresher, B. (2011), 'The Phoneme', in M. Van Oostendorp, C. Ewen, E. Hume and K. Rice (eds), *The Blackwell Companion to Phonology*, 241–66, Oxford: Wiley-Blackwell.

Ellis, S. and Moss, G. (2014), 'Education Policy and Research: The Phonics Question Reconsidered', *British Educational Research Journal*, 40 (2): 241–60.

Flores, M. and Ganz, J. (2009), 'Effects of Direct Instruction on the Reading Comprehension of Students with Autism and Developmental Disabilities', *Education and Training in Developmental Disabilities*, 44 (1): 39–53.

Florit, E. and Cain, K. (2011), 'The Simple View of Reading: Is It Valid for Different Types of Alphabetic Orthographies?' *Educational Psychology Review*, 23 (4): 553–76.

Fodor, J. (1974), 'Special Sciences (or: The disunity of science as a Working Hypothesis)', *Synthese*, 28 (2): 97–115.

Gergen, K. and Gergen, M. (1986), 'Narrative form and the Construction of Psychological Science', in T. R. Sarbin (ed.), *Narrative Psychology: The Storied Nature of Human Conduct*, New York: Praeger

Goodman, K. (1967), 'Reading: A Psycholinguistic Guessing Game', *Journal of the Reading Specialist*, 6: 126–35.

Gough, P., Hoover, W. and Peterson, C. (2013), 'Some Observations on a Simple view of Reading', in C. Cornoldi and J. Oakhil (eds), *Reading Comprehension Difficulties: Processes and Intervention*, 1–13, London: Routledge.

Grabe, W. and Stoller, F. (2011), *Teaching and Researching Reading*, Abingdon: Routledge.

Hacking, I. (1999), *The Social Construction of What?* Cambridge, MA: Harvard University Press.

Hacking, I. (2006), 'Kinds of People: Moving Targets', British Academy Lecture http://www.britac.ac.uk/pubs/src/_pdf/hacking.pdf (accessed7 May 2015).

Hank, P. (2000), 'Do Word Meanings Exist?' *Computers and the Humanities,* 34: 205–15.

Hirsch, E. (2015), 'The Annual Education Lecture with E.D. Hirsch', http://www.policyexchange.org.uk/modevents/item/the-annual-education-lecture-with-e-d-hirsch (accessed 9 October 2015).

Hirst, P. (1967), 'Logical and Psychological Aspects of Teaching', in R. S. Peter (ed.), *The Concept of Education*, London: Routledge and Kegan Paul.

Hjetland, H., Brinchmann, E., Solveig-Alma, H., Hagtvet, B. and Melby-Lervåg, M. (2014), 'Preschool Predictors of Later Reading Comprehension Ability: A Systematic Review', https://www.campbellcollaboration.org/library/preschool-predictors-of-later-reading-comprehension-ability-a-systematic-review.html (accessed 14 January 2017).

Holliman, A. and Hurry, J. (2013), 'The Effects of Reading Recovery on Children's Literacy Progress and Special Educational needs Status: A Three-year follow-up Study', *Educational Psychology*, 33 (6): 719–33.

Honeybone, P. and Watson, K. (2006). 'Phonemes, Graphemes and Phonics for Liverpool English', *Education Committee of the Linguistics Association of Great Britain*, www.phon.ucl.ac.uk/home/dick/ec/accents.htm (accessed 3 November 2013).

Hruby, G. (2012), 'Three Requirements for Justifying an Educational Neuroscience', *British Journal of Educational Psychology*, 82: 1–23.

Hurst, B. (1980), 'Teaching, Telling and Changes in Belief', *Journal of Philosophy of Education*, 14 (2): 215–24.

Johnston, R. S. and Watson, J. (2004), 'Accelerating the Development of Reading, Spelling and Phonemic Awareness', *Reading and Writing*, 17 (4): 327–57.

Khalidi, M. (2013), *Natural Categories and Human Kinds Classification in the Natural and Social Sciences*, Cambridge: Cambridge University Press.

Labov, W. (1973), 'The Boundaries of Words and their Meanings,' in Charles-James Bailey and Roger W. Shuy (eds), *New Ways of Analysing Variation in English*, 340–73, Washington: Georgetown University Press.

Machin, S., McNally, S. and Viarengo, M. (2016), '"Teaching to Teach" Literacy', CEP Discussion Paper No 1425, London: London School of Economics and Political Science.

MacIntyre, A. (1981), *After Virtue*, London: Duckworth.

May, H., Sirinides, P. and Gray, A. (2015), 'Evaluation of the i3 Scale-up of Reading Recovery', https://appam.confex.com/appam/2015/webprogram/Paper13033.html (accessed 7 October 2015).

McDowell, J. (1994), *Mind and World*, Cambridge, MA: Harvard University Press.

Moats, L. (2014), 'What Teachers don't know and why they aren't Learning it: Addressing the Need for Content and Pedagogy in Teacher Education', *Australian Journal of Learning Difficulties*, 19 (2): 75–91.

Modern Languages Association (2016), http://www.dictionary.com/browse/word (accessed 14 January 2017).

No Child Left Behind Act of 2001, Pub. L. No. 107-110, 115 Stat. 1425. Part A, Subpart 1, Sec. 1111, 2[c], https://www2.ed.gov/policy/elsec/leg/esea02/index.html (accessed 14 January 2017).

Oancea, A. and Pring, R. (2008), 'The Importance of Being Thorough: On Systematic Accumulations of "What Works' in Education Research", *Journal of Philosophy of Education*, 42 (1): 15–39.

Odom, S., Brantlinger, E., Gersten, R., Horner, R., Thompson, B. and Harris, K. (2005), 'Research in Special Education: Scientific Methods and Evidence-Based Practices', *Exceptional Children*, 71 (2): 137–48.

Ofsted (2010), *Reading By Six*, https://www.gov.uk/government/uploads/system/uploads/attachment_data/file/379093/Reading_20by_20six.pdf (accessed 14 January 2017).

Ofsted (2014), 'Getting them Reading Early', https://www.gov.uk/government/uploads/system/uploads/attachment_data/file/379490/Getting_20them_20reading_20early.pdf (accessed July 24 2015).

Ormell, C. (1967), 'The Problem of Curriculum Sequence in Mathematics', in Glenn Langford and D. J. O'Connor (eds), *New Essays in the Philosophy of Education*, 216–33, London: Routledge.

Ouellette, G. and Shaw, E. (2014), 'Oral Vocabulary and Reading Comprehension: An Intricate Affair', *L'Année psychologique*, 114 (04): 623–45.

Phillips, D. (1995), 'The Good, the Bad, and the Ugly: The Many Faces of Constructivism', *Educational Researcher*, 24 (7): 5–12.

Pinnell, G. (1994), 'An Inquiry-Based Model for Educating Teachers of Literacy', *Literacy, Teaching and Learning*, 1: 9–21.

Plag, I., Arndt-Lappe, S., Brann, M. and Schramm, M. (2015), *Introduction to English Linguistics*, Berlin and Boston: Walter de Gruyter GmbH.

Popper, K. (1963), *Conjectures and Refutations: The Growth of Scientific Knowledge*, New York: Harper & Row.

Rapaport, W. and Kibby, M. (2007), 'Contextual Vocabulary Acquisition as Computational Philosophy and as Philosophical Computation', *Journal of Experimental & Theoretical Artificial Intelligence*, 19 (1): 1–17.

Rawls, J. (1955), 'Two Concepts of Rules', *The Philosophical Review*, 64 (1): 3–32.

Ricoeur, P. (2010), *Time and Narrative*, Chicago: University of Chicago Press.

Robins, R. (2014), *General Linguistics* London: Routledge.

Rudd, A. (2012), *Self, Value, and Narrative: A Kierkegaardian Approach,* Oxford: Oxford University Press.

Savage, R., Burgos, G., Wood, E. and Piquette, N. (2015), 'The Simple View of Reading as a Framework for National Literacy Initiatives: A Hierarchical Model of Pupil-Level and Classroom-Level Factors', *British Educational Research Journal*, 41 (5): 820–44, Early View.

Schwartz, R. and Gallant, P. (2011), 'The Role of Self-Monitoring in Initial Word-Recognition Learning', in C. Wyatt-Smith , Elkins J., Gunn S. (eds), *Multiple Perspectives on Difficulties in Learning Literacy and Numeracy*, 235–53, London: Springer Science.

Searle, J. (1969), *Speech Acts*, Cambridge: Cambridge University Press.

Searle, J. (1995), *The Construction of Social Reality*, London: Penguin.

Sellars, W. (1956), 'Empiricism and the Philosophy of Mind', in Herbert Feigle and Michael Scriven (eds), *The Foundations of Science and the Concepts of Psychology and Psychoanalysis*, 253–315, Minnesota: University of Minnesota Press.

Share, D. (2008), 'On the Anglocentricities of Current Reading Research and Practice: The Perils of Overreliance on an "Outlier" Orthography', *Psychological Bulletin*, 134 (4): 584–615.

Shulman, L. (1999), 'Taking Learning Seriously', *Change*, 31 (4): 10–17.

Smith, F. (1999), 'Why Systematic Phonics and Phonemic Awareness Instruction Constitute an Educational Hazard', *Language Arts*, 77 (2): 50–155.

Snel, M., Terwelb, J., Aarnoutsec, C. and Leeuwec, J. (2012), 'Effectiveness of Guided Co-Construction versus Direct Instruction for Beginning Reading Instruction', *Educational Research and Evaluation*, 18 (4): 353–74.

Stevenson, L. (2003), 'Twelve Conceptions of Imagination', *British Journal of Aesthetics*, 43 (3): 238–59.

Strawson, G. (1997), 'The self', *Journal of Consciousness Studies*, 4 (5–6): 405–28.

Stuart, M. (2014), 'Government Imposition of Synthetic Phonics is "damaging able readers" really?', http://educationmediacentre.org/blog/government-imposition-of-synthetic-phonics-is-damaging-able-readers-really/ (accessed 10 August 2015).

Taylor, C. (1979), 'Interpretation and the Sciences of Man', in Paul Rabinow and William M. Sullivan (eds), *Interpretative Social Science: A Reader*, 28, Berkeley, CA: University of California Press.

Torgerson, C. J., Brooks, G. and Hall J. (2006), *A Systematic Review of the Research Literature on the Use of Phonics in the Teaching of Reading and Spelling*, London: DfES.

Tunmer, W. (2014), 'How Cognitive Science has Provided the Theoretical Basis for Resolving the "Great Debate" over Reading Methods in Alphabetic Orthographies', in Saths Cooper and Kopano Ratele (eds), *Psychology Serving Humanity: Proceedings of the 30th International Congress of Psychology Volume 2*, 228–39, London: Psychology Press.

Van Der Hulst, H. (2013), 'Discoverers of the Phoneme', in K. Allan (ed.), *The Oxford Handbook of Linguistics*, Oxford: Oxford University Press.

Watt, D. (2003), 'Phoneme-grapheme Correspondences and a Newcastle Accent', *Education Committee of the Linguistics Association of Great Britain*, www.phon.ucl.ac.uk/home/dick/ec/accents.htm (accessed 3 November 2013).

Wellington, J. (2015), *Educational Research: Contemporary Issues and Practical Approaches*, London: Bloomsbury.

Wetzel, L. (2009), *Types and Tokens; on Abstract Objects*, Cambridge, MA: The MIT Press.

Williams, B. (2007), 'Life as Narrative', *European Journal of Philosophy*, 17 (2): 305–14.

Winch, P. (1990), *The Idea of a Social Science and its Relation to Philosophy*, London: Routledge.

Index

Lightning Source UK Ltd.
Milton Keynes UK
UKHW022003140619
344431UK00003B/116/P